THE
COMPUTER CONCEPTS
COLORING BOOK

THE COMPUTER CONCEPTS COLORING BOOK

by Barry M. Glotzer

Illustrations by
Cinthea Vadala

BARNES & NOBLE BOOKS
A DIVISION OF HARPER & ROW, PUBLISHERS
New York, Cambridge,
Philadelphia, San Francisco, London,
Mexico City, São Paulo, Singapore, Sydney

Barry M. Glotzer is Chairperson of the Department of Business Administration at Bramson ORT Technical Institute. He has taught mathematics and computer science at the prestigious Stuyvesant High School in New York City, Polytechnic Institute of New York, and New York City Technical College. In addition, he has authored manuals, monographs, and syllabi in computer science and mathematics for school systems and private corporations. He has developed and taught teacher training seminars in computer science, programming languages, and computer applications programs.

Cinthea Vadala received her education at Music and Art High School and Hunter College. She is the illustrator of The Zoology Coloring Book. She is now a free-lance scientific illustrator living in the San Francisco area.

This book was produced by Coloring Concepts, Inc.
PO Box 324, Oakville, CA 94562
The book editor was Joan W. Elson
The copy editor was Scott Amerman
Type was set by ComCom
Page makeup and production coordination was by C. Linda Dingler
The proofreader was Bernie Borok

THE COMPUTER CONCEPTS COLORING BOOK. © 1985 by Coloring Concepts, Inc. All rights reserved. Printed in the United States of America. No part of this book may be used or reproduced in any manner whatsoever without written permission except in the case of brief quotations embodied in critical articles and reviews. For information address Harper & Row, Publishers, Inc., 10 East 53rd Street, New York, NY 10022. Published simultaneously in Canada by Fitzhenry and Whiteside Limited, Toronto

FIRST EDITION

ISBN 0-06-460308-3

85 86 87 88 89 10 9 8 7 6 5 4 3 2 1

To my parents, Jack and Mollie, who provided me with my first microcoding. To my wife, Eileen, and children David, Lisa, and Jonathan, who, through their patience and encouragement, provided peripheral and auxiliary support.

TABLE OF CONTENTS

Preface

How to Use This Book: Coloring Instructions

PLATE

1. Introduction
2. The Computer
3. The Keyboard and Video Display
4. Printers
5. The Disk System
6. The Main Computer Board
7. Parts of a Central Processing Unit
8. Information Flow in the Central Processing Unit
9. The Operating System
10. The Operating System and Programming
11. Computers Talking to Computers
12. Communications: Timesharing and Networking
13. Flowcharting
14. Creating a Program

15 Outline of a BASIC Program

16 The PRINT Instruction

17 The Assignment Instruction

18 The INPUT Instruction

19 The INPUT and GOTO Instructions

20 The IF . . . THEN . . . Instruction

21 Sample Programs: Tax Table and Counting Amoebas

22 Sample Program: Cash Register

23 The READ/DATA Instructions

24 The FOR/NEXT Instructions

25 The DIM Instruction and Subscripted Variables

26 Two-Dimensional Arrays

27 Sample Program: Plane Ticket Reservations

28 The SQUARE ROOT and INTEGER Functions and DEFINE FUNCTION Instruction

29 The Random Number Instruction

30 The GOSUB and RETURN Instructions

31 Low-Resolution Graphics

32 Low-Resolution Graphics at Work

33 Video Display Graphics in Finer Detail

34 Turtle Graphics: LOGO

35 Vector Graphics and Plotters

36 Word Processing Programs

37 Data Base Management Programs

38 Music Synthesis

39 Voice Synthesis

40 A System for Artificial Intelligence

41 Introduction to Robotics

42 Computer Games and Simulations

43 Intelligence Simulating Games

44 The Future of Computers

APPENDIX

A1 Number Systems and Binary Numbers

A2 Octal and Hexadecimal Numbers

A3 Building a Microchip

A4 Logic Blocks

A5 Logic Blocks: Binary Addition

A6 Analog and Digital Computers

A7 Sorting

Conversion Table

Glossary

Index

PREFACE

Almost every facet of our everyday lives involves computers. Computers serve in the background whenever we do ordinary things such as call long distance, make a plane reservation, cash a check, use a credit card, or send a letter. They are rapidly entering our places of work and our homes. We may be expected to operate a computer on our jobs or we may acquire one to aid us in any number of personal ways. Whatever our involvement, we should know enough about computers to feel on easy terms with them and to appreciate their problem-solving abilities.

The Computer Concepts Coloring Book is designed to provide the basic knowledge that leads to computer literacy. Each plate with its supporting text presents an aspect of understanding the microcomputer. Through the coordinated activities of reading and coloring, you form a clear conception of how computers receive, process, and display information. You also gain insight into what it means to create a computer program. The BASIC language is introduced and illustrated by simple programs. Individual plates explain computer applications such as word processing, computer games, music synthesis, computer graphics, artificial intelligence, and robotics. In the coloring format, flowcharting, timesharing, and networking are easily grasped. Fundamental skills and knowledge are presented through a discussion of number systems, logic blocks, computer generations, and computer techniques for processing information.

At first glance, some of the plates may appear quite complex. However, they are designed to be processed (not just looked at) step by step. By simply coloring titles and related structures/instructions, in order, from A toward Z, and reading the brief related text, you will learn the contents of these plates. The plates are a result of numerous experiments with many students. The vast majority of my students, as young as five and as old as seventy-five, learn more rapidly by interacting with (coloring) a diagram at the same time as they follow a lecture or read a text. This coloring activity provides a lasting impression for the learner.

First and foremost I would like to thank Joan Elson for an outstanding job of patient editing of this manuscript. She displayed the professional understanding and ability that was necessary for the creation of this book. I also wish to thank Cinthea Vadala, who as illustrator provided wonderful renditions of the coloring plates. I thank William Carr and Dr. Theodore Tracewell for their conscientious and proficient review of the manuscript. Janet Muth provided a careful coloring check of the plates. Grateful acknowledgment is due Ken Christensen, Bob Hopton, Frank Thompson, and Robin Tanny, who provided helpful information, and to Stuart Boynton, who provided editing advice on many preliminary plates.

HOW TO USE THIS BOOK:
COLORING INSTRUCTIONS

1. This is a book of illustrations (plates) and related text pages. You (the colorer) color each structure indicated the same color as its name (title), both of which are linked by identical letters (subscripts). In doing this, you will be able to relate identically colored names and structures at a glance. Structural relationships become apparent as visual orientation is developed. These insights, plus the opportunity to display a number of colors in a visually pleasing pattern, provide a rewarding learning experience.

2. You will need coloring instruments. Colored pencils or colored felt-tip pens are recommended. Laundry markers (with waterproof colors) and crayons are not recommended: the former because they stain through the paper, and the latter because they are coarse, messy, and produce unnatural colors.

3. The organization of illustrations and text is based on the author's overall perspective of the subject and may follow, in some instances, the order of presentation of a formal course of instruction on the subject. To achieve the maximum benefit, you should color the plates in the order presented, at least within each group or section. Some plates may seem intimidating at first glance, even after reviewing the coloring notes and instructions. However, once you begin coloring the plate in order of presentation of titles and reading the text, the illustrations will begin to have meaning and the relationships of different parts will become clear.

4. As you come to each plate, look over the entire illustration and note the arrangement and order of titles. The number of colors needed (CN) appears in the upper right corner. Scan the coloring instructions (printed in boldface type) for further guidance. Be sure to color in the order given by the instructions. Most of the time this means starting at the top of the plate with (A) and coloring in alphabetical order. Contemplate a number of color arrangements before starting. In some cases, you may want to color related forms with different shades of the same color; in other cases, contrast is desirable. One of the most important considerations is to link the structure and its title (printed in large outline or blank letters) with the same color. If the structure to be colored has parts taking several colors, you might color its title as a mosaic of the same colors. It is recommended that you color the title first and then its related structure. If the identifying subscript lies within the structure to be colored and is obscured by the color used, you may have trouble finding the related title unless you colored it first.

5. In some cases, a plate of illustrations may require more colors than you have. Forced to use a color twice on the same plate, you must take care to prevent confusion in identification and review by employing them on separate areas well away from one another. On occasion, you may be asked to use colors on a plate that were used for the same structure on a previous related plate. In this case, save the colors until you reach the appropriate title.

6. Symbols used throughout the book are explained below. Once you understand and master the mechanics, you will find room for considerable creativity in coloring each plate. Now turn to any plate and note:

   a. Areas to be colored are separated from adjacent areas by heavy outlines. Lighter lines represent background, suggest texture, or define form and (in the absence of "don't color" symbols) should be colored over. Some boundaries between coloring zones may be represented by dotted lines. These represent a division of names or titles and indicate that an actual boundary may not exist or, at best, is not clearly visible.

b. As a general rule, large areas should be colored with light colors and dark colors should be used for small areas. Take care with very dark colors: they obscure detail, identifying subscripts, and texture lines or stippling. In some cases, a structure will be identified by two subscripts (such as A + D). This indicates you are looking at one structure overlying another. In this case, two light colors are recommended for coloring the two overlapping structures.

c. Any outline-lettered word followed by a small capitalized letter (subscript) should be colored. In most cases, there will be a related structure or area to color. If not, the word functions as a heading and is colored black (●) or gray (★).

d. In the event structures are duplicated on a plate, as in left and right parts or serial parts, only one may be labeled with a subscript. Without boundary restrictions, or instructions to the contrary, these like structures should be given the same color.

e. In looking over a number of plates, you will see some of the following symbols:
- ● = Color black; generally reserved for headings.
- ★ = Color gray: generally reserved for headings.
- $-\!\!\mid\!\!-$ = Do not color.
- ( ) = Set next to title's subscript; for example, A( ) signals that this structure is composed of parts listed below with the same letter but different exponents and receives same color; only its parts are labeled in illustration.
- A^1, A^2 = Identical letter with different exponents implies that parts so labeled are sufficiently related to receive the same color or shades of the same color.

7. The title of a structure to be colored on the related (facing) plate is set in italics where it first appears in the text. This enables you to quickly spot in the text the title of a structure to be colored.

THE
COMPUTER CONCEPTS
COLORING BOOK

1 INTRODUCTION

What costs 500 to 1000 times less and does more than its predecessors did 40 years ago? One of the very few answers to this question is the modern computer.

Color the Cost of a Computer System heading in gray. Color titles A through F using light colors and the bars A through F representing the decline in computer cost. Then, color the Computer Generations heading in gray, titles G, H, and I, and the vertical bars showing the generations of the computer.

The very first electronic computers were beyond the economic reach of the average individual. Not until the last ten years has the purchase price of a computer approached that of a small television set. Nowadays, computers have more capabilities and greater ease of use than those of the 1940s and 1950s. They are no longer solely in the province of governments and large corporations.

There are three generation classifications of the electronic computer, each characterized by a significant technological advance. The *first generation,* extending from the late 1930s to the middle of the *1950s,* is that of the vacuum tube. The computer at this time was room sized and required an equally large air cooling system to prevent heat buildup. The number of calculations performed was on the order of 1000 per second. The earliest of the vacuum tube computers required the user to set a series of switches and insert wires into panels. Each new task required new switch settings and wiring.

With the invention of the transistor in the late *1940s,* the *second computer generation* was born. The transistor could conduct electricity more efficiently than a vacuum tube. No large air cooling unit was required. The size and price of the computer came down, and the number of calculations per second was increased tenfold. During this generation, high-level programming languages such as FORTRAN, COBOL, PL/1, and BASIC were created. The user could write programmed instructions that directed the computer, in effect, to set its own switches and wiring.

The *third generation,* that of the microchip, began in the early *1970s.* The microchip is an electronic device that contains thousands of transistors but is no bigger than your fingertip. This generation heralded the availability of a very small cost computer having the capabilities of its larger and costlier predecessors. The speed of computation increased another tenfold to one hundred-fold with the use of the microchip. Programming languages were so refined that programs became interchangeable among different computers.

Watches, electronic typewriters, automobile electronic ignition systems, televisions, stereos, and games are some of the devices that make use of the third generation computer.

Color the Number of Computers in Use heading and the related bars, A through F, in colors to correspond with those chosen for A through F above.

As the cost of computers goes down, the number of computers in use increases. The earliest electronic computers were few in number. At the beginning of the 1940s there were less than a dozen electronic computers. Each had a different configuration, designed to perform a specific task. In the middle of the 1950s, the number of computers increased to approximately two thousand. At this point, computers were created as families. Each family had many members of the same type and capability. The *1960s* saw thousands of computers in use. Today, in the *1980s,* the number of computers produced and sold each month is in the hundreds of thousands. There are approximately 160 different manufacturers producing small computers alone.

Color the Computer Processing Power heading, titles J through N, and the related diagram.

Computers are generally classed as *mainframes, minicomputers,* or *microcomputers.* The classification depends on the amount of information (data) managed, the memory available, and the *speed of processing.* The large, expensive mainframe is capable of processing huge amounts of data and storing millions of characters. Characters are printed symbols such as letters, numbers, and punctuation marks. Except for some experimental models, the mainframe computer was all that existed until the minicomputer arrived in the 1960s.

The minicomputer does not process the same volume of data or store as many characters as the mainframe. Typically, storage is about one or two million characters. Minicomputers cost much less than mainframes.

The microcomputer is the smallest of the electronic computer family. It is the computer most often used by a small business person, classroom teacher, and home user. The amount of storage available is usually less than 100,000 characters (roughly 16,000 words). Sophisticated processing is possible with a microcomputer, and the cost is within the means of the average person.

With this book you can learn the ins and outs of the small giants, the microcomputers.

INTRODUCTION.

COST OF A COMPUTER SYSTEM ★
1940s A   1970s D
1950s B   1980s E
1960s C   1990s F

COMPUTER GENERATIONS ★
FIRST G
SECOND H
THIRD

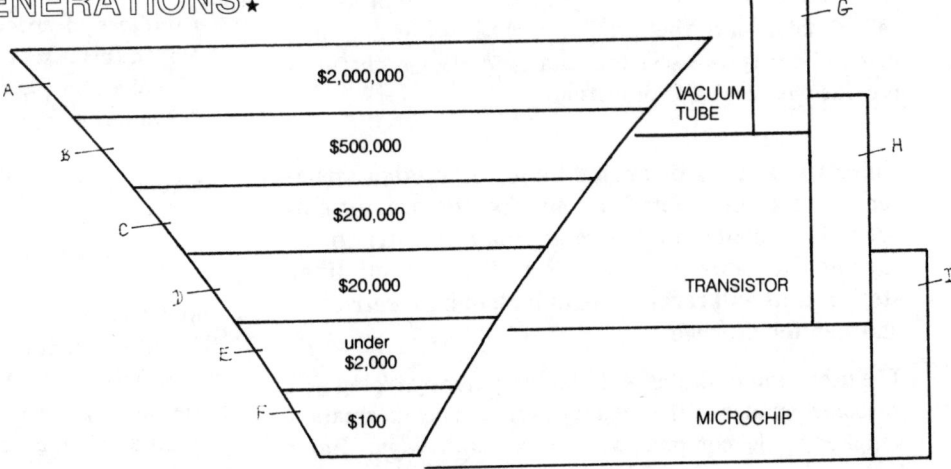

- A — $2,000,000
- B — $500,000
- C — $200,000
- D — $20,000
- E — under $2,000
- F — $100

G — VACUUM TUBE
H — TRANSISTOR
I — MICROCHIP

NUMBER OF COMPUTERS IN USE ★

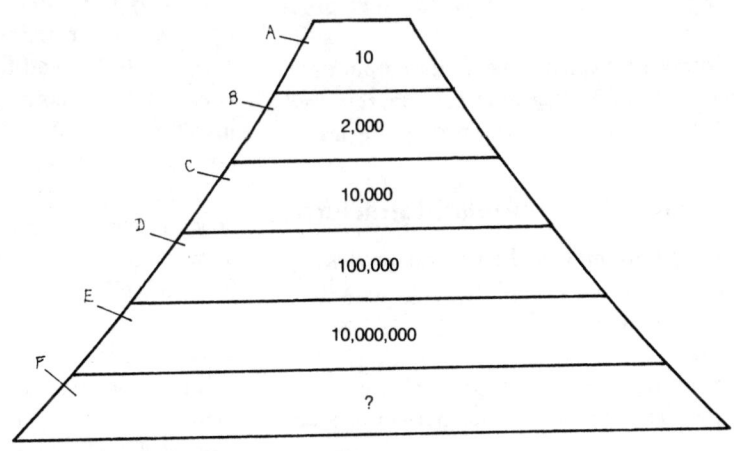

- A — 10
- B — 2,000
- C — 10,000
- D — 100,000
- E — 10,000,000
- F — ?

COMPUTER PROCESSING POWER ★
   MEMORY STORAGE J
   SPEED OF
      PROCESSING K
MAINFRAME
   COMPUTER L
MINICOMPUTER M
MICROCOMPUTER N

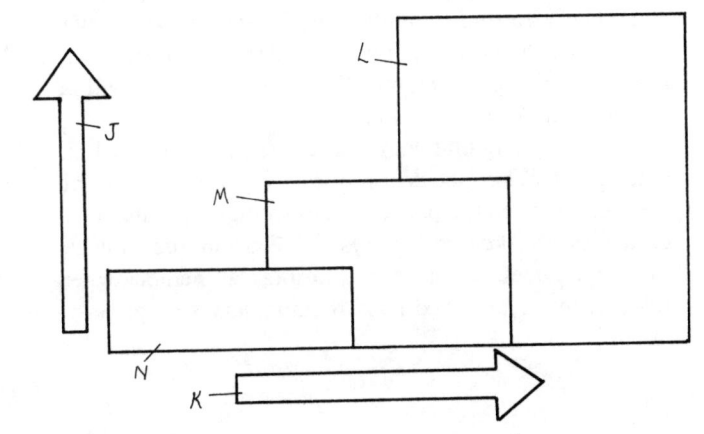

2 THE COMPUTER

A computer is a device which can receive, process, and display information. It is not a single piece of equipment, but a system of many components. These components include input units, the processing unit, and output units. Input units allow the user (you) to enter information, called data, into the computer. The processing unit manipulates (processes) the data, and the output units provide the results of processing.

Color titles A ( ) through A⁴ and the related structures and arrows. The User and its title are not colored. Use shades of the same color for structures sharing the same subscript. Note that the auxiliary storage unit will receive two colors; one for retrieval, another for storage.

The user communicates with the computer by typing at a *keyboard* similar to that of a typewriter. The information supplied by the computer's user is called the *input*. Input includes instructions and information to be processed. The set of instructions is called a program. The other information, input data, consists of numbers or words to be processed by the program.

An *auxiliary storage unit* can also be used to input data. Previously stored data and programs can be *retrieved* from the storage device for use by the processing unit.

Color titles B through B² and the related structures.

The *main processing unit* houses the central processing unit, or *CPU*, and the *internal* (main) *memory*, as well as other circuitry. This main unit is the "computing" part of the computer system. All other components (keyboard, auxiliary storage, video display, and printer) are called peripherals because they operate around (peri-) the processing unit.

The CPU is the operational center of the computer. It consists of electronic circuits wired for specific tasks, such as doing arithmetic, making logical decisions, remembering data and controlling the other units. The CPU will be explained in Plates 7 and 8.

The processing unit continually scans the keyboard for a key press. When the user presses a key at the keyboard, the computer reads a particular electronic code value generated by the key and places the code in the internal memory. Codes are also stored in internal memory when information is retrieved from the auxiliary storage unit.

Color titles C ( ) through C⁶ and the related structures and arrows.

A character or symbol typed at the keyboard is usually displayed on the *video display screen*. However, when one of a number of special keys is pressed, nothing is displayed. In this case, the computer may perform a specific task involved in processing data or operating the units. Plate 3 describes the keyboard and key function in greater detail.

In addition to displaying information typed at the keyboard, the video display screen (CRT, cathode ray tube, or monitor) is used when the computer displays the results of its calculations or decisions. Results produced by the computer are called *output*.

The information that has been entered and processed is retained only as long as the computer remains on. In order for the user to turn off the computer and still save the program and input or output data, two types of devices can be used: the *printer* and the *auxiliary storage unit*.

A printer is a keyboardless typewriter which is controlled by the CPU. Permanent copies of programs and processed information are printed on paper in a format designed to be read by people. The output of the printer is called "hard copy," because the user can take it away, intact and readable, from the computer. Printers are discussed on Plate 4.

If the user wants to save data and programs, an auxiliary storage unit can be used for *storage*. The most common auxiliary storage units are the floppy disk unit (shown) and the hard disk unit. Both make use of specially prepared recording surfaces. You have seen that the stored programs and data can subsequently be used as input (retrieving, arrow A⁴), bypassing the need to type them in at the keyboard again. Storage and retrieval are discussed on Plate 5.

When the user intends to print or store the programs and data, specific instructions must be typed at the keyboard. The processing unit then directs the printer or auxiliary storage unit to perform the appropriate operation.

In review, the user can enter input via the keyboard or via the auxiliary storage device. Then, the user has the option of viewing the output on the video display screen, printing a written record with the printer, or storing the information with an auxiliary storage unit.

THE COMPUTER.

USER[A⊹]
INPUT UNITS[A()]
KEYBOARD[A1]/INPUT[A2]
AUXILIARY STORAGE
  UNIT[A3]/RETRIEVAL[A4]

MAIN PROCESSING UNIT[B]
  CPU[B1]
  INTERNAL MEMORY[B2]

OUTPUT UNITS[C()]
VIDEO DISPLAY[C1]/OUTPUT[C2]
PRINTER[C3]/OUTPUT[C4]
AUXILIARY STORAGE
  UNIT[C5]/STORAGE[C6]

3 THE KEYBOARD AND VIDEO DISPLAY

Now that you understand the general organization of the computer, the individual units will be discussed in more detail. In this plate you will learn more about the keyboard and video display.

Color the Information Flow heading, titles A, B, and C, and the related structures to review the relationships of the keyboard, processor unit, and video display. The shapes used are standard computer symbols and will be seen in several plates of this book.

When the user types at the *keyboard,* input passes into the *processor unit.* The processor unit can then send information on to the *video display* screen as output.

Color the Keys heading, titles D through F, and the representative keyboard at the right. Use light colors. Leave the H key uncolored for now.

The organization of the keyboard of the computer is similar to that of an ordinary typewriter. The *alphanumeric* (alphabet and number) *keys* are positioned in the standard QWERTY configuration. (Q, W, E, R, T, and Y are the first six letters at the left of the second row of keys from the top in standard typewriters). In addition to standard symbol keys (>, <, /, etc.), there are *special purpose keys* on the computer keyboard. These special purpose keys are used to signal the computer to perform a specific task. For example, when a program or data line is completed, the special purpose *Return key* (or on certain models, the Enter or Endline key) is pressed. The Return key acts like a carriage return of a typewriter, but with a difference. As soon as it is pressed, the computer performs in response to the line's meaning.

The actual arrangement of the keyboard can vary from model to model. Some keyboards feature a numeric pad in which the number keys are arranged like those of a calculator.

Color the H key, titles F and G, and the related representations in the drawing. Use a light color for F.

The keys of the keyboard are switches that, when pressed, send a signal to the electronic circuits of the processor unit (in some cases, to circuits in the keyboard itself). When a key is pressed, such as the alphabet key, H, in the middle diagram, a signal is transmitted. This signal is a specific *electronic code number.* For H, the code is 11001000. The most common code list is called ASCII (pronounced "as-key") or American Standard Code for Information Interchange, shown in the Conversion Table. The computer stores the *keyboard code* in a specific internal memory location in the processor unit, identifies the key (in this case, H), and, when required by the CPU, sends the code number to the video display circuits.

Color titles H through L and the related representations. Use light colors for H and I.

The video display screen is like a television without a channel tuner (selector). When the video display is turned on, a *language prompt symbol* and a *cursor* present on the screen indicate that the computer is ready to receive information from the user. The language prompt symbol indicates the instruction language to be entered. An example of a language prompt symbol is "]"; in other models, " < " and "*" are used. The cursor is usually a blinking box or a single underscore line, and shows the position on the screen where the next typed character is going to be displayed.

When a key is pressed, the computer identifies the keyboard code. If the symbol is not of a special type, the code is sent to video display circuits. These circuits send a signal to the video display, causing portions of the screen to light. The result is that the letter the user has typed (in this case, H) is displayed at the cursor position. The cursor moves to the right to the next screen position.

Color the Dot Matrix heading, title K[1], and the dot pattern of the letter H. Leave the other dots uncolored.

The video display screen has an invisible grid of *dots* that can be *lighted* or left dark. Each keyboard character can be displayed by illuminating a specific combination of dots in a single dot matrix. A dot matrix is a rectangle of dots arranged in rows and columns (frequently seven rows by five columns). The video display circuits control the illumination of these dots, guided by the character's code number. The letter H appears on the screen. It appears to be solid but it is actually a collection of lighted dots in the "H" shape. Video graphics are explained in Plates 31 to 35.

THE KEYBOARD AND VIDEO DISPLAY.

INFORMATION FLOW ★
  KEYBOARD A
  PROCESSOR UNIT B
  VIDEO DISPLAY C

KEYS ★
  ALPHANUMERIC D
    H KEY D'
  SPECIAL PURPOSE E
    RETURN KEY E'
KEYBOARD CODE F
PROCESSOR UNIT G
VIDEO CIRCUIT CODE H
VIDEO DISPLAY SCREEN I
LANGUAGE PROMPT
  SYMBOL J
LETTER H K
CURSOR L
DOT MATRIX ★
  LIGHTED DOTS K'

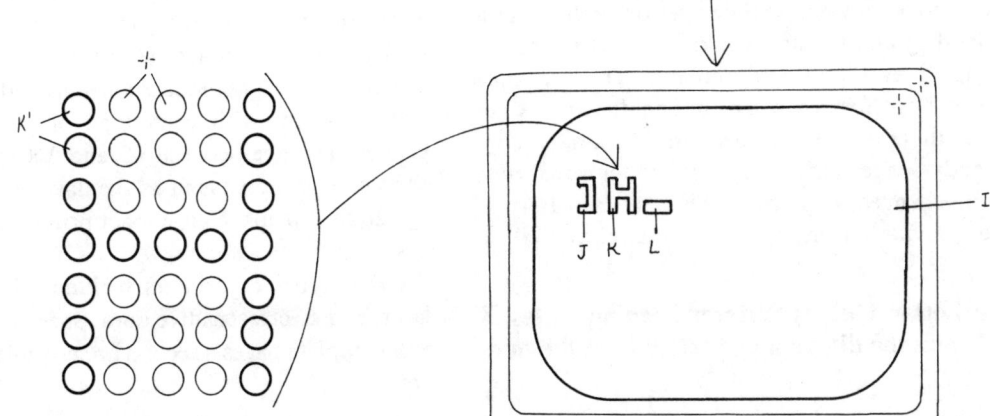

KEYBOARD AND VIDEO DISPLAY
CN 12

4 PRINTERS

In the previous plate, output was displayed on the video screen. When a permanent copy ("hard copy") of the output is desired, the printer is used.

Color the Information Flow heading, titles A through D, and the related representations in the top diagram.

When a character is to be printed, the *central processing unit* (CPU) sends the code for the character to the *printer* circuits. These circuits activate the printer display mechanisms to produce the desired symbol on paper. In the example, the ASCII code for the letter H is sent to the printer to display the *letter on paper*.

The major distinction among printers is the way in which the characters are formed on the paper. The printer display mechanism for most computers falls into one of two categories, impact and non-impact.

Color the Impact Printers and Dot Matrix Printer headings, titles E through J, and the related representations in the diagram at the upper right. Use a light color for E.

An impact type printer uses a method similar to that of the typewriter to display a letter on paper. A typeface configured to a particular pattern is pressed against a ribbon and paper to produce the desired symbol.

The dot matrix printer produces the symbol using dots in a closely spaced grid (matrix). A typical matrix pattern consists of seven rows of five dots each. The *print head* has a vertical line of seven closely spaced *wires* (pins). The end of each wire can be made to strike the *ribbon* and *paper* by a signal from the computer to the printer circuits. One vertical column of the matrix pattern for each symbol is printed at a time. The letters are formed by moving the print head horizontally across the paper one column at a time. In the diagram, the first stroke of the H is printed by activating all seven wires in the column. The three dots in the crossbar are formed when the middle wire is activated three times as the print head moves horizontally.

A major advantage of the dot matrix printer is that type fonts can be changed very easily. The matrix pattern is changed to provide for any type of character desired.

Color the Letter Quality Printer heading, titles K through L, and the diagram and letter H at the middle left.

The *daisy wheel* printer mechanism is a second example of impact printers. In this case, a fully formed letter is pressed against a ribbon in order to transfer the design to the paper. Each *end* of a *spoke* of the wheel (petal of the "daisy") has a symbol embossed on the side that faces the ribbon. The wheel spins at a rapid rate. When the wheel is in the correct position, the printer circuits send a signal to the print head *hammer*. The hammer strikes the end of the spoke to produce the impression of the symbol on the paper. The symbol printed on the paper is fully formed, not made up of a series of dots. The resulting hard copy looks as if it was printed on a typewriter. For this reason, the output from such a printer is called letter quality. A disadvantage of this type of printer is that in order to change the type font, the entire daisy wheel has to be changed.

Color the Non-Impact Printer and Thermal Printer headings, title M, and the diagram at the bottom right, along with the dot matrix pattern of the letter H.

Non-impact printers produce a symbol without directly touching the paper. The thermal printer is an example. *Heating elements* are arranged in one column in the print head. However, unlike the wires of the dot matrix printer, the heating elements do not actually touch the paper. The printer circuits send a signal to the print head to apply power to the required heating elements. The heat produced activates a heat-sensitive dye embedded in a specially coated paper. The result is the appearance of a dot pattern in the shape of the desired symbol. The print head moves horizontally across the paper until the entire line of text is printed. The major advantage of thermal printers is that the printer is quiet and has few moving parts. A disadvantage is that the paper is sensitive to heat. Even sunlight could ruin a page of text.

The number of characters per second (cps) that can be printed varies with each type of printer. Dot matrix printers average between 60 and 160 cps. Fully formed character printers (such as the daisy wheel printer) average 20 to 100 cps. Non-impact printers average 80 to 120 cps.

Other types of printers include ink jet, electrostatic, laser, and electrosensitive ones. Speeds ranging up to several complete pages a second are possible with some printers.

PRINTERS.

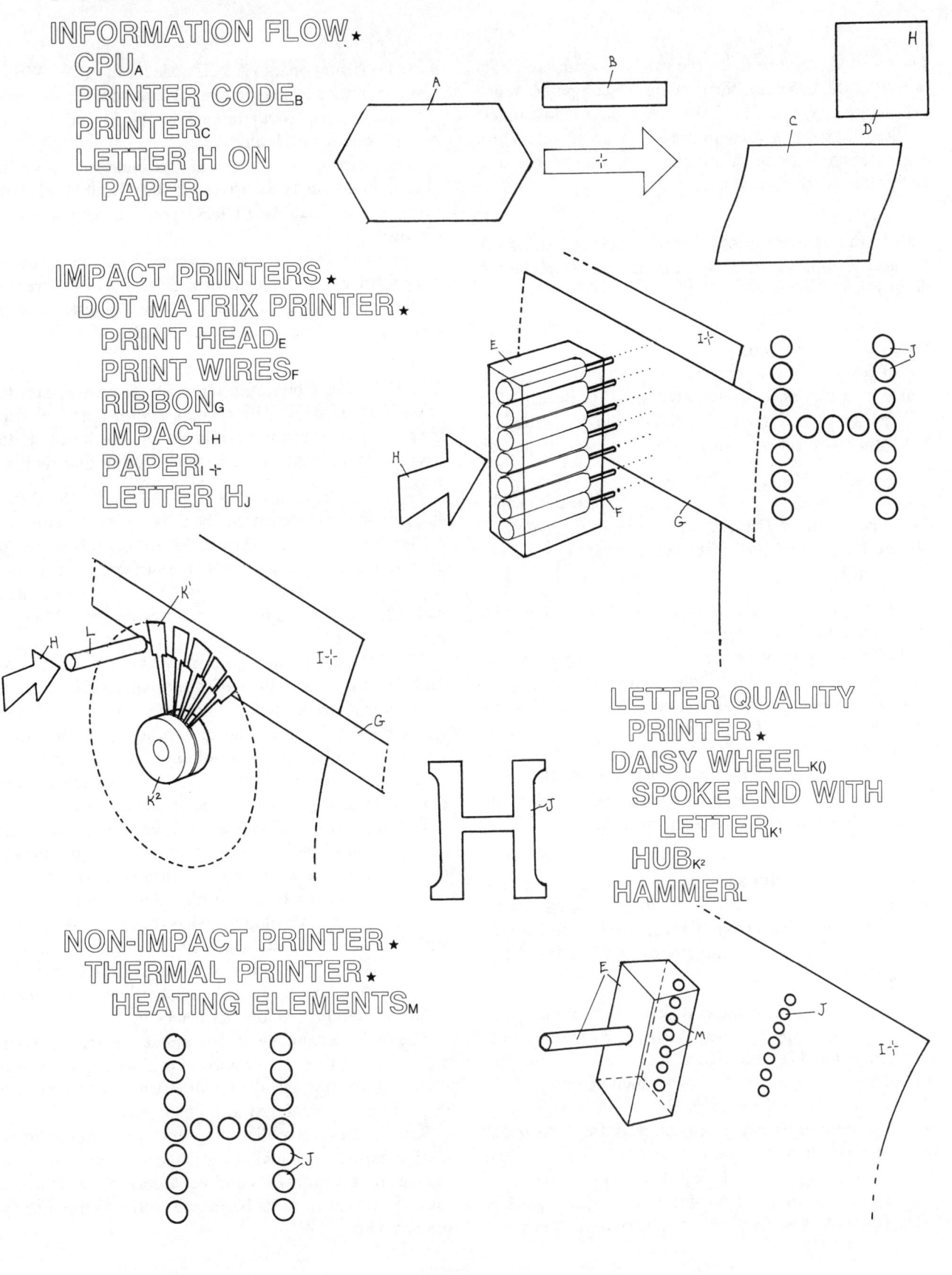

INFORMATION FLOW ★
- CPU_A
- PRINTER CODE_B
- PRINTER_C
- LETTER H ON PAPER_D

IMPACT PRINTERS ★
DOT MATRIX PRINTER ★
- PRINT HEAD_E
- PRINT WIRES_F
- RIBBON_G
- IMPACT_H
- PAPER_I ✦
- LETTER H_J

LETTER QUALITY PRINTER ★
- DAISY WHEEL_K()
- SPOKE END WITH LETTER_K1
- HUB_K2
- HAMMER_L

NON-IMPACT PRINTER ★
THERMAL PRINTER ★
- HEATING ELEMENTS_M

4
PRINTERS
CN 12

5 THE DISK SYSTEM

The internal memory holds the user's program and data as well as the programs for running the computer. When the computer is turned off, the user's input is lost unless auxiliary storage is used to make a permanent record. Most personal computer systems make use of the disk system for auxiliary storage.

Color the Information Flow heading, titles A through D, and the related representations in the top diagram.

The disk system permits information to be transferred from the *processor unit* onto a *floppy disk* for *storage*. It is also possible for the processor unit to retrieve information from a disk and use it in processing (retrieval). This information can be the user's, stored from an earlier session, or a manufacturer's disk with a program already on it.

Color the Floppy Disk Structure heading, titles E, H, and I only, and the related structures. Use a light color for I.

A floppy disk is a circular piece of plastic which has been coated on both sides with magnetic material, usually iron oxide. The plastic is very thin and flexible (floppy), somewhat like audio recording tape flattened into a disk. Floppy disks come in two standard sizes, 5¼ inches and 8 inches in diameter. The plastic disk is permanently covered by an *envelope* for protection and support. A lint-free *inner jacket* cleans the disk as it rotates inside the envelope. Windows in the envelope and inner jacket allow access to the magnetic surface of the disk.

Color the Disk Drive heading, titles F and G, and J through Q, and the structures in the Floppy Disk Structure and Disk Drive diagrams. The read/write head is actually below the floppy disk in the Disk Drive diagram.

The *alignment slots* on the envelope assure proper positioning of the floppy disk when it is placed into the disk drive *entry slot*. The disk drive hub goes through the *hub hole*. The drive motor (not shown) spins the disk inside the envelope at over three hundred revolutions per minute when information is being read or recorded. The *read/write window* allows the *read/write head* to contact the disk surface. Information is read from and written onto the disk surface by the read/write head. Reading takes place when the read/write head translates the magnetic particle orientation into ASCII code for the CPU. Writing is accomplished by magnetizing the iron oxide particles on the disk surface to correspond to the 0s and 1s of the ASCII code for each character.

Data are read and written onto the underside only of the disk in single-sided disk drives (shown). Double-sided disk drives use two read/write heads, one on each surface of the disk.

The *write protect notch,* when covered with tape on 5¼-inch disks, or left uncovered on 8-inch disks, prevents writing onto the disk. *Index holes* on the disk guide the disk drive mechanism in organizing the information.

Color the Disk heading, titles R, S, and T, and the related structures. The tracks, sectors, and characters are not actually visible when one looks at the disk surface. Part of a 5¼-inch floppy disk is illustrated.

Information is recorded on the floppy disk in concentric circles, called *tracks.* The tracks are organizational regions of the disk, not grooves in the surface. Usually, there are at least thirty-five tracks. Tracks are divided into units called *sectors.* Typically, one sector can contain 256 *characters* of data.

The disk surface is organized by "hard" sectors or by "soft" sectors. When the hard sector approach is used, an index hole indicates the beginning of each sector. By sensing the index holes as the disk rotates, the disk drive circuits control arrangement of information on the track. In the soft sector method, the location of each sector is marked by a specially recorded track segment.

Depending on the number of tracks and sectors, the disk size, and whether or not the disk is single-sided or double-sided, a range of ninety thousand to over one million characters can be stored on a floppy disk.

An alternate to the floppy disk is the hard disk, consisting of a platter of metal coated with magnetic particles. The tracks of hard disks are condensed (more concentric circles per unit area); consequently, hard disks are capable of storing several million characters.

The major advantage of disk systems is that access to data is direct; that is, any portion of the disk can be read without going through all previous data. Access time to an item of data is measured in milliseconds.

Some computers utilize magnetic tape, similar to recording tapes, as an auxiliary storage medium. The disadvantage of tape storage is indirect access to data (the tape must be played from its beginning to the location of the desired data).

THE DISK SYSTEM.

INFORMATION FLOW ★
- PROCESSOR UNIT A
- STORAGE B
- RETRIEVAL C
- DISK SYSTEM D

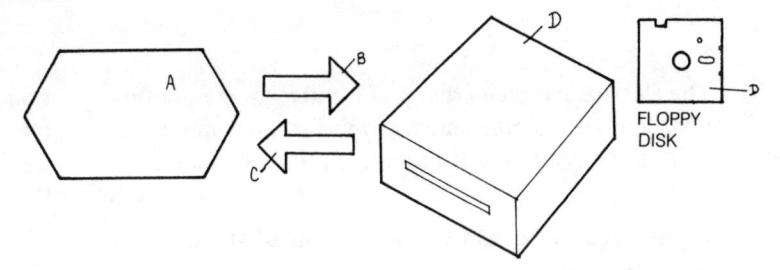

FLOPPY DISK STRUCTURE ★
- PLASTIC DISK E
- HUB HOLE F
- INDEX HOLES G
- INNER JACKET H
- ENVELOPE I

READ/WRITE WINDOW J
INDEX HOLE WINDOW K
HUB HOLE WINDOW L
WRITE PROTECT NOTCH M
ALIGNMENT SLOT N

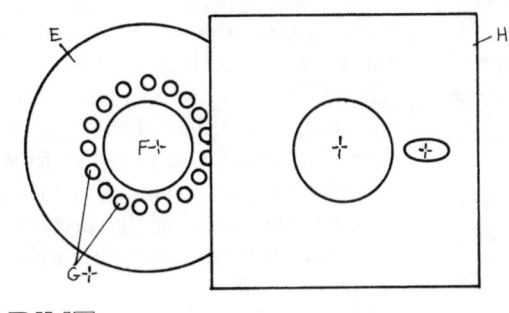

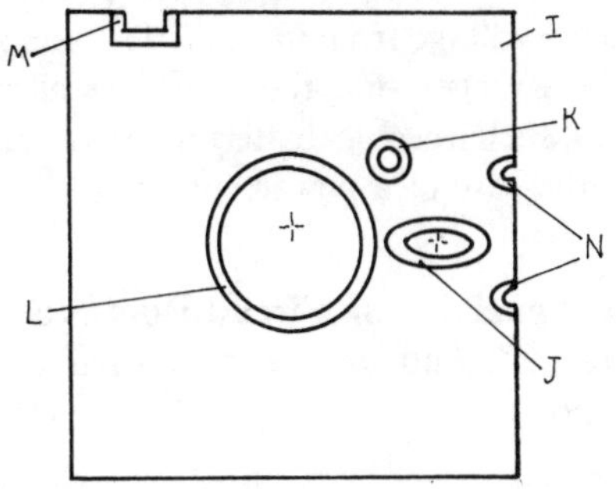

DISK DRIVE ★
- ENTRY SLOT O
- HUB P
- READ/WRITE HEAD Q

DISK ★
- TRACK R
- SECTOR S
- CHARACTER T

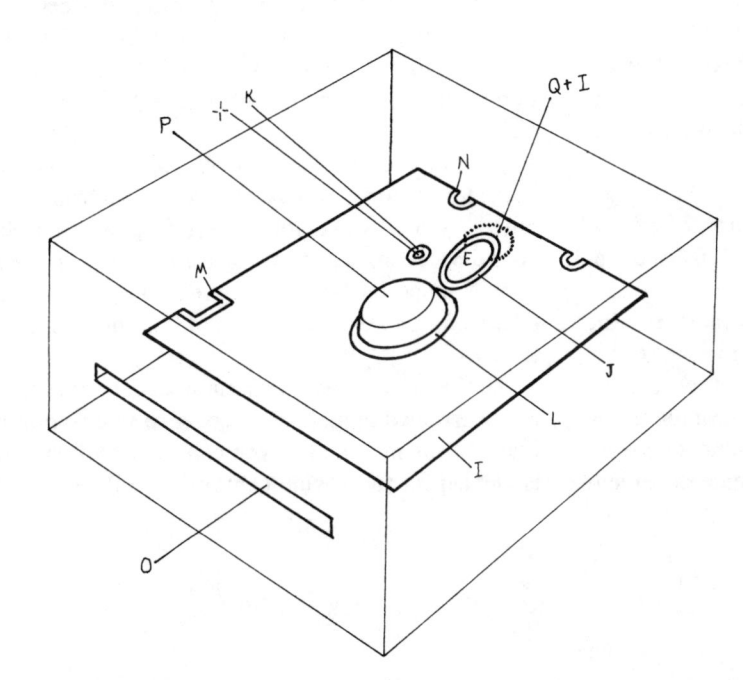

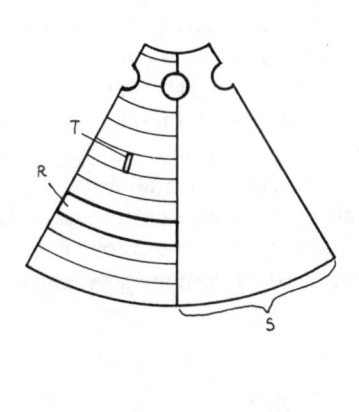

6
THE MAIN COMPUTER BOARD

The electronic circuits that perform the computing functions and provide the actual power for the computer are built into circuit boards inside the processor unit.

Color titles A, B, and C and the related structures in the top illustration.

The *parent computer board* contains many electronic circuits connected by traces (wires). *Sockets* in the parent board accommodate and connect other circuit boards. The electrical *power supply* used to run all the circuit boards must be of precise and constant voltage. There must be no interference from outside devices, such as a surge of electricity from turning an electrical motor on or off. There are auxiliary devices that can protect the circuit boards from overvoltage (surge). The power source takes the standard voltage from the electrical line and converts it into the voltages that the computer circuits require. Sometimes rechargeable batteries are used to provide power in the case of a power outage.

Color the Special Task Circuit Boards heading, titles D through F², and all the structures of the lower illustration.

Each of the special task circuit boards is constructed and wired to perform a specific function. All of these boards, when interconnected to the parent board, form the main computer board. The placement of each of the special task circuit boards varies with different computers. There are three general arrangements. In the first, boards are separate and plug into the parent board (illustrated). In the second arrangement, the boards are not separate but are sections of special circuits on the parent board itself. The third type is a combination of the first two board arrangements.

The central processing unit (CPU) forms the *central processing board*. The CPU is actually composed of several circuits encased on one or more microchips (see Appendix Plate 3 for microchip structure). The two fundamental divisions of the central processor unit are the *arithmetic and logic unit (ALU)* and the *control unit (CU)*. These circuits perform all arithmetic calculations, make all logical decisions, control access to the computer by input and output devices, provide the instructions to store and retrieve data from memory, and coordinate the execution of a program. See Plate 7 for the structure of a one-microchip CPU.

The *memory board* contains those circuits used to store the programs currently being executed as well as the data required or created by their execution. This type of memory is called main memory. (Recall that auxiliary or mass memory devices were discussed in Plate 5. These auxiliary devices are used to store programs, data, or segments of both that are not immediately required by the CPU or that simply cannot be accommodated by the main memory.)

Although main memory may look like one unit, it actually consists of two types of circuits, RAM and ROM. *Random access memory* or *RAM* (pronounced "ram") can be either read or written; that is, information can be taken from or stored in it. The user's program, when entered and executed, is kept in RAM. RAM loses the stored information when the power is removed. Information stored in *read only memory* or *ROM* (pronounced "rhom") circuits can only be read; no data can be written into it after insertion of the first program. Usually programs and data to be stored in ROM are entered by the manufacturer; for example, the computer's program responsible for scanning the keyboard is stored in ROM. ROM retains the stored information independent of external power.

The *input/output board* contains the circuits that send coded information to the input/output devices. The coding is the result of instructions received from the CPU. For example, the coding for positioning characters on the video display is the responsibility of these circuits. The special signals to the auxiliary storage devices to retrieve information pass through this circuit board for interpretation. The interpretation may result, for example, in positioning the read/write head over a particular track of a disk.

The input/output board may also control communications; for example, it may receive signals from other computers by modem (Plate 11), send signals to special-purpose devices, such as those operating lights in your home, control a special type of output device, such as a plotter (Plate 35), or execute any one of a number of other functions.

All the circuit boards communicate with each other in predetermined sequences and over special communication lines. In the next plates, you can see how this interaction is carried on to provide computing abilities.

THE MAIN COMPUTER BOARD.

PARENT COMPUTER BOARD A
SOCKETS (SLOTS) B
POWER SUPPLY C

SPECIAL TASK CIRCUIT BOARDS ★
  CENTRAL PROCESSING BOARD D
    ALU D1
    CU D2
  MEMORY BOARD E
    RAM E1
    ROM E2
  INPUT/OUTPUT BOARD F
    AUXILIARY STORAGE F1
    COMMUNICATIONS F2

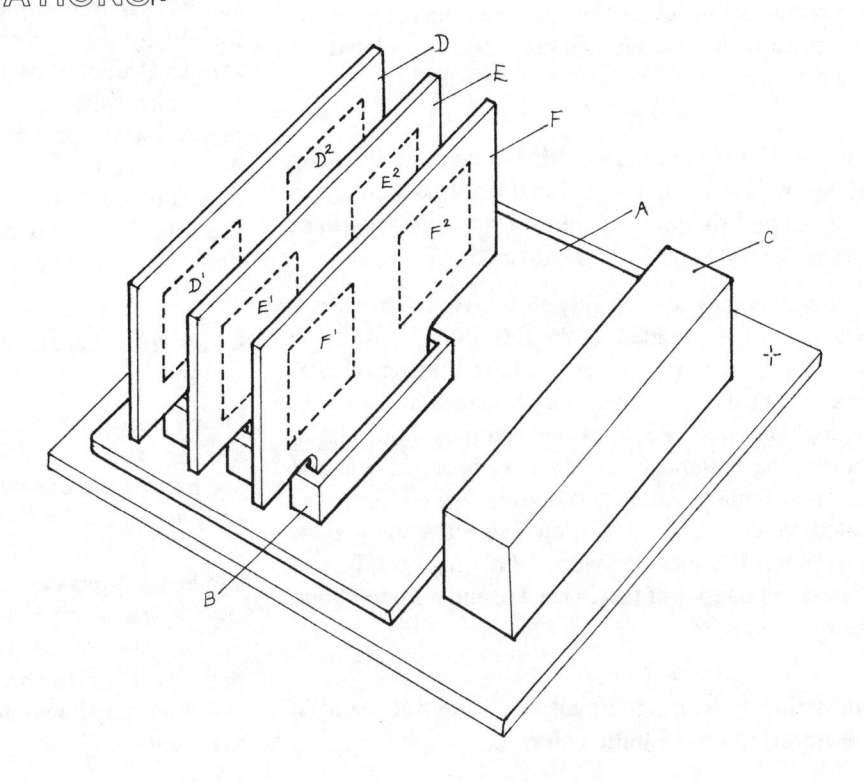

7 PARTS OF A CENTRAL PROCESSING UNIT

The most important component of the computer is the central processing unit (CPU). This unit performs the calculations and processing of data according to the instructions given in the program. The CPU is usually implemented on a single microchip (see Appendix Plate 3).

Color the Microchip Package heading, titles A, B, and C, and the related structures of the drawing at the top of the plate. Use a light color for A.

When you look at any of the circuit boards inside a processor unit (see Plate 6), you see many small rectangular boxes mounted into a complex network of wires. Each of the hard plastic or ceramic boxes contains a microchip, no bigger than a fingernail. Usually, the largest box is the central processor. The *CPU microchip's* circuits are connected to the other microchips and computer components by tiny wires attached to *pins* that extend outside the box. The pins emerge from the case in two parallel rows. Hence, the term *dual in-line pins (DIP)* is used to refer to the package containing the microchip. Most CPU DIPs have at least sixteen pins.

The parts of the CPU microchip are circuits at several levels which cannot be completely visualized without special optical devices. In the diagram of the CPU microchip illustrated in the lower part of the plate, the components are represented by discrete units to enhance understanding of function.

Color the CPU heading and titles D through E^2 using light colors. With color A, color the actual size of the microchip and the part labeled A on the enlargement diagram. Color structures D through E^2.

The *connector pads* serve as tie points between the microchip wires to the outside and the DIP pins.

During the execution of a program, arithmetic calculations and logical comparisons are performed by the *arithmetic and logic unit* (ALU) as the data passes through it. Typically, the arithmetic operations include addition and subtraction (multiplication and division are performed as repeated addition and subtraction, respectively). Typical logic comparisons include logical AND, logical OR, and various combinations of these (see Appendix Plates 4 and 5 for logic blocks).

Color titles F through F^3 and H^1 and the related representations with light colors.

The *control unit* (CU) has several functions. The major function is *sequencing* operations so that all the parts of the computer can work together to perform a task. Operations include the *fetching* and *decoding* of successive instructions of a program stored in main memory. Sequencing these operations insures that a particular instruction, result, or data item is used in the proper order.

Fetching an instruction or data value involves reading that item from a portion of main memory. Decoding consists of identifying the instruction to be performed and locating the data in memory (RAM or ROM) to be used by this instruction, if required. The CU makes use of a particular memory location, the *program counter* (PC). The program counter is a special part of main memory, usually found on the CPU microchip itself (as shown), that keeps track of the location, in RAM, of the next program instruction. You can think of its function as a bookmark that keeps track of where you are to begin reading after putting down your book.

Color title G and the related structure.

The *clock unit* generates timing pulses. These timing pulses are the electronic equivalent of the ticks of a metronome used by a musician to keep correct tempo. The timing pulses are measured in microseconds (1/1,000,000 second). In the computer system, the operations performed by the various system components may have to wait until another part of the CPU microchip performs its task. The timing pulses serve as signals to each unit to perform a certain function. For example, the ALU must wait for the CU to fetch data from memory. The ALU may wait, say four ticks, before performing addition on the data that it expects the CU to have provided at that time.

Color titles H, H^2, and H^3 and the related representations.

Other important units of the CPU microchip are two *memory areas*. These *RAM* and *ROM* areas of the CPU are part of the computer's main memory but are physically separated from the other main memory microchips on the circuit boards. The CPU memory areas store data and instructions that are being used by the ALU, CU, and clock units at a particular phase in program execution. Certain parts of the RAM sections of the CPU are called registers. In the next plate you will see how the registers and other CPU components actually execute a particular instruction.

PARTS OF A CENTRAL PROCESSING UNIT.

PARTS OF A CENTRAL
PROCESSING UNIT
CN 8

MICROCHIP PACKAGE.★
  CPU MICROCHIP_A
  DIP_B
  PINS_C

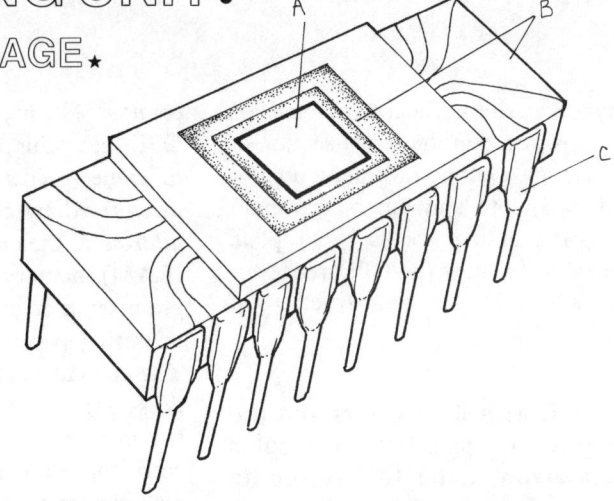

CPU.★
  CONNECTOR PADS_D
  ARITHMETIC LOGIC UNIT_E
    ARITHMETIC_{E1}
    LOGIC_{E2}
  CONTROL UNIT_F
    SEQUENCING_{F1}
    FETCHING_{F2}
    DECODING_{F3}
    CU MEMORY/PROGRAM COUNTER_{H1}
  CLOCK UNIT_G
  MEMORY_{H()}
    CPU RAM_{H2}
    CPU ROM_{H3}

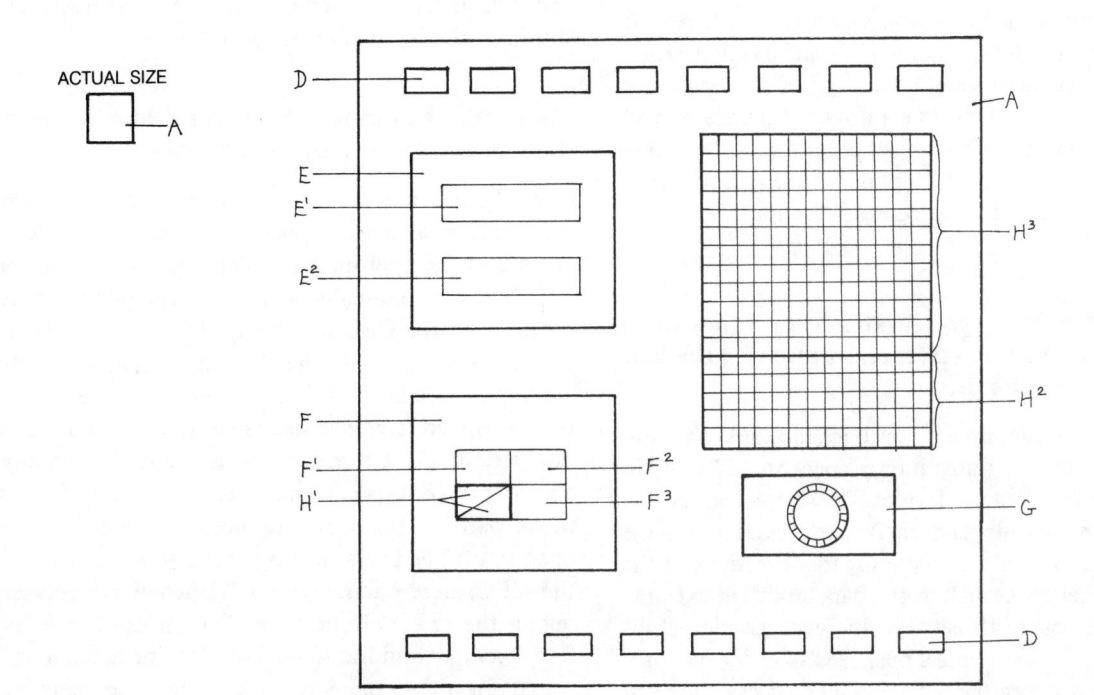

ACTUAL SIZE

8
INFORMATION FLOW IN THE CENTRAL PROCESSING UNIT

When a program is typed at the keyboard or retrieved from auxiliary storage, it is stored in the RAM section of the computer's main memory. Getting information (program instructions and data) into and out of the main memory for processing is an exacting process. In this plate you will see, in simplified form, how the CPU retrieves, processes, and stores data by following the instructions in your program.

Color titles A through E with light colors and the related representations at the upper left. Then color title F and the related arrow. Color title G and its structure at upper center. Color the Object Program heading, titles B[1] through E[1], and the related object code binary equivalent in RAM only.

The program that you type at the keyboard is the *source program*. It is usually written in a programming language, such as BASIC. However, the CPU cannot process a program written in this kind of language. Before processing the source program, the CPU executes another program, either an interpreter program or a compiler program (Plate 10 explains translation with these two programs). Either program *translates* the source program into machine code (translation). The resulting machine code (language) program is called the *object program*. It takes the form of a series of binary numbers (0s and 1s) that represent both the operations and data required by the source program instruction. One line of source program may correspond to many lines of object program. In this plate, the single instruction to add 5 plus 7 and assign the sum to the variable A is translated into the machine codes shown in *RAM*.

Color title H and its representation gray. Color titles I, J, and K and the related representations at the left. Use a light color for K.

A bus is a set of communication lines (circuits) that are grouped by function. Buses interconnect the CPU main memory and input/output devices. The address bus begins at the CPU microchip and carries addresses (numbers corresponding to memory locations) to all sections of the computer. Other buses include the data bus, used to transmit data back and forth between the various microchips of the system, and the control bus, used to carry synchronizing signals between the CPU and all devices connected to the bus.

When the object code program has been written to memory, a signal is sent from the *operating system* (discussed in Plate 9) to the CPU to begin processing the program. When the first instruction is stored in RAM, it must simultaneously be correlated with the *program counter*. The program counter, a portion of RAM on the CPU microchip, is automatically set to a starting number or value (predetermined by the manufacturer) which is interpreted by the operating system as the number or *address* of the object code of the first instruction in main (RAM) memory. As each address is processed, the program counter automatically increments and directs the operating system to locate the next object code in RAM. The current contents of the program counter (here, address 35) are sent out on the *address bus* to RAM where the memory location is selected. A special read circuit reads the contents (here, 00101011) of the selected memory address (35).

Color titles J[1] and L and the related representations on the right side of RAM. Also color the operation code on the bus the same color used for E[1] in RAM. Use a light color for L.

The contents of the selected address, usually a value stored in one byte or eight binary numbers, are sent along the *data bus* to the *instruction register*, a portion of RAM on the CPU microchip. In this example, the selected address is the *operation code* (00101011) for the source program "add" instruction. In effect, then, the add instruction is stored in the instruction register.

Color titles M through N and the related representations in the lower part of the plate.

Once the instruction is stored in the instruction register, it is further decoded by means of a *programmable logic array* and the appropriate signals are sent by the *control unit*. The programmable logic array is a portion of ROM memory on the CPU microchip. It is used to encode or decode logic signals in the form of comparisons between the object code instruction and a predetermined manufacturer-supplied reference set. The result is execution of the instruction. The control unit is a circuit for sending out control pulses at specific time intervals to activate or deactivate parts of the CPU. If the instruction involves an operation to be performed by the *arithmetic logic unit* of the CPU, here adding 5 and 7, then it is necessary to obtain the required operands. The operands are fetched from memory and transferred in the same manner as illustrated for the add instruction. When the required operands are fetched from memory, the arithmetic logic unit can perform the required operation (find the sum, 00001100, of 00000101 and 00000111; or 12 = 5 + 7). More complicated instructions require many more fetching, decoding, and execution steps until the desired computation is complete.

INFORMATION FLOW IN THE CENTRAL PROCESSING UNIT.

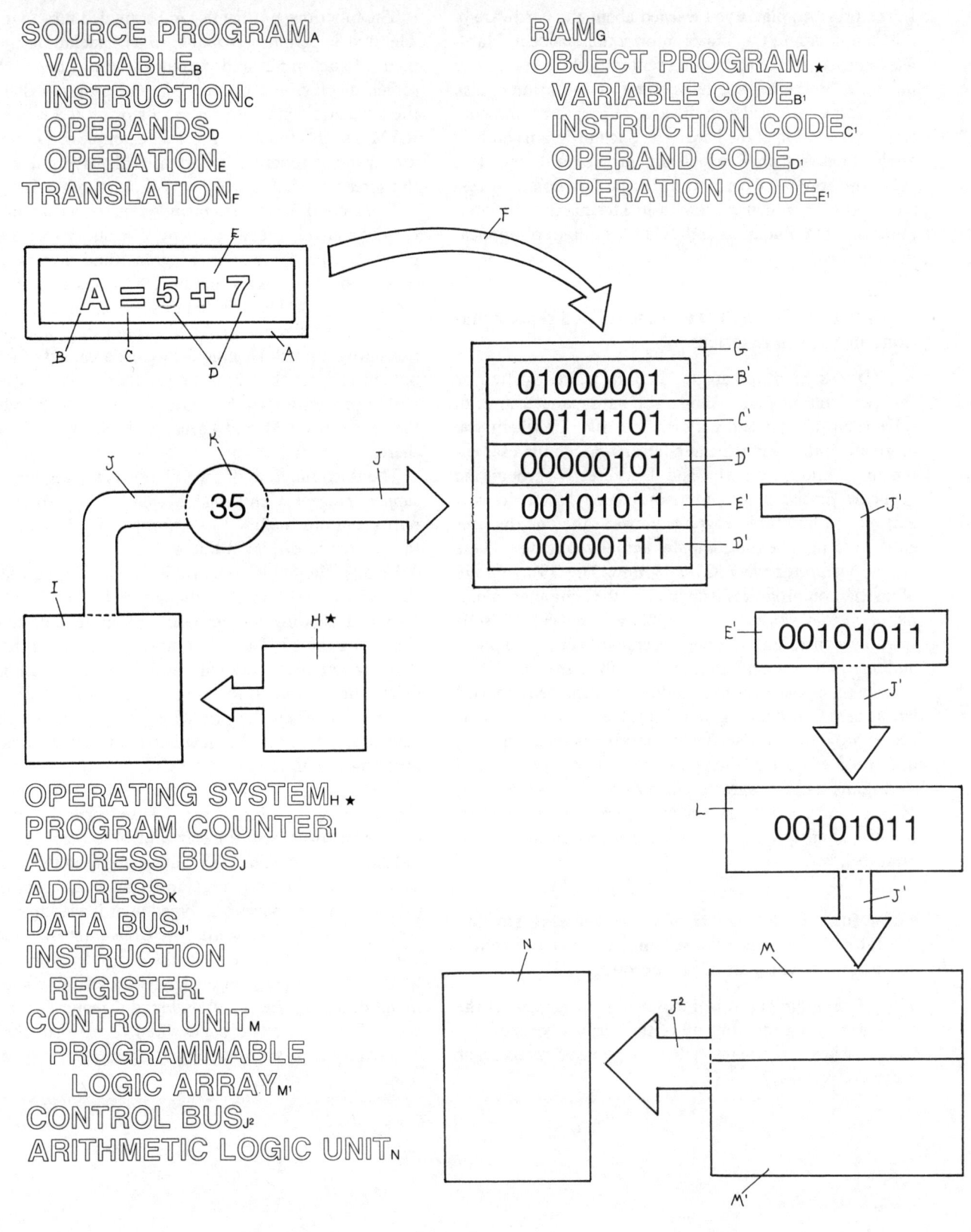

SOURCE PROGRAM A
  VARIABLE B
  INSTRUCTION C
  OPERANDS D
  OPERATION E
TRANSLATION F

RAM G
  OBJECT PROGRAM ★
  VARIABLE CODE B'
  INSTRUCTION CODE C'
  OPERAND CODE D'
  OPERATION CODE E'

OPERATING SYSTEM H ★
PROGRAM COUNTER I
ADDRESS BUS J
ADDRESS K
DATA BUS J'
INSTRUCTION REGISTER L
CONTROL UNIT M
  PROGRAMMABLE LOGIC ARRAY M'
CONTROL BUS J²
ARITHMETIC LOGIC UNIT N

9
THE OPERATING SYSTEM

In the previous plates you learned about the hardware of the computer and the flow of information inside it. Hardware consists of the computing center itself (the processor unit) and its peripheral units, such as the printer, disk drive, and video display. Software are programs that control the operation of the hardware. Such programs include applications software, which are programs designed to make the computer perform a specific function, and systems software, which are responsible for making the computer operate. Plates 36 and 37 are examples of applications software.

Color titles A through D and the related representations in the top diagram.

Applications programs are sets of instructions written by the user (you) or designed by a software manufacturer to solve the problems and perform the tasks for which you originally purchased the computer. Although the user enters applications programs and data directly through the keyboard or disk drive into main memory, there are several unseen layers of programs between the one the user enters and the one the computer actually executes. These are the *operating system (OS) programs*. The OS is a family of instruction programs (supplied by the computer manufacturer) that control and support all applications software by controlling the computer hardware. *Compilers* and *interpreters* are programs that perform the translation of your set of instructions into those that can be processed by the central processing unit. Once the compiler or interpreter program is chosen by the user (or manufacturer) it is considered part of the operating system. *Systems software* consists of programs and processing routines that activate and control the computer *hardware*. It includes the operating system functions expanded on in the diagram below.

Color titles C through H of the lower diagram and the related representations. Color in gray the representations at the end of the arrows.

The OS program controls the overall management of the computer by coordinating all of the various types of system software. It is usually called a supervisor, monitor, or executive routine.

The functions of the OS can be divided into four areas. The first is *peripherals management,* including management of such input and output devices as the keyboard, screen display, and printer. The OS program that scans the keyboard for a keypress and stores the key's code in RAM is such a function. Another example of a peripherals management function is correctly displaying a letter on the screen so that it will not overlap another letter.

The second function is *memory management,* in which the OS controls the assignment of memory to the source program (the application program) and any associated data, and the object program (the translated program; recall Plate 8). The OS memory management programs determine how space in RAM is budgeted. The applications program will be assigned to one area, data for it will be sent into another, and the results that come from the CPU's processing will be sent to a third. The OS allocates the space in RAM and keeps track of where things are there.

The third function of the OS directs the reading of any *support programs* and their placement in memory. Support programs include those that provide instructions to the printer to display a line of text.

Finally, the OS is responsible for scheduling the CPU to perform tasks in a particular order (*CPU management*), depending on the user's program requirements. Managing the CPU's time is most important. If the computer system is to work efficiently, the CPU must be kept busy. The OS might, for example, direct the CPU to use the interval when the printer is printing the result of a calculation to start the next series of calculations, thus avoiding idle time for the CPU.

It is a straightforward process to set the operating system programs to begin. When the user turns the computer on, the hardware will transfer control to the first location in ROM memory. The OS program begins at this location. The fact that the program is in ROM means that the OS programs do not have to be typed in or loaded from auxiliary storage. In other words, the OS is immediately available on power up. Otherwise, the computer would need a hardware set to perform the keyboard scanning and command decoding. Early computers did require such hardware. They had to be hand wired to perform the most elementary task, such as reading a particular switch position.

THE OPERATING SYSTEM.

USER A
APPLICATION SOFTWARE B
OPERATING SYSTEM C()
   COMPILER C1
   INTERPRETER C2
   SYSTEMS SOFTWARE C3
HARDWARE D

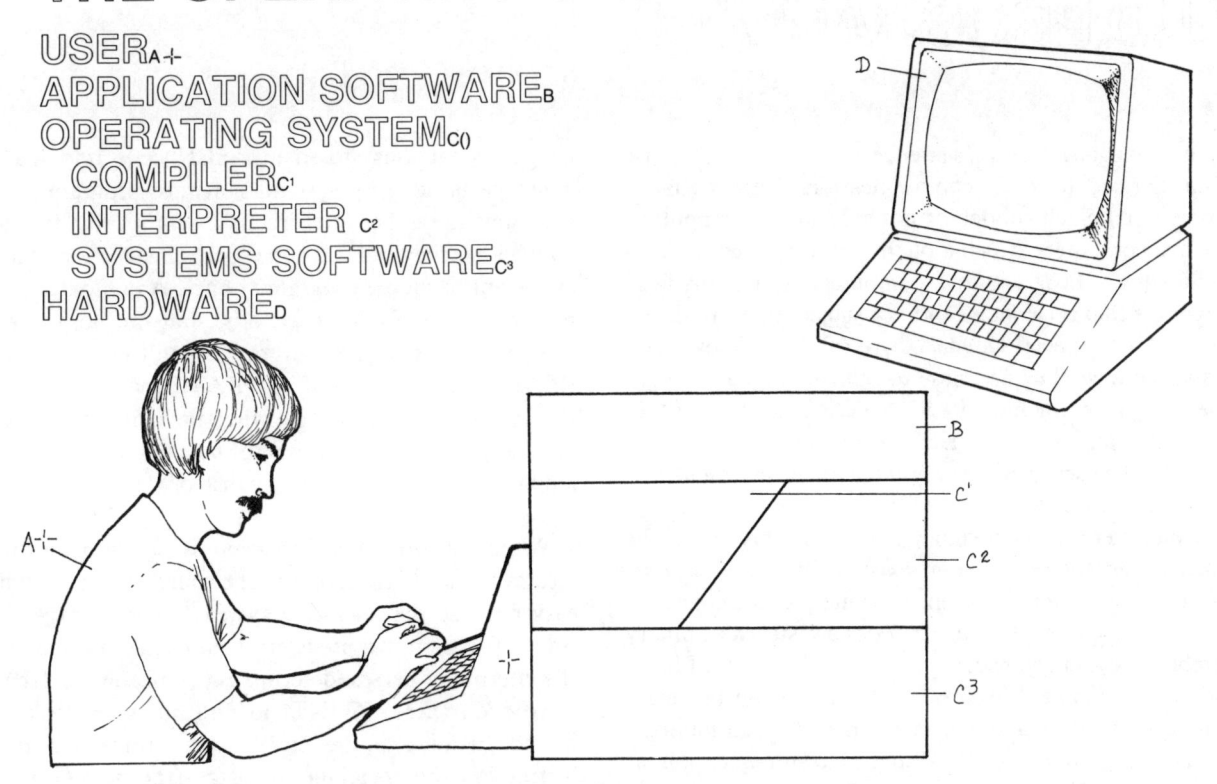

OPERATING SYSTEM/ROM MICROCHIP C
   PERIPHERALS MANAGEMENT E
   MEMORY MANAGEMENT F
   SUPPORT PROGRAM USAGE G
   CPU MANAGEMENT H

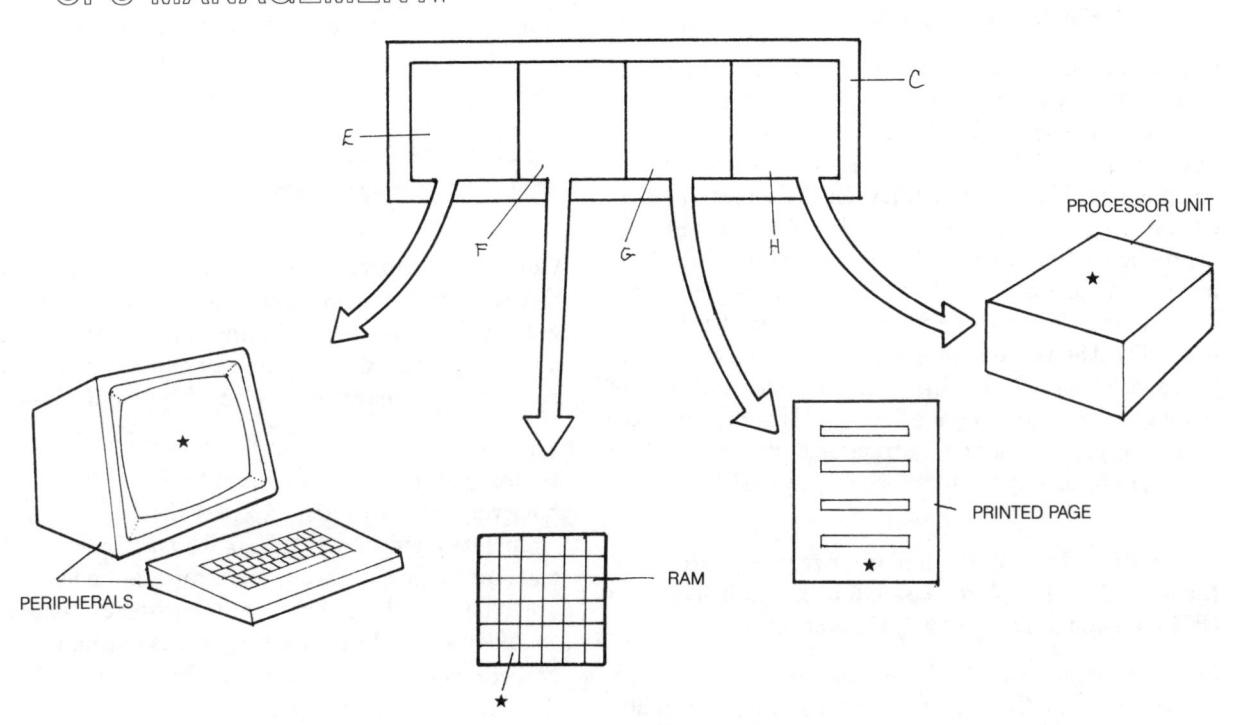

PROCESSOR UNIT
PRINTED PAGE
RAM
PERIPHERALS

10 THE OPERATING SYSTEM AND PROGRAMMING

Human languages have sentence complexities that are often clarified by body communications (such as facial expressions). Such subtlety is not available to computers, nor are computers capable of interpreting intent. Communicating a program to a computer requires artificial languages that are concise and not subject to misinterpretation. These special languages are called high-level languages because they are close to human language. High-level languages include BASIC, FORTRAN, COBOL, PL/1, Pascal, and more than 150 others.

Before the user's source program, written in a high-level language, is executed by the CPU (Plate 8), it is stored in the computer's main memory RAM. At this point, the untranslated source program exists in memory as a sequence of character codes, one code number per character typed. You will recall that the codes are stored as binary numbers (0s and 1s), usually in the ASCII system. Binary code (for example, 00100000, not shown) can be represented in literature and conversation as decimal numbers (here, 32 in source line C) to enhance communication, as is done here. (See Appendix Plate 2.)

Color the Source Program, Computer One, and Computer Two headings, titles A through G, and the related representations in the source line at upper center, and within RAM (G) in Computer One only. Use light colors for B through F. Note that C is not to be colored in the source line.

Certain key (reserved) words indicating predetermined operations may be stored as a single code number rather than as a sequence of ASCII codes representing each letter. For example, PRINT is a reserved word instructing the computer to display information on the screen. This requires a sequence of operations, keyed by the PRINT instruction. Often, the PRINT instruction is represented in memory as one code number (decimal equivalent, 186) rather than as five separate codes, one for each letter of the word. The ASCII codes for space (32), numeral 5 (53), plus (43) and numeral 7 (55) form the remainder of the *RAM storage* of the source program line. The high-level language source program must now be translated into the machine language object program for processing by the CPU.

Color titles H through K and their representations on the left side of the plate. Also color the 1st instruction (B) in the upper bus. Use a light color for J.

Machine language is the binary coding that is actually processed by the CPU. The conversion of high-level language instructions stored in ASCII code into machine language is done by systems software programs. These programs are either interpreters or compilers, depending on whether they translate one source instruction at a time or the entire source program at once. A computer system will make use of one or the other but not both at once.

The interpreter program may be built in as part of the ROM memory or loaded into RAM from auxiliary storage by the operating system when the computer is turned on. The latter method allows the user to change high-level language by simply changing a disk or tape in an auxiliary storage unit.

When the *interpreter program* is set into motion, it locates the *first instruction* of the source program. This is easy because the operating system began storage of the source program in a predetermined RAM location. Then, the interpreter parses (determines the meaning of) the first instruction (here, PRINT) to find out what task is required. In doing so, the interpreter has translated the first instruction into machine language (the *object code*). It then calls on another part of the operating system to execute the line's meaning. A subordinate processing routine is given control to do whatever operation is specified. Then, the *second source instruction* is located, and the process repeats until all source lines have been executed. Each source program instruction is translated into machine language and executed before the next instruction is translated and executed. If there are any errors in the instruction's syntax, they are brought to the user's attention immediately because the instruction will not execute. All during this processing, the operating system has made use of the CPU and associated computer components as needed for line interpretation and execution.

Color the source program instructions stored in RAM of a different computer at upper right. Then color titles L through M¹, and the rest of the diagram at right, representing the compiler program and related representations. Use a light color for M.

The *compiler program* can be part of ROM or stored in auxiliary storage as with the interpreter. The compiler, however, translates and executes the entire source program as one unit. As it does so, it translates each line into machine language, checks for errors, and compares it to other lines in the program for consistency. Because the compiler works the source program as one unit, the *object program* contains many *binary codes,* corresponding to all the lines of the source program.

THE OS AND PROGRAMMING.

SOURCE PROGRAM ★
  SOURCE LINE_A
  1ST INSTRUCTION_B
  2ND INSTRUCTION_C
3RD INSTRUCTION_D
4TH INSTRUCTION_E
5TH INSTRUCTION_F
RAM_G

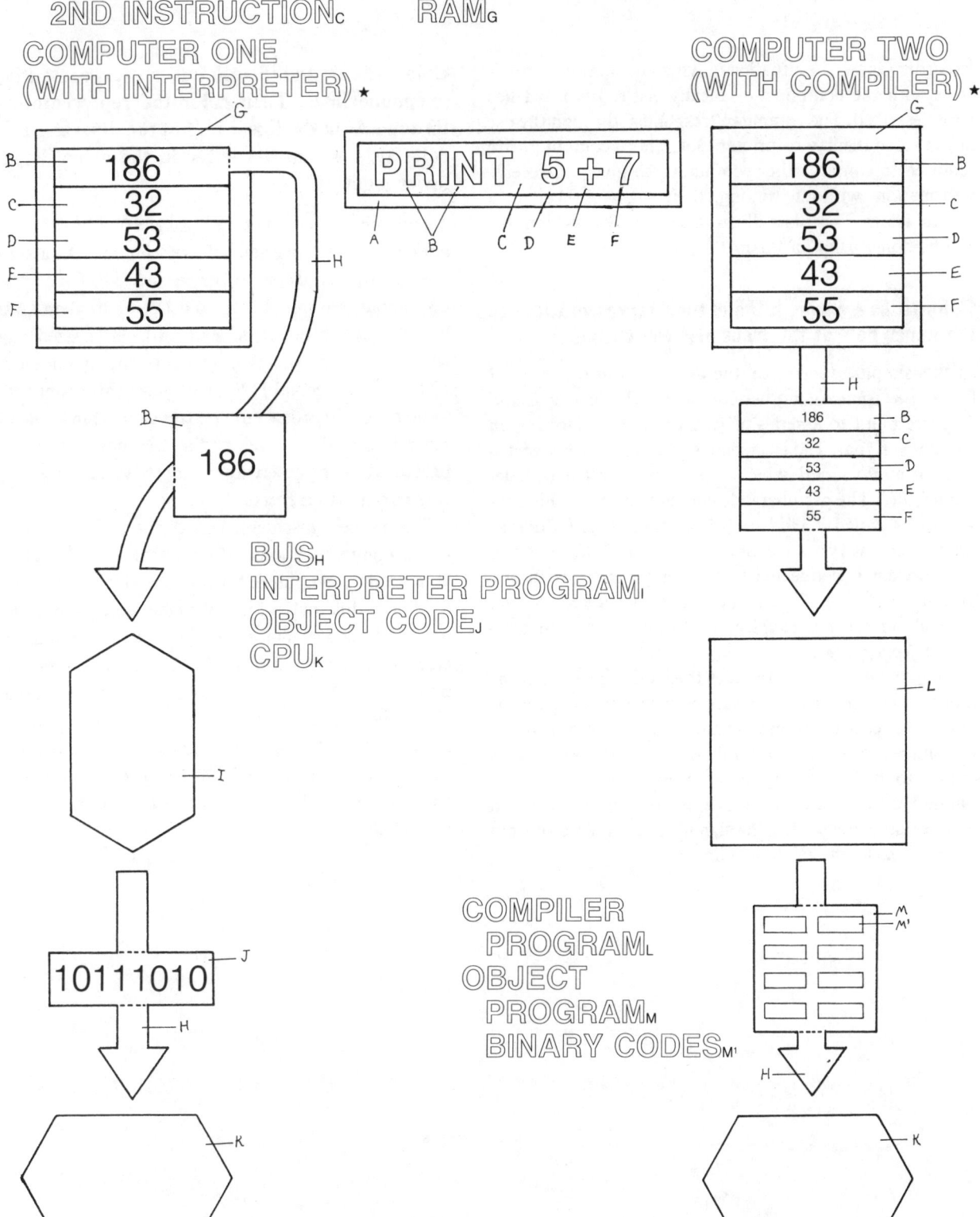

COMPUTER ONE
(WITH INTERPRETER) ★

COMPUTER TWO
(WITH COMPILER) ★

BUS_H
INTERPRETER PROGRAM_I
OBJECT CODE_J
CPU_K

COMPILER PROGRAM_L
OBJECT PROGRAM_M
BINARY CODES_M'

11 COMPUTERS TALKING TO COMPUTERS

In earlier plates, the situation in which the user communicates with the computer by means of the keyboard has been described. The computer "responds" through the use of the video display or printer. Sometimes computers are required to contact other computers, to give and receive information without routing their signals through a human being. This plate illustrates one way in which this can be done, using ordinary telephone lines.

Color titles A through D and their representations in the upper half of the transmission scheme.

In this simplified example, the user types in the *letter H* for *transmission* to another computer. The *binary 0s and 1s* correspond to a series of voltage changes forming an electronic signal. The electronic signal must be converted into an *audio signal* which can be transmitted by telephone lines. The peripheral device that performs this conversion is called a *modem* (MOdulator; DEModulator; modulate: to vary a wave for transmission of information). The modem is connected to the computer, as with any peripheral device. The audio signal generated is sent through an *acoustic coupler* and "spoken" into an ordinary *telephone receiver*.

The acoustic coupler receives the audio signal from the modem and provides a mechanical means of securing the telephone receiver so that the audio signal can be directly transmitted to it. It is not unlike a radio speaker with a cradle to hold the telephone receiver. Sometimes the phone handset and acoustic coupler are eliminated and a connection made so that the signal can pass directly from the modem to the telephone line.

Color title D^1 and the related arrow representing the telephone lines. Then color the representations D through A^1 in the lower half of the diagram. Finally, color title A^3 and its letter in the video display at lower right.

Telephone lines conduct the signals from the sender's telephone to the telephone at the destination. At a standard rate of 110 bits (0s or 1s) per second (110 baud) it would take about two minutes to transmit by modem all of the words that are double-spaced on a letter-sized page. A faster rate of transmission by a different type of modem is 1200 bits per second (1200 baud). At this faster rate, the same page of words would be transmitted in about eleven seconds. Signals received by the destination telephone are processed by the receiving computer system. Receiving is carried out as the reverse of sending.

The process just described is not unlike human telephone communications. When you talk on the telephone, your brain (computer) transmits a signal to your vocal cords (modulator), which produce words (an audio signal). The handset's receiver converts your sounds into an electronic signal in a form that can be sent over the telephone lines. At the other end the process is reversed. The electronic signal is converted into audio waves which are directed into the ear (demodulator) of the listener and converted into nerve impulses (binary codes) that are interpreted by the brain and "appear" as conscious awareness of the message.

COMPUTERS TALKING TO COMPUTERS.

LETTER TRANSMITTED A
BINARY REPRESENTATION A¹
MODEM B
AUDIO SIGNAL A²
ACOUSTIC COUPLER C
TELEPHONE D/LINES D¹
LETTER RECEIVED A³

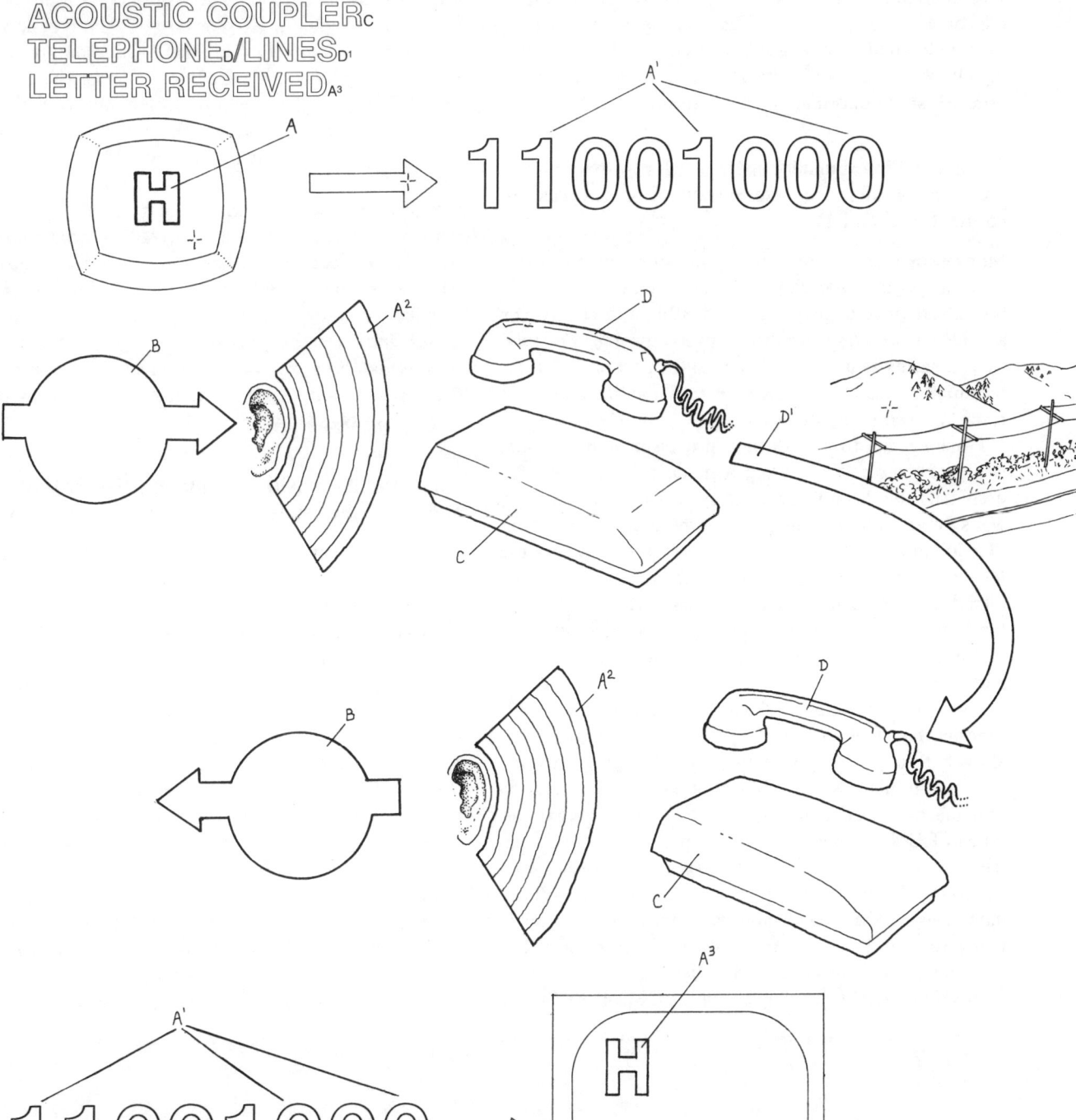

12 COMMUNICATIONS: TIMESHARING AND NETWORKING

In schools and in the business world, an individual often shares a computer with another user. In this plate you will learn how two or more people can make use of one or several computers at the same time. There are two methods of accomplishing this. Timesharing allows two or more individuals to have access to a single CPU. Networking allows two or more computers to be interconnected in order to share information or programs.

Color the Timesharing heading, titles A through G[1], and their related representations. Use contrasting colors for C and D.

Many people can share a single *processor unit* in a timesharing system. All each person needs is a *terminal* (keyboard and video display only) and either a direct wire or a *modem connection* to a distant processor unit. For each user, it seems as if the processor unit is part of his or her terminal. Actually, the processor unit may be in another room or even many miles away.

Hooking up to the distant processor unit is quite straightforward. When using a modem connection, the user dials the distant computer system's phone number, waits for an audible signal (in effect the computer is saying "Hello" and "Who is this on the line?"), then places the telephone handset in the acoustic coupler, and waits for an introductory message on the video display. Then the user types his or her name (or sometimes an account number) and is cleared to use the distant processor unit as his or her own.

Suppose that you and a friend are using a system with timesharing. The CPU and operating system programs allow both of you to type in *programs*. The programs will be stored in main RAM memory of the distant processor unit, starting at different locations. Now suppose that you type in RUN (a signal to start your program) before your friend does. The processor unit begins to execute your program. However, sometimes the CPU has to wait for data from RAM. Meanwhile, your friend's program is ready to run. The operating system will start the CPU working on that program during the wait for data from your program. This juggling act in the CPU is performed by the control unit against a background of timing pulses from the clock unit.

This is one aspect of timesharing, but there are others. Suppose that execution of your program is finished and your *printer* is being used for output. The processor unit is now free to complete your friend's program. A printer's speed is very slow compared with that of the processor unit. What holds the processor unit output while the printer works it off is the *buffer*. The buffer is a set of RAM chips that act, under an auxiliary CPU, as a "holding tank." The data from the distant processor unit is transferred to this "holding tank" (either in your printer or in your terminal) until the printer is ready to print a line. The buffer's CPU can sense when a line has been printed and when the printer is ready to receive more data. When your friend's program is finished, the output is fed into the buffer until it can be printed out. By this time a third person may be using the processor unit. The only major drawback to timesharing is that if the processor breaks down, all usage stops.

Color the Networking heading, titles H through K, and all of the representations of the lower diagram.

In the networking system, each user has a complete computer system that does whatever processing is required. A user can communicate with another user by connecting to the *communication processor* (by means of a modem or direct wire). The communication processor is like a telephone switchboard. After the usual "sign on" procedure (similar to the timesharing sign on) the user enters the name of the person or computer that he or she wishes to contact. The communication processor directs the hookup through the telephone or direct wire lines. Of course, if the requested computer is not connected or turned on (on line), then an appropriate message will be returned to the user. A user can specify that he or she wants to use a *large computer system* that is connected to the network, for example to gain access to a library of information stored in that computer system's memory. The larger computer searches its memory for a particular item and transmits it to the user's computer for further processing.

COMMUNICATIONS.

12
COMMUNICATIONS:
TIMESHARING AND NETWORKING
CN 11

TIMESHARING ★
   TERMINAL ONE_A
   TERMINAL TWO_A1
   MODEM/CONNECTION_B
   PROGRAM ONE_C
   PROGRAM TWO_D
   PROCESSOR UNIT_E

BUFFER ONE_F
BUFFER TWO_F1
PRINTER ONE_G
PRINTER TWO_G1

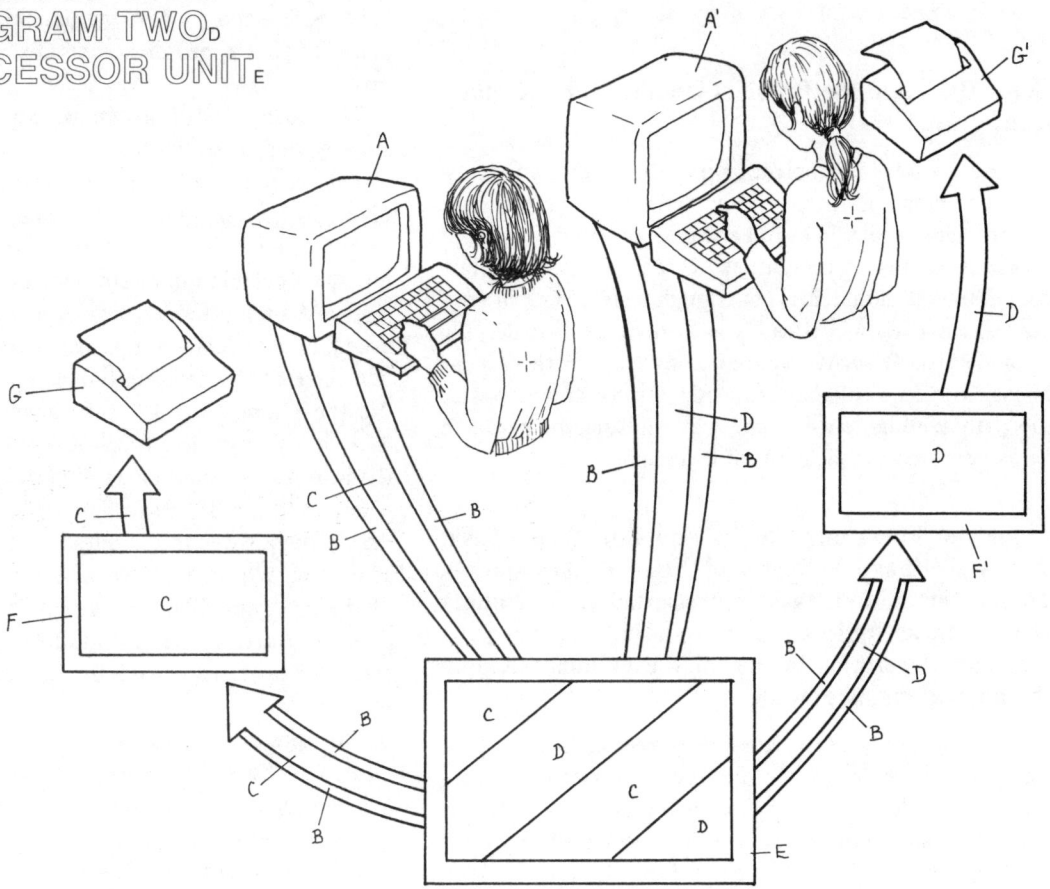

NETWORKING ★
   COMPUTER SYSTEM ONE_H
   COMPUTER SYSTEM TWO_I
   COMMUNICATION PROCESSOR_J
   LARGE COMPUTER PROCESSOR UNIT_K

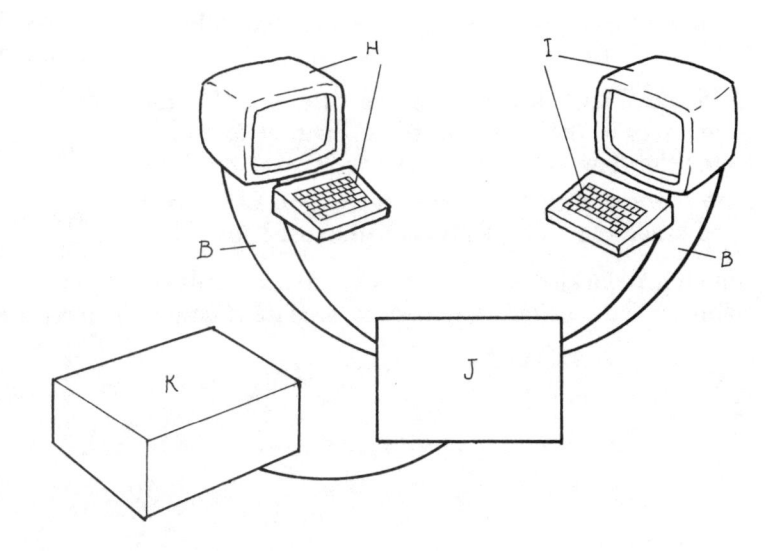

13 FLOWCHARTING

When you wish to give a computer a problem to solve or a task to perform, it is necessary to do some careful thinking beforehand. The computer must be given a set of logical and explicit instructions. The majority of computers cannot understand nuances of the spoken language nor make inferences from a set of sentences.

Color the State the Problem heading and the statement gray.

In order to solve a problem or perform a task, you must clearly understand the program. The first step is to define the problem or task in as full a way as possible. Leave out no requirements or limitations. When you must guide a person to your house, it is not enough to say, "Get in your car and drive here." Instead, you have to list, in order, the right, left, or U-turns required to follow a path to your house. Or, you would have to send your visitor a map with the path highlighted in some way. Stating the problem helps you create a clear set of directions.

Color the Flowchart Shapes and Functions, Task, and Algorithm headings and titles B through D¹. Then color the four tasks represented in the column at far left, as well as the circle adjacent to each of the four algorithms in the middle column, reading the algorithms as you do.

A common human task, answering the telephone, illustrates the principles involved in creating concise instructions to complete a problem. After the problem or task is defined by stating the problem, one makes a list, in everyday language, of all the steps needed to solve the problem. The series of steps which are followed to produce a desired result is called an algorithm (pronounced *al*-go-rith-im).

Color the Flowchart heading and title A. Color the perimeters of the shapes in the column at far right. Color the flow paths (arrows) gray except the NO path marked with a no color sign (–|–). Leave NO uncolored, and color YES the color used for C¹.

A flowchart is a kind of map that shows the operations the computer must perform in order to produce a desired result. In addition, the flowchart shows the order (flow) in which the operations are to be performed. The box shapes represent the type of computer operation that is to be performed. You write in whatever steps apply to your particular problem. These boxes are standard symbols used in flowcharts. Just by glancing at a flowchart, you can see what types of actions are planned and in what order.

The flattened *oval* box shows where to *start* or *end* the step-by-step instructions.

The *rectangular* box means that an *operation* is to take place. In the diagram the first operation is to listen for a ringing phone. In real computer programs the operation may be a calculation or storage of a particular data item.

The *diamond-shaped* box is used for a question to be asked, or a *decision*/comparison to be made. For example, you see that the decision box could contain the question, "Is the phone ringing?" The answers may be "yes" or "no" in this case. Each possible answer is placed outside the box at a different point or vertex of the diamond. The program flow will pass to the next series of boxes, depending on the answer to the question. In this program, if the answer was "no," the arrow would go directly to the end of the program. If the answer is "yes," as shown in the plate, the arrow goes to another rectangular box. This time, the operation inside the box could be "Pick up the receiver."

The *keystone* or trapezoid-shaped box indicates information to be supplied to or provided by the computer *(input/output)*. In the illustration, this box could tell the human to output (say) "hello."

These are the major flowchart shapes.

More complicated tasks may require a series of flowcharts. Each chart is written for a portion of the task, and all are finally assembled into a large and complete diagram.

The primary aim of the flowchart is to outline an algorithm for performing a task. In general, a flowchart will not be different for each type of computer. It is possible to create one for many different computers.

How each flowchart step is actually translated into the language of the computer will be discussed in the following plates.

FLOWCHARTING.
STATE THE PROBLEM.

PICK UP THE PHONE AND SAY "HELLO" WHEN IT RINGS.

FLOWCHART SHAPES AND FUNCTIONS.
OVAL_A: START/END_A
RECTANGLE_B: OPERATION_{B1/B2}
DIAMOND_C: DECISION_{C1}
KEYSTONE_D: INPUT/OUTPUT_{D1}

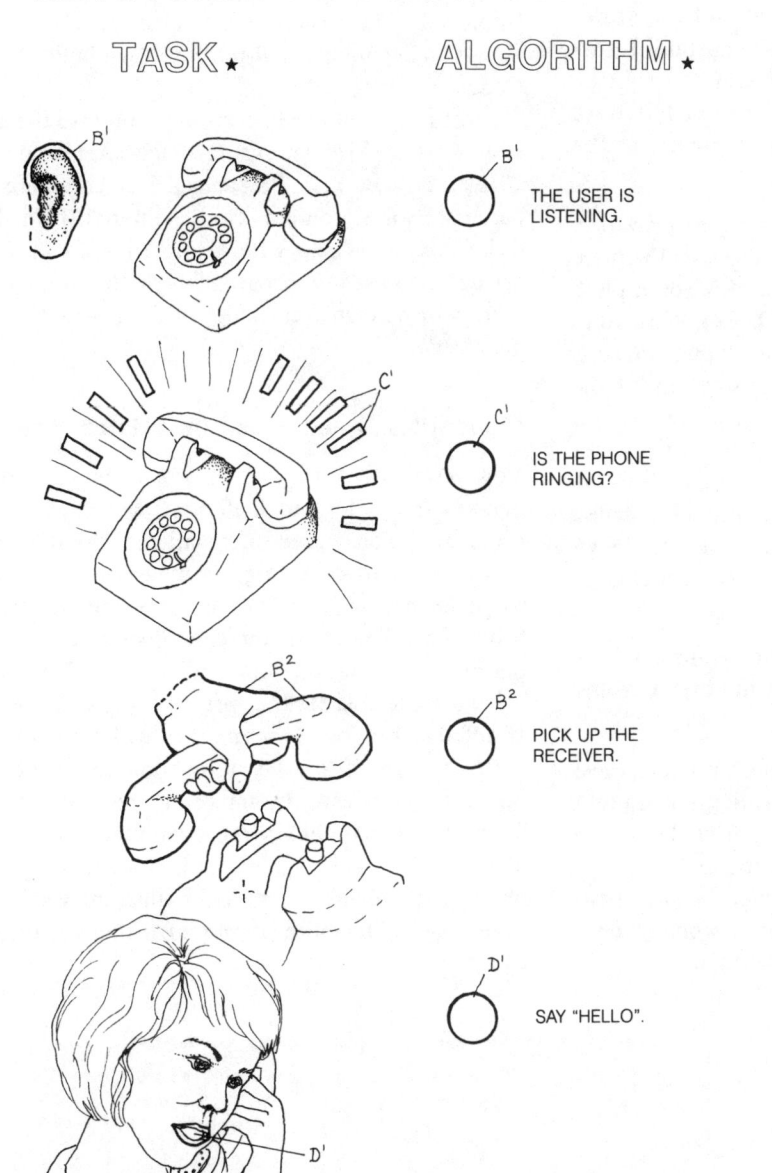

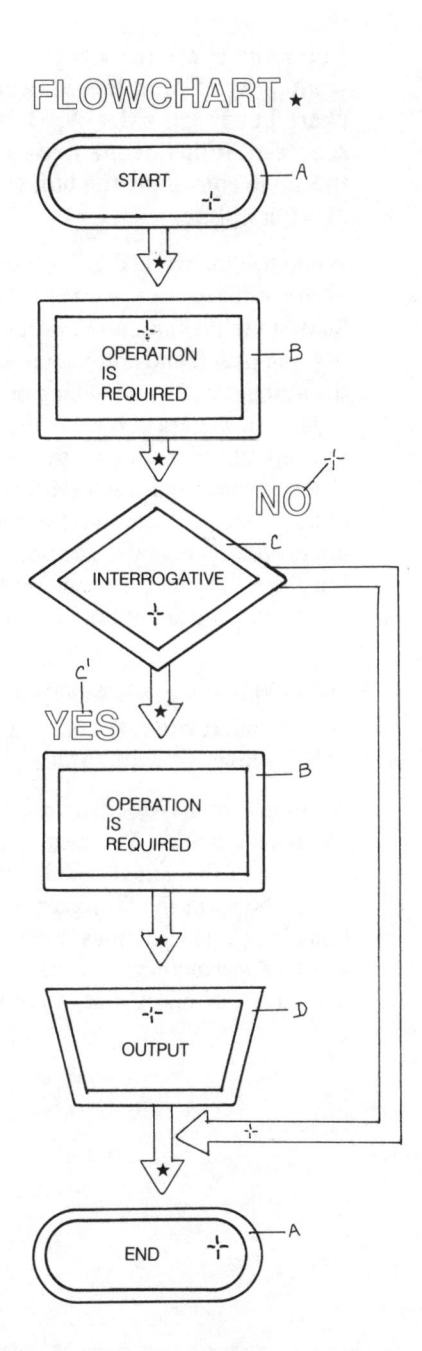

TASK

ALGORITHM

THE USER IS LISTENING.

IS THE PHONE RINGING?

PICK UP THE RECEIVER.

SAY "HELLO".

FLOWCHART

START

OPERATION IS REQUIRED

INTERROGATIVE — NO

YES

OPERATION IS REQUIRED

OUTPUT

END

14 CREATING A PROGRAM

A computer program is a series of instructions that are written in the language of the computer. The computer will carry out the instructions in order to perform a task or to solve a problem. We have already seen a good first step in computer program design—preparing a flowchart. In order to learn how to present the instructions to the computer, we will first take a look at another flowchart.

Color the State the Problem heading and the statement gray. Color the Flowchart Boxes and Flowchart headings, titles A, B, and C, and the related representations of the flowchart column at left. Use the same colors for the box symbols as you did in the previous plate.

While reading the text below, supply the selling price (say $4.98) at the correct point alongside the chart on the price line), do the computation of the tax (say 8%) on a piece of scrap paper, and add your answer ($0.3984, or $0.40 to the nearest cent) to the selling price. Display the total cost.

This flowchart shows a step-by-step solution to the problem of computing a cost (selling price plus sales tax) of a particular item. A keyboard input was required (get selling price), calculations were performed (find 8% of the price, add the result to the price), and a solution reached (display total cost). The answer (output) would be shown on the video display (and optionally on the printer).

Color the Program heading and the column of instructions at the right gray. Each of the instructions will be discussed in future plates.

Although you have been able to follow the flowchart, most computers cannot. The next step in creating a computer program is the actual coding (translation) of the design steps, shown in the flowchart, into a particular programming language. You must input (type in at the keyboard) a list of instructions that represent the flowchart steps. Such a list of instructions may look like this:

```
10   REM COMPUTATION OF COST
20   INPUT A
30   B = A * .08
40   C = A + B
50   PRINT "THE COST IS"; C
60   END
```

The exact syntax (vocabulary and punctuation) depend on the particular computer and programming language employed. The program language used here is called BASIC (Beginner's All-purpose Symbolic Instruction Code).

Most users enter their own program into the computer system via the keyboard using a high-level language (Plate 10), such as BASIC. Prepackaged or commercially prepared software programs can be entered (loaded) from a disk (or tape). Whether the keyboard or an auxiliary storage device is used for program entry, the computer system then does its own translating of the instructions into binary code.

Color titles D and E and the related structures.

Your computer program is stored in the computer's main memory along with all other data (the selling price, for example) or needed information (a tax rate table, perhaps). One part of a program may instruct another part to perform a task and store the result in memory for future use. The computer can process information and perform computations for varying tasks. For you, it will calculate the cost (selling price plus tax) for some item. If different programs are input, it can compute the orbit path of a space shuttle or operate the lights in your home. It is this capacity for being *programmable* for different tasks that makes the computer system versatile. The toaster, on the other hand, is a single purpose machine. It performs one task (or different versions of the same task). Therefore, it is said to be a *dedicated machine*.

CREATING A PROGRAM.

STATE THE PROBLEM.

INPUT A PRICE FROM THE KEYBOARD, COMPUTE A TAX, AND DISPLAY THE TOTAL PRICE.

FLOWCHART BOXES.

START/END_A   INPUT/OUTPUT_B   OPERATION_C

FLOWCHART.

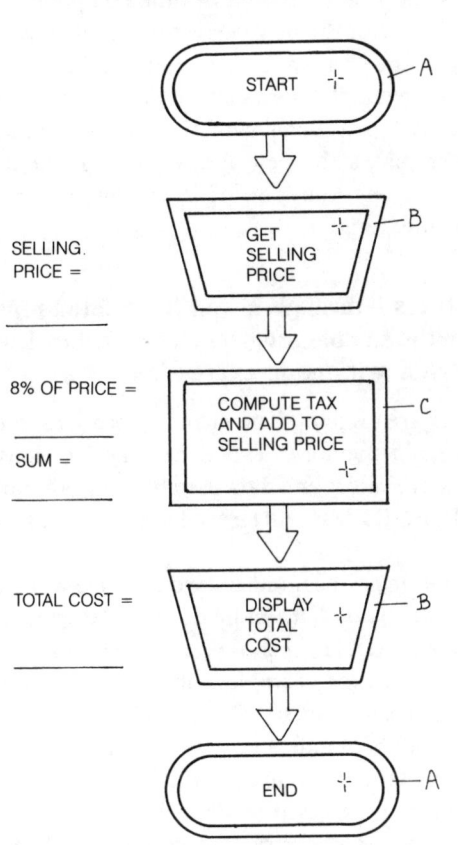

- START — A
- GET SELLING PRICE — B
- COMPUTE TAX AND ADD TO SELLING PRICE — C
- DISPLAY TOTAL COST — B
- END — A

SELLING PRICE = ___

8% OF PRICE = ___

SUM = ___

TOTAL COST = ___

PROGRAM.

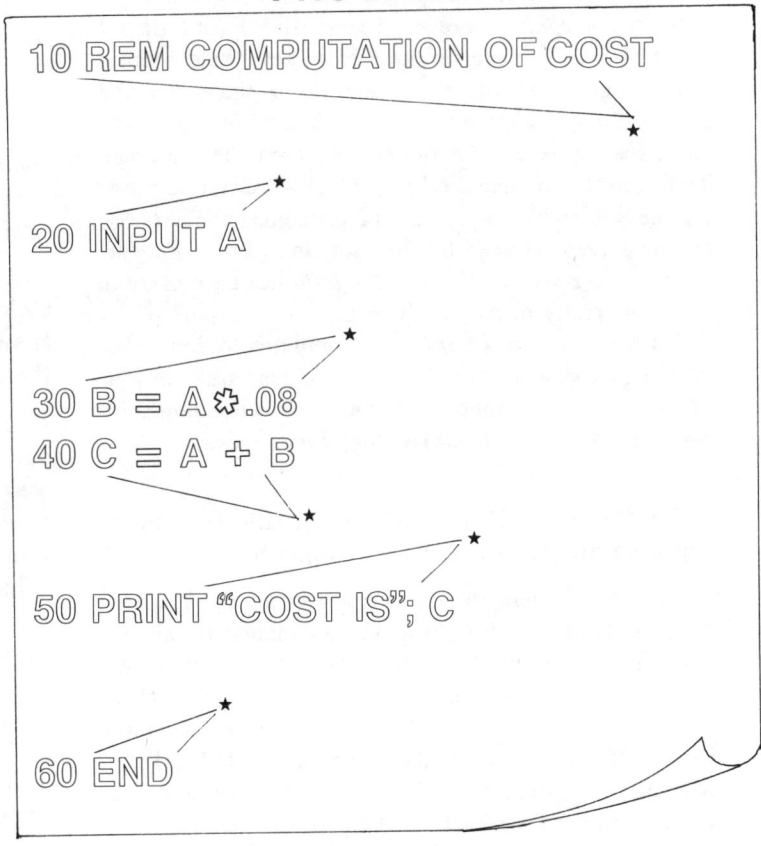

```
10 REM COMPUTATION OF COST
20 INPUT A
30 B = A * .08
40 C = A + B
50 PRINT "COST IS"; C
60 END
```

PROGRAMMABLE MACHINE_D

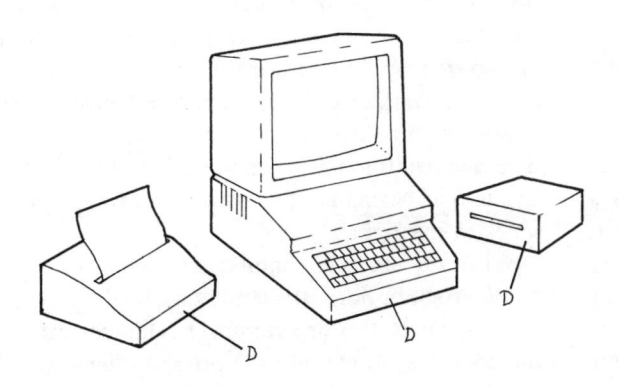

DEDICATED MACHINE_E

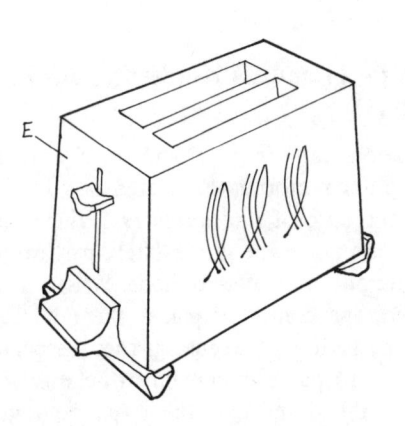

15 OUTLINE OF A BASIC PROGRAM

You are now ready to look at the characteristics of a program written in the BASIC computer language.

Color the System Commands heading, titles A through F, and their related representations in the diagram at the top.

System commands, used as adjuncts to BASIC commands, perform the housekeeping needed to prepare the computer to receive your program. When the user types in the *system command reserved word* HOME (or CLEAR or CLS) and then presses the Return key, the computer immediately clears the display and places the *cursor* and the *language prompt* symbol at the home position of the video display screen (at the upper left in the example). Typing in the command NEW (or SCRATCH) and pressing the Return key causes the cursor to go to the next line on the screen. Unseen by the user, the part of internal memory reserved for the new program has been cleared. It is now ready to receive the program.

System commands vary from computer to computer. Although the words used for a particular task may be different, each computer has equivalent commands for performing system (housekeeping) commands.

Color the Basic Program heading, title G, and its representations in the sample program.

A word that is part of the special vocabulary of system commands and BASIC program commands is called a *reserved* (key) *word*. When a reserved word is used, the computer performs a predetermined operation (such as clearing the screen for HOME). BASIC reserved words include REM, used for making comments (REMarks) in a BASIC program; INPUT, used to have the computer receive information; PRINT, used to have the computer output information; and END, sometimes used to end a BASIC program. These commands are discussed in future plates.

Color title H and its representations in the sample program.

As each command is typed and the Return key pressed, the computer performs the related task immediately, except in the case of *line numbers*. When the steps in a program are not to be immediately performed, the commands are put into deferred mode. When such commands are typed, the computer places them in main memory without performing (executing) their associated task.

In order to put a command in deferred mode, a line number is typed and then the actual command is typed.

Of course, the user presses the Return key to signal the computer that the program line is completed. Line numbers must be non-negative integers (0, 1, 2, . . .). The computer stores and executes (when instructed) the deferred program lines in the order of increasing line number. Notice that it is common practice to number the lines as multiples of 10. If the user makes a mistake or wishes to change a program line in deferred mode, the line number is retyped, followed by the corrected program line. Pressing the Return key causes the computer to replace the old line with the new correct one (not shown). Additionally, if the user wants to place a line between lines 60 and 70, for example, then a line number between these two (say 65) is typed along with the added command. The computer places the new line in the correct numerical sequence. Using multiples of 10 for line numbers facilitates such editing.

Color titles I through L and the related representations in the sample program. Then, color title M and the related arithmetic expression.

Variables are used to name memory locations in the computer's main memory. These memory locations can be used to store values and data used by your program. In the example, ENGLISH will be used to store a student's grade value.

In addition to line numbers and reserved words, BASIC uses *special symbols* to indicate that the computer is to perform a particular operation, punctuate a line of output (";",":" or "," for example), or designate a variable as having a special value ("$" or "%" for example). The "=" symbol here indicates that an assignment of a value is to be made to a variable. Variables and the assignment command are discussed in Plate 17.

Arithmetic *operation symbols* are used when a calculation is to be performed. The standard order of operations is used by the computer to evaluate an *arithmetic expression*. Expressions inside parentheses are evaluated first. Exponentiation operations (raising a number to a power symbolized by "↑" before the exponent value) are performed next, then multiplication (symbolized by "∗") and division (symbolized by "/") operations, and finally, addition and subtraction (symbolized by "+" and "−"). Evaluation begins at the left of the expression and proceeds to the right.

When the user has completed the entry of the deferred mode program lines, the command RUN is typed in immediate mode (no line number). This command signals the computer to execute the program lines that the user has stored.

OUTLINE OF A BASIC PROGRAM.

SYSTEM COMMANDS ★
KEYBOARD A
SYSTEM COMMAND
  RESERVED WORD B
VIDEO DISPLAY C
  LANGUAGE PROMPT D
CURSOR POSITION
  AFTER "HOME" E
CURSOR POSITION
  AFTER "NEW" F

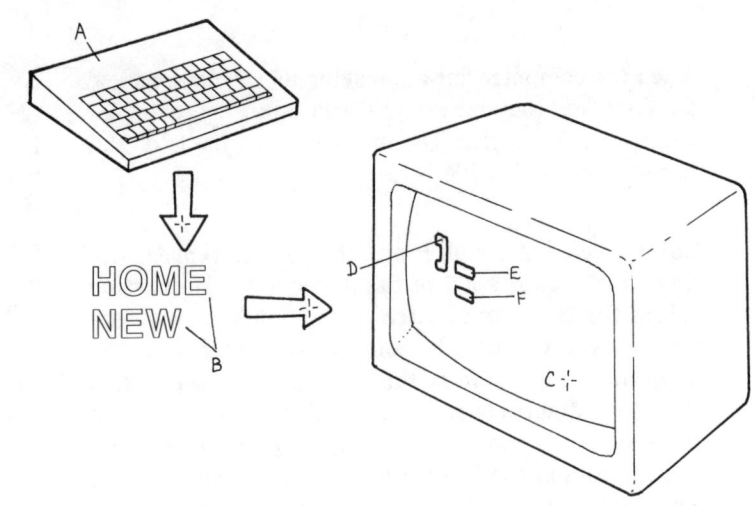

BASIC PROGRAM ★
BASIC COMMAND
  RESERVED WORD G
LINE NUMBER H
VARIABLE NAME I
SPECIAL SYMBOL J
OPERATION K
TEXT L
ARITHMETIC
  EXPRESSION M

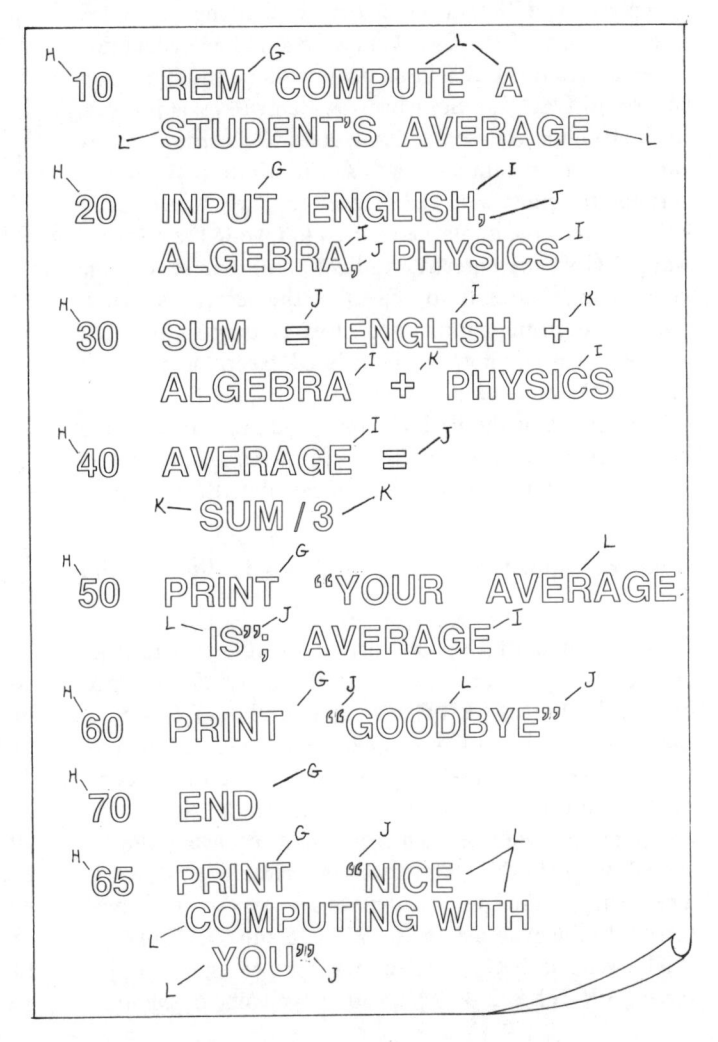

```
10 REM COMPUTE A STUDENT'S AVERAGE
20 INPUT ENGLISH, ALGEBRA, PHYSICS
30 SUM = ENGLISH + ALGEBRA + PHYSICS
40 AVERAGE = SUM / 3
50 PRINT "YOUR AVERAGE IS"; AVERAGE
60 PRINT "GOODBYE"
70 END
65 PRINT "NICE COMPUTING WITH YOU"
```

$19.5 = 11 + (5-3) * 3/4 + 2 \uparrow 3 - 1$

16
THE PRINT INSTRUCTION

When the computer finishes making its calculations and decisions, you want the results shown on the video display screen and/or printer. The reserved word used for this output command is PRINT.

Color titles A through E and the related representations in the diagram 1 at the upper left. Contrasting colors for B, C, and E are recommended. Note the screen itself is not to be colored. While working the diagram, read carefully the related text. In this and the other diagrams to be colored, start mentally at the keyboard, and color step by step as though you were typing in the instruction at the keyboard and it was appearing on the video display screen.

When you type PRINT on the *keyboard,* it appears on the screen as part of the BASIC instruction. The instruction in the diagram is typed in immediate mode (no line number; recall Plate 15). So, when the *Return key* is pressed, the instruction is executed immediately. The *display* may vanish for an instant and, in this example, only the words between the *quotation marks* reappear. The words or symbols (between the quotation marks) following the reserved word PRINT are entered into RAM and then sent to the video display circuits to appear in the screen as *output display.* Anything within quotes (except quotes), whether it makes sense or not, will be printed exactly as typed in the PRINT command.

The results of the PRINT command are shown in the lower screen: the word HELLO is printed and, on the next line, 5 + 6 is printed (no sum is calculated).

Color the upper right diagram 2 as you did diagram 1.

If you want a PRINT instruction executed so that an arithmetic expression is evaluated, the instruction is typed differently. In this PRINT instruction, PRINT 5 + 6, in the upper screen, the expressions are not enclosed by quotation marks. This makes quite a difference to the computer. Omitting the use of quotation marks signals the computer to evaluate each expression following the reserved word PRINT. The arithmetic circuits go to work. The results of the computation are displayed on the lower screen. In the example, the sum 11 of 5 and 6 is displayed.

The second PRINT instruction shown in the upper screen, PRINT 9/2 + 6 * 4, causes the value of the more complicated expression to be calculated and displayed (28.5, shown in the lower screen). Because the expression has been typed without quotation marks, it will also be handled as an arithmetic problem. Remember, the asterisk is the symbol for multiplication. Multiplication and division are calculated first (from left to right), then addition and subtraction (also working from left to right). Here is how the arithmetic looks when taken a step at a time (by the computer's arithmetic unit):

9/2 = 4.5
6 * 4 = 24
4.5 + 24 = 28.5

Color the lower left drawing 3 as you did before.

The PRINT instruction here has two parts. The first is an expression in quotes and the second is an arithmetic problem. The semicolon (;) is called a delimiter and separates the two items. The first item is an expression that is displayed exactly as written since it is enclosed in quotation marks. The second item is an arithmetic expression whose value is calculated by the computer and then displayed. Because the semicolon is used as a delimiter, the two items' display will appear right next to each other (see lower screen). See Plate 17 for more on delimiters.

Color the lower right diagram 4 as you did before.

In the previous three examples, the PRINT instruction was written in immediate mode. When the Return key was pressed, the instruction was immediately executed. Here the use of line numbers puts the instructions into deferred mode. The computer delays execution until the immediate command RUN is entered. Until then, the instructions are stored in main memory. As long as the program lines remain unchanged, you can type RUN as many times as you like. Each time, the computer will display HELLO FRIEND.

Because the primary display device is the video screen, all output is shown here. If output is to go to a printer, each computer system will have a separate scheme for doing so. Most require a command in addition to PRINT. For example, you may have to use the reserved word PR#1 or OPEN 1 at the point where you want output to go to the printer.

THE PRINT INSTRUCTION.

KEYBOARD A
INPUT DISPLAY B
QUOTATION MARKS C

RETURN KEY D
OUTPUT DISPLAY E

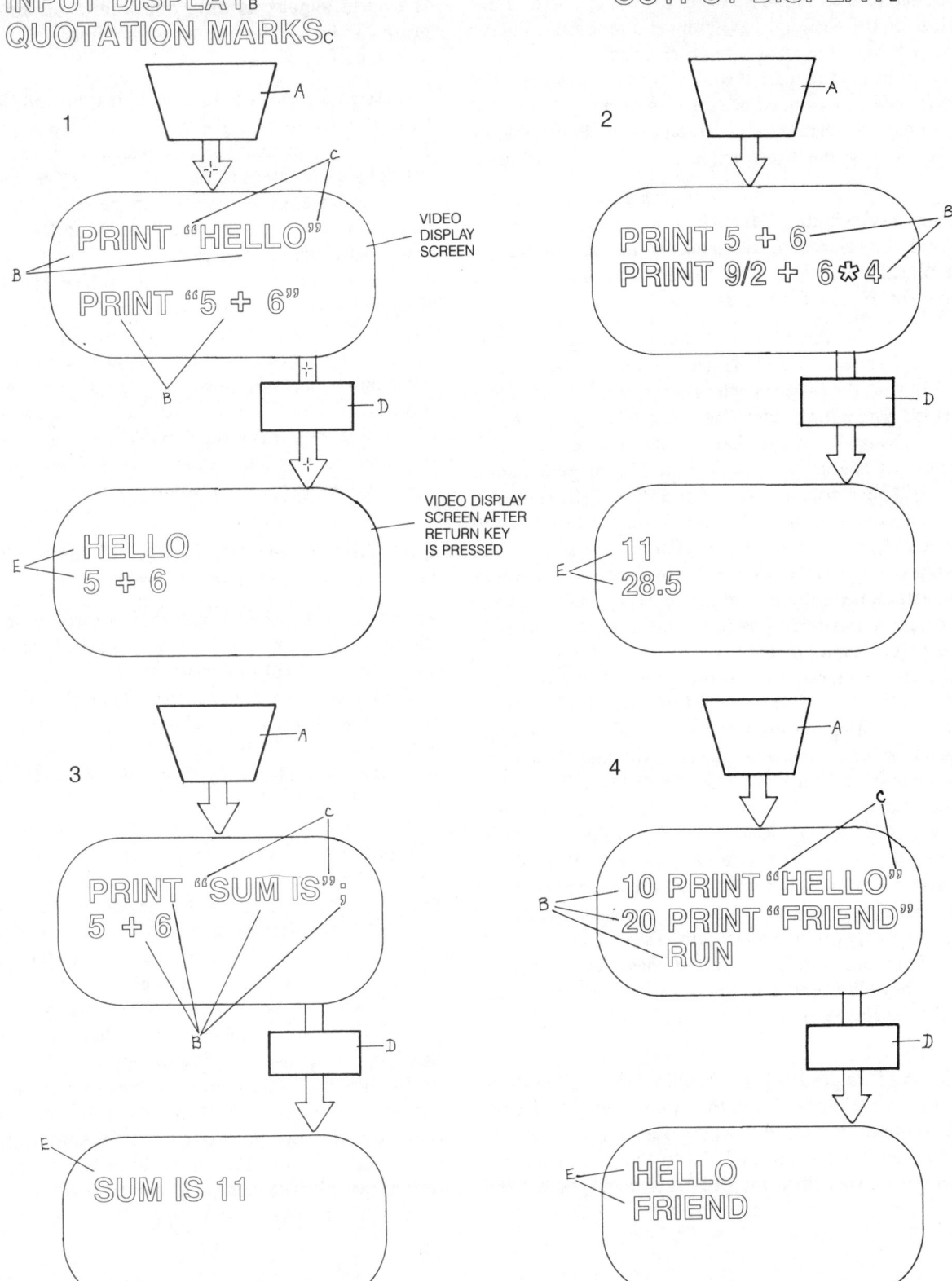

1

PRINT "HELLO"
PRINT "5 + 6"

VIDEO DISPLAY SCREEN

HELLO
5 + 6

VIDEO DISPLAY SCREEN AFTER RETURN KEY IS PRESSED

2

PRINT 5 + 6
PRINT 9/2 + 6✱4

11
28.5

3

PRINT "SUM IS"; 5 + 6

SUM IS 11

4

10 PRINT "HELLO"
20 PRINT "FRIEND"
RUN

HELLO
FRIEND

17 THE ASSIGNMENT INSTRUCTION

The PRINT instruction is used in BASIC to display a line of text or the answer to an arithmetic problem. Suppose that you want the answer to be retained in memory for later use by another part of your program. Perhaps several individuals' names must be stored in memory to be used by a program segment. This storage is made possible by using an assignment instruction.

Color the Assigning Values heading, titles A through C, and the related representations in the top part of the plate. You might want to use four shades of one color for B, B^1, B^2, and B^3.

A *variable* is a symbol to which a value is assigned. In the *keyboard* shown, A and B$ are the symbols and 5 and HELLO are the assigned values being typed. The value 5 is called a *numeric datum*. The value HELLO is called a *string datum*. A string datum value can contain any "string" of characters (letters, numerals, or punctuation marks). The instructions A = 5 and B$ = "HELLO" are *assignment instructions*. One does not have to know the address in memory where 5 or HELLO are stored. The operating system takes care of this by first storing them in a predetermined location and then creating a table of variable names and addresses (not shown). One need only refer to the names of the variables A or B$ in order to make use of the value assigned to them, as shown in the simplified representation of RAM *(simplified RAM table)*.

The operating system's method of allocating storage depends on what value is assigned to a variable. If the value is not numerical, but a string like "HELLO", the variable name must contain the suffix $ to indicate that a series of characters (a "string") is involved. If the value is numeric, it either has no suffix, as in the example A, or if its value is always an integer, % is used as a suffix. The variable names must begin with a letter of the alphabet, contain no reserved words, or other special symbols (such as "!", "+", "?", etc.). Some versions of BASIC have further restrictions. They allow only a letter, two letters, or a letter and number (exclusive of suffix) for variable names.

Color the Sample Program heading, lines 10 to 40 of the Sample Program, and the simplified RAM variable value table at middle right. Leave the arrows to RAM locations uncolored. Note that program line 30 requires two lines for illustrative purposes here.

It should appear as only one line in an actual program. This is true for program lines on following plates as well.

The assignment instruction is executed in a precise order. First, the side to the right of the equals sign is processed. The value of the expression is evaluated. If the value on the right is a constant (such as .08 or 1000, in lines 10 and 20), no calculation is required. If the right side contains an arithmetic expression, as in lines 30 and 40, the arithmetic logic unit is called on to perform the indicated calculation. In the example, the values of PRICE * RATE (1000 * .08) and PRICE + TAX (1000 + 80) are computed. Then, the computed value is assigned to the variable (TAX or PAY, respectively) that appears on the left side of the assignment instruction. In the case of RATE and PRICE in lines 10 and 20, the constant (.08 or 1000) is assigned to the variable name. The values are stored in memory and variable names placed in the variable value table by the operating system.

Color titles D and D^1, the PRINT instruction (line 50), and the video display screen.

Execution of the *PRINT instruction* causes the *display* of the values assigned to the listed variables. Line 50 causes 1000, 80, and 1080 to appear on the screen.

The programmer has control of the display of the values of particular variables. In addition to listing the variables whose values are to be shown, the delimiters separating the names indicate the type of spacing to be used. The portion of the operating system that sends signals to the video display or printer causes variable's values to be placed in predetermined columns on the screen. The values may be separated by ten or fifteen columns (character positions) automatically when the delimiter comma (,) is used between variable names (shown here; 1000, 80, and 1080 are each in their own column). If the delimiter semicolon (;) is used, then the spacing between values may be 0 (values are printed with no separation between) or 1 (one character space) between them (Plate 16). The actual number of columns' spacing depends on the particular operating system convention used by its creator.

Several dialects of BASIC have built-in reserved words that allow the user to specify exact column positions for each variable's value. The reserved words perform just like setting the tab positions on a typewriter.

THE ASSIGNMENT INSTRUCTION.

ASSIGNING VALUES ★
KEYBOARD_A
ASSIGNMENT INSTRUCTION_B
   VARIABLE_{B1}

NUMERIC DATUM_{B2}
STRING DATUM_{B3}
SIMPLIFIED RAM TABLE_C

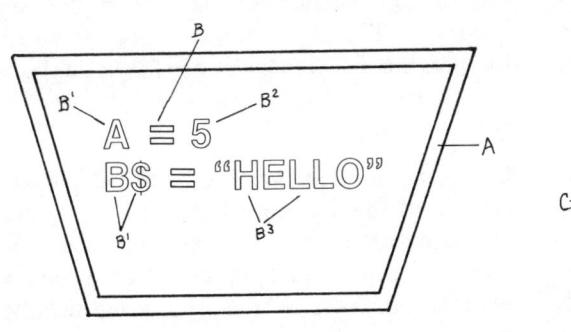

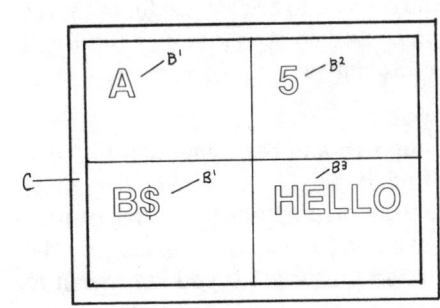

```
A = 5
B$ = "HELLO"
```

A	5
B$	HELLO

PRINT INSTRUCTION_D
   DISPLAY_{D1}

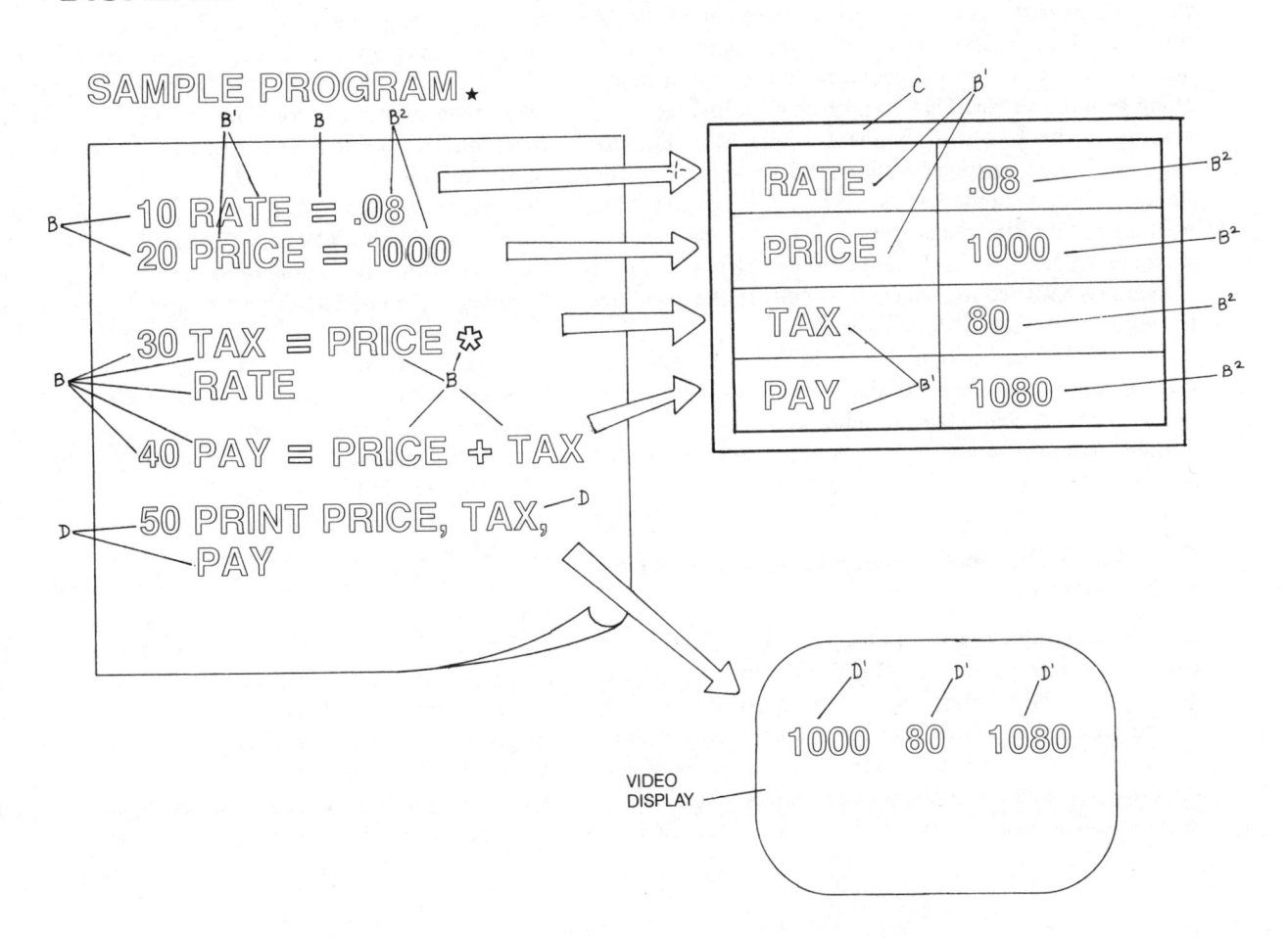

SAMPLE PROGRAM ★

```
10 RATE = .08
20 PRICE = 1000
30 TAX = PRICE * RATE
40 PAY = PRICE + TAX
50 PRINT PRICE, TAX, PAY
```

RATE	.08
PRICE	1000
TAX	80
PAY	1080

1000 80 1080

VIDEO DISPLAY

18
THE INPUT INSTRUCTION

In the last plate, the values of the variables were assigned by statements written as part of the program, A = 5 or B$ = "HELLO." In this plate, you will learn how values can be assigned to variables by the user during the execution of the program. If the tax and cost calculation program in the previous plate was going to be used for many items, several lines might have to be changed for each new item. Perhaps the tax rate would change as well as the cost of the item. Greater flexibility in the program is necessary.

Color titles A through D[1] and the upper sample program. You may find it helpful to retain the same color for an instruction throughout the series of program plates. For example, if you used green for the assignment instruction in Plate 17, you may wish to color it green here (C) and where it appears in the following plates. Color the display on the top video screen.

An *INPUT instruction* allows the user to enter a value of the listed *variable* while the program is executing. When the INPUT instruction is executed, the computer halts and displays a *prompt symbol,* usually a question mark, along with the cursor. This is a prompt to the user to enter a *value* at the *keyboard.* In the example, after line 10, INPUT X, is executed, a question mark (?) appears on the screen. The user inputs 3 at the keyboard. When the value is entered, it is displayed on the screen next to the question mark. When the Return (Enter or Endline) key is pressed, the value is assigned to the listed variable. In the example, the value 3 is assigned to the variable X.

The INPUT instruction allows the user's program to process more than one set of data. The X variable could be assigned any value the user chooses.

Lines 20 and 30 multiply X by X and display the result on the screen.

Color the INPUT instruction and the video display at the center of the diagram.

Line 10 illustrates that if more than one value is to be entered, the reserved word INPUT is followed by the list of variables whose values are to be supplied by the user during program execution. The comma between variables serves as a delimiter to separate the variable names. When the prompt symbol appears, the user enters values at the keyboard. The user enters the first value (here, JANE) followed by a comma, and then the next value (here, 25). The comma serves again as the delimiter between values. The user can mix variable types (numeric and string) in one INPUT instruction. In the example, the user types in a name and age of an individual. Note the suffix dollar symbol ($) indicating that the value of the variable name is a string. The values of these variables may be used by the program for a calculation; for example, to find if a person (name variable) is old enough (age) to vote.

Color the program segment and video display at the bottom of the diagram. For line 60, you can apply A and D colors to all the letters or alternate colors A and D. Line 60 is both an INPUT and a PRINT instruction. Note that several program lines require two lines for illustrative purposes. They should appear as one line in an actual program.

Just imagine one using this tax program for the first time without line 10. When the program is executed, a question mark appears on the screen. There is no indication of what type of value is to be entered. A good programming technique is to provide a prompt (help) message to explain what type of value is required by the program at that moment. The use of a *PRINT instruction* to *display* a line of explanation (such as line 10) provides the needed information. Then, the INPUT instruction (line 20) causes the computer to halt and query (?) as before. This time the user has some indication of what value (here, .08 and 1000) is to be entered. Lines 30 and 40 are assignment instructions, which should be familiar from Plate 17.

Some implementations of BASIC allow the user to combine the PRINT instruction with the INPUT instruction. Lines 60 and 70 of the sample program segment provide the prompt and wait for values. INPUT "WHO ARE YOU" causes WHO ARE YOU to be printed on the screen and the prompt symbol to appear as well. Remember, N$ is a variable name for a string value, JANE, supplied at the keyboard by Jane. Line 70 ends the program.

The INPUT instruction provides for interaction between the user and computer during the execution of a particular program. This type of activity is the basis for interactive programming. The user no longer writes a program, enters it, and waits for the computer to complete the work. The user can change the action of a program by entering information during its execution.

THE INPUT INSTRUCTION.

INPUT INSTRUCTION_A
   VARIABLE_A1
   PROMPT SYMBOL_A2
KEYBOARD_B
   PROMPTED VALUE_B1
ASSIGNMENT INSTRUCTION_C
PRINT INSTRUCTION_D
   DISPLAY_D1

```
10 INPUT X
20 T = X * X
30 PRINT T
```

```
10 INPUT NAME$, AGE
```

```
10 PRINT "ENTER
   RATE, PRICE"
20 INPUT RATE, PRICE
30 TAX = PRICE * RATE
40 PAY = PRICE + TAX
50 PRINT "YOU OWE"; PAY
60 INPUT "WHO ARE YOU"; N$
70 PRINT "GOODBYE;
   N$"
```

Display 1:
```
? 3
  9
```

Display 2:
```
?  JANE, 25
```

Display 3:
```
ENTER RATE,
PRICE
? .08 1000
YOU OWE 80
WHO ARE YOU?
JANE
GOODBYE JANE
```

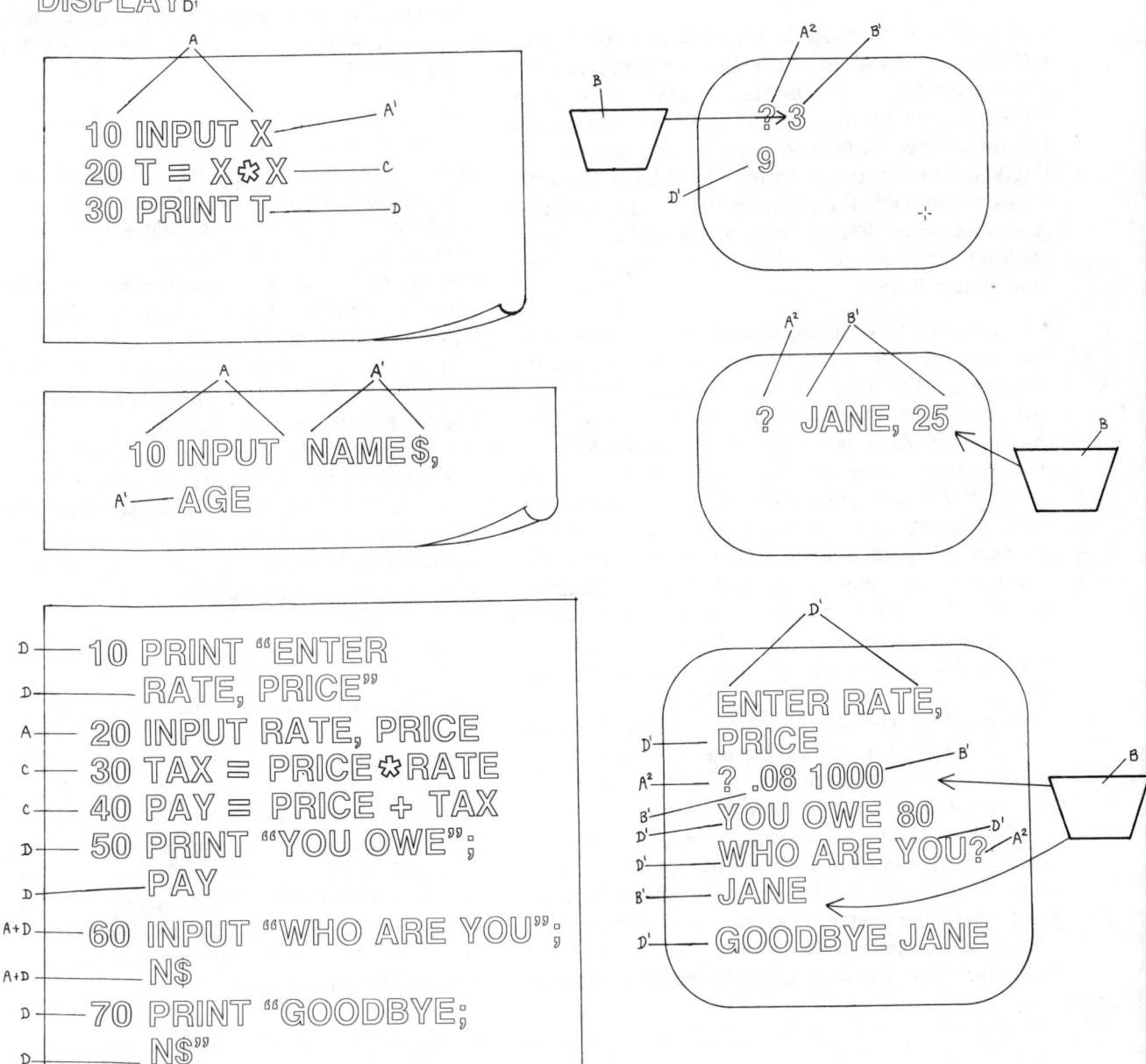

19 THE INPUT AND GOTO INSTRUCTIONS

In this plate, a method to have a program re-execute itself is presented. This method uses the GOTO instruction to make your program easier to use (more "user friendly") for people who do not know how to write or run one themselves.

Color titles A through G. Use a light color for C. Color lines 10 and 20 of the Cost Calculation Program, then color video display diagram 1. Go back and forth between the Cost Calculation Program and the appearance on the screens after execution of the line(s) colored in the program. Color lines 30 to 90. Be sure you color the program lines and screen and read about each diagram before you continue. Color the keyboard input (C) and the Return key (D) at the appropriate points.

This program concerns calculating the cost of an item once the selling price and tax rate are known. Like the programs on the last plate, it is constructed so that the user supplies the tax rate and price each time it runs. Once the whole program has been entered, and the *RUN instruction* typed, the screen will first appear as in diagram 1. Line 10 of the program caused the prompt RATE OF TAX to be *displayed*. The *INPUT instruction* of line 20 generates the question mark prompt on the screen. The user types in the requested value at the *keyboard* (diagram 2). The *Return* (Enter or Endline) *key* is pressed, and the program's execution advances to the next lines (30 and then 40). WHAT PRICE? appears on the screen (diagram 3).

By including two INPUT instructions (lines 20 and 40), the programmer has required the user to enter data in a specific order. At the same time, the user is *prompted* by lines 10 and 30 as to what value to enter.

After the price (1000) has been entered from the keyboard and the Return key pressed (diagram 4), the program goes on to the next line. Lines 50 and 60 are *assignment instructions* that calculate the value of the tax and total price to be assigned to the variables TAX and PAY, respectively. The *display* produced by the *PRINT instruc-*

tions (lines 70, 80, 90) makes the output easier to understand.

Color the GOTO instruction (line 100) of the Cost Calculation Program and the arrow which represents the function of returning to line 30; it does not appear on a written program. Color the RUN instruction as well.

Recall that a program is usually executed line by line from the lowest to the highest numbered line. At times it is desirable to direct the flow out of sequence, either backward or forward, to another line in the program. Here, after line 100, the program flow goes back to line 30 ("branches to line 30"). At that point, WHAT PRICE appears as well as the question mark prompt from the INPUT instruction (bottom two lines of diagram 5). The input and computation processes begin all over again. It is as if you had restarted the program with line 30. The *GOTO instruction* directs the program flow to the indicated line (in this case, line 30). In this example, lines 10 and 20 are not re-executed; thus, the rate of tax remains unchanged in the subsequent calculations.

The GOTO instruction causes what is called unconditional branching (the program flow always goes to the indicated line). In this way new prices can be input and costs computed for any number of items. The information that is showing on your screen will scroll (move) upward as more values are added.

By now you probably have realized that the above program has no end. The cost computation program will keep on prompting for another price as long as the computer is not asked to make a decision capable of ending the process. The term for this kind of program flow is looping. The user can interrupt the loop by turning off the computer or pressing a special purpose key. But the program itself does not end at any predetermined point. A more elegant method is to build in a condition, which is a decision step within the program, that offers a way out. The IF . . . THEN . . . instruction described in the next plate explains this conditional branching.

THE INPUT AND GOTO INSTRUCTIONS.

PRINT INSTRUCTION_A
  DISPLAY_{A¹}
INPUT INSTRUCTION_B
  DISPLAY_{B¹}
PROMPTED INPUT/
  KEYBOARD_C
  DISPLAY_{C¹}
RETURN KEY_D
ASSIGNMENT INSTRUCTION_E
GOTO INSTRUCTION_F
  ARROW_{F¹}
RUN INSTRUCTION_G

COST CALCULATION PROGRAM ★

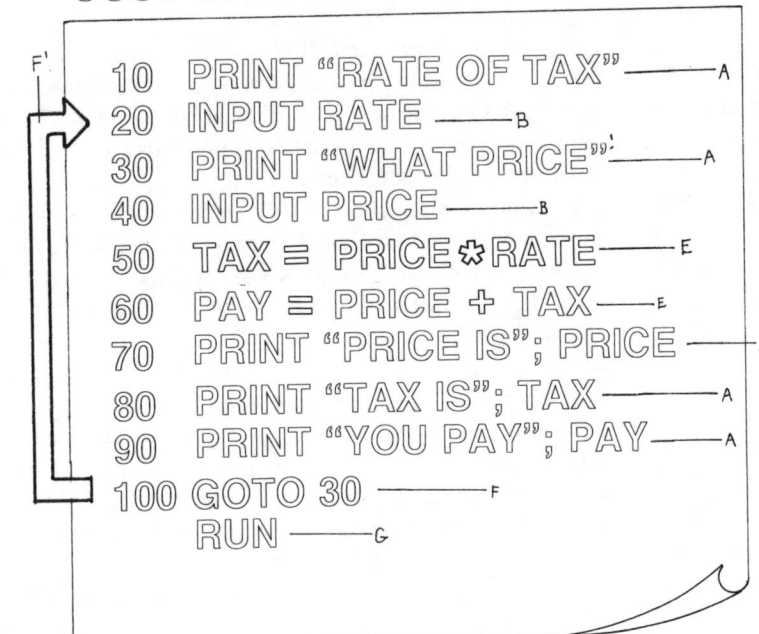

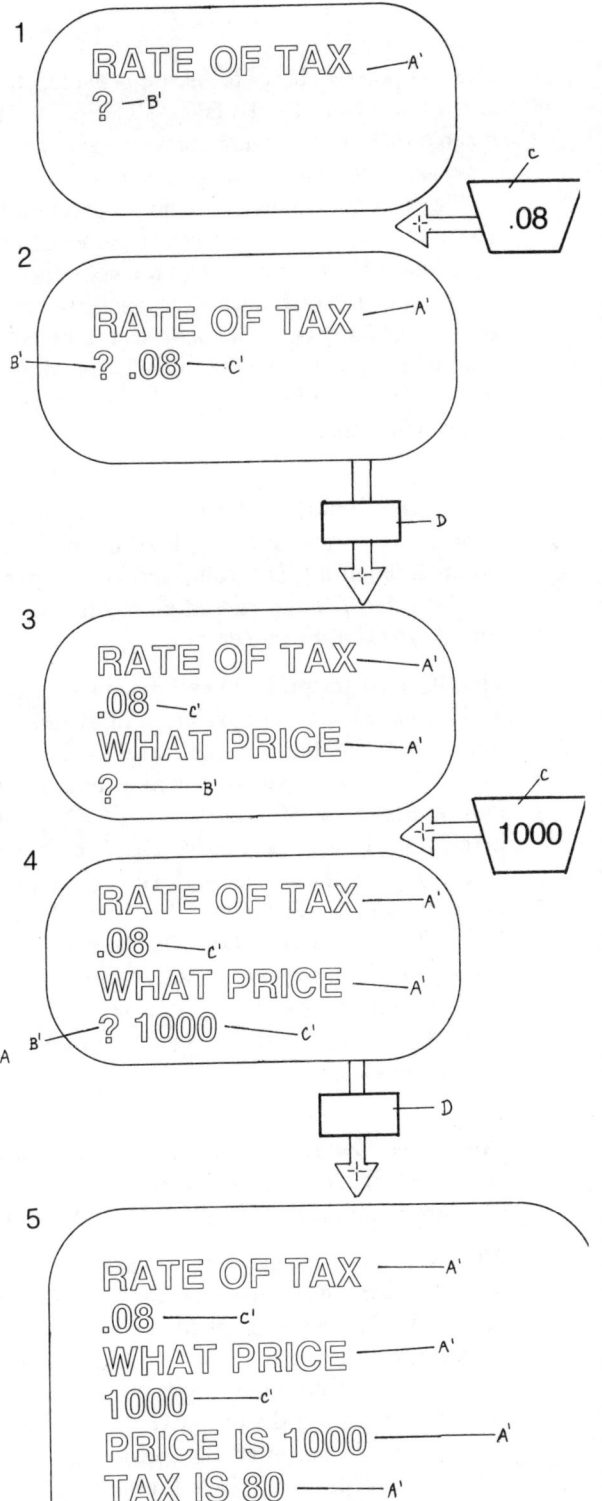

```
10   PRINT "RATE OF TAX"         ── A
20   INPUT RATE                  ── B
30   PRINT "WHAT PRICE"          ── A
40   INPUT PRICE                 ── B
50   TAX = PRICE * RATE          ── E
60   PAY = PRICE + TAX           ── E
70   PRINT "PRICE IS"; PRICE     ── A
80   PRINT "TAX IS"; TAX         ── A
90   PRINT "YOU PAY"; PAY        ── A
100  GOTO 30                     ── F
     RUN                         ── G
```

1
RATE OF TAX ── A'
? ── B'
            ⇐ .08 ── C

2
RATE OF TAX ── A'
B' ── ? .08 ── C'

D

3
RATE OF TAX ── A'
.08 ── C'
WHAT PRICE ── A'
? ── B'
            ⇐ 1000 ── C

4
RATE OF TAX ── A'
.08 ── C'
WHAT PRICE ── A'
B' ── ? 1000 ── C'

D

5
RATE OF TAX ── A'
.08 ── C'
WHAT PRICE ── A'
1000 ── C'
PRICE IS 1000 ── A'
TAX IS 80 ── A'
YOU PAY 1080 ── A'
WHAT PRICE ── A'
? ── B'

20 THE IF...THEN...INSTRUCTION

The computer's ability to decide between alternatives is called into action by the IF ... THEN ... instruction. It can be used to end a looping program like the one in the previous plate, but it can do much more.

The programmer must set up a condition for testing. The computer decides between the alternatives, and, depending on the outcome, the flow continues to the next line or is directed (branches) to another line in the program. Branching brought about by a test of a condition is conditional branching. (The looping caused by the GOTO instruction of the last plate was an example of unconditional branching.)

Color the Conditional Branching heading, titles A through D[1], lines 10 through 40 of the upper Conditional Branching Program, and the numerals 1 to 5 on the video display screen at right. The arrows are for illustrative purposes only.

Line 10 starts the program with an initial value for M (M = 1). Line 20 causes the value, 1, of M to appear on the screen. Line 30 adds 1 to the current value of M (2 = 1 + 1). M is said to be incremented by one. The test condition occurs in line 40. The IF ... THEN ... instruction here asks, "Is the value of M less than or equal to 5?" When M = 2, the IF clause is true, so the program flow passes back to line 20 (arrow D[1]). That is, IF 2 is less than (<) 5 (true), THEN GOTO 20. The new value, 2, of M appears on the screen as a result of line 20. One is added to M again (line 30) and the IF clause truth is tested again. The program will continue looping until the screen looks as you have colored it.

Color the Conditional Branching Program shown below the first one. This illustrates the first program at a later time. Color the ALL DONE on the screen.

When the current value of M is 5 at line 20, the number is displayed on the screen. Then, at line 30, 1 is added to M so that the new value of M is 6. This time the value of M is greater than 5, so that the IF clause is false. The THEN clause instruction is ignored (arrow C[1]) and program flow passes to the line after the IF ... THEN ... instruction. The line after this decision instruction causes the printing of the ALL DONE phrase and the program terminates because the last line has been executed.

The statement in the IF clause can be any algebraic sentence that may make use of the following relations:

equal to = less than or equal to <=
less than < greater than or equal to >=
greater than > not equal to <> or #

Not all decisions must lead to branching actions in the THEN clause. It is possible to stop the looping program using the reserved word STOP as the instruction in the THEN clause (IF ... THEN STOP). STOP is a reserved word in BASIC that halts execution of a program. It can be used anywhere it is needed logically in a program.

Color the Menu Program heading, titles E through F[1], and the entire Menu Program, the video display screen, and the related keyboard input.

In this program, the first two *PRINT instructions* (lines 10 and 20) cause the screen to display a simple lunch menu. A prompt appears on the screen.

The *INPUT instruction* (line 30) halts the computer so that it will wait for you to type in a number (representing your choice) at the *keyboard*. Remember, you can choose item 1 or 2 only. The next two statements (lines 40 and 50) instruct the computer to perform a particular task, depending on your choice of C. Depending on its value, the cost of the item will be *displayed* as either $15 or $10. Let's take a closer look at what happens when the IF ... THEN ... instructions are executed. Suppose that you choose item 2, fish. You have typed in 2 at the keyboard. In the first IF ... THEN ... instruction (line 40) this value is compared to 1. As the statement "C = 1" is false, the THEN clause PRINT instruction is ignored. The program flow passes (arrow C[1]) to line 50, the second IF ... THEN ... instruction. In this case, the statement "C = 2" is true, so the PRINT instruction in that line is executed and the screen displays COST IS $10.00.

The last line in the program will display HEARTY APPETITE. If you chose 1, the PRINT instruction in line 40 would execute and the one in line 50 would be ignored.

In both programs, the IF ... THEN ... instruction leads to a decision about the value of a variable. The outcomes are quite different, however, giving you an idea of the versatility of the IF ... THEN ... instruction.

THE IF...THEN...INSTRUCTION.

CONDITIONAL BRANCHING ★

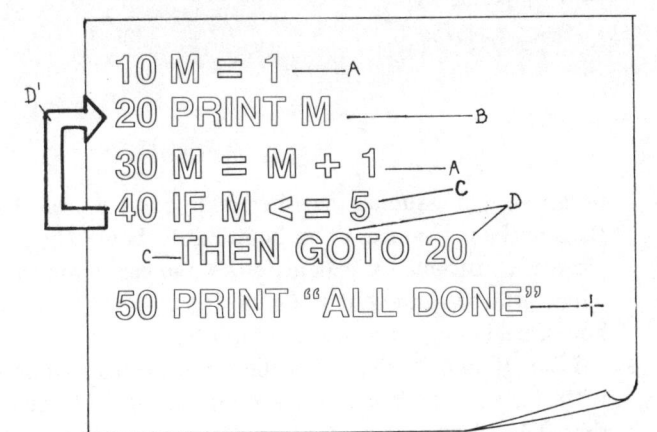

```
10 M = 1              —A
20 PRINT M            —B
30 M = M + 1          —A
40 IF M <= 5          —C    —D
   THEN GOTO 20
50 PRINT "ALL DONE"
```
(D')

ASSIGNMENT INSTRUCTION_A
PRINT INSTRUCTION_B
  DISPLAY_B'
IF...THEN...INSTRUCTION_C
  ARROW_C'
GOTO INSTRUCTION_D
  ARROW_D'

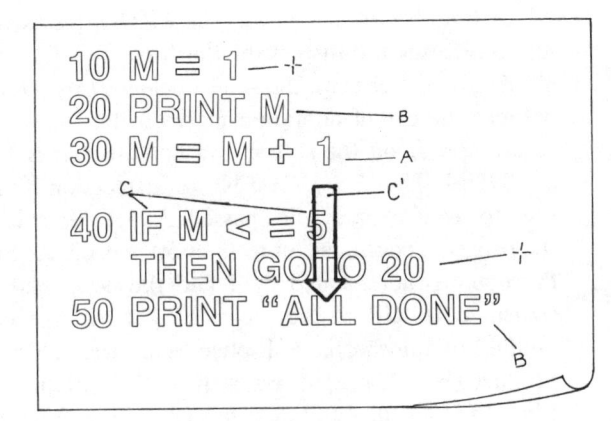

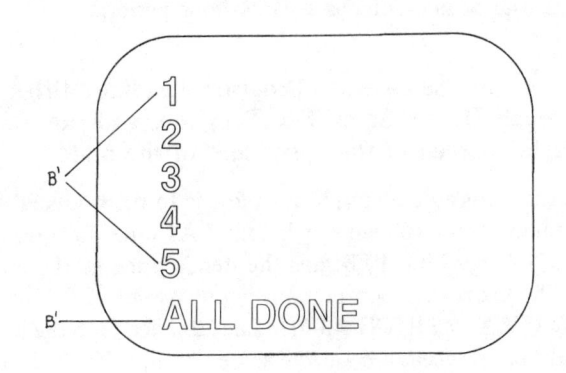

```
10 M = 1
20 PRINT M            —B
30 M = M + 1          —A
                 C—    —C'
40 IF M <= 5
   THEN GOTO 20
50 PRINT "ALL DONE"
                      —B
```

Display (B'):
```
1
2
3
4
5
ALL DONE
```

MENU PROGRAM ★

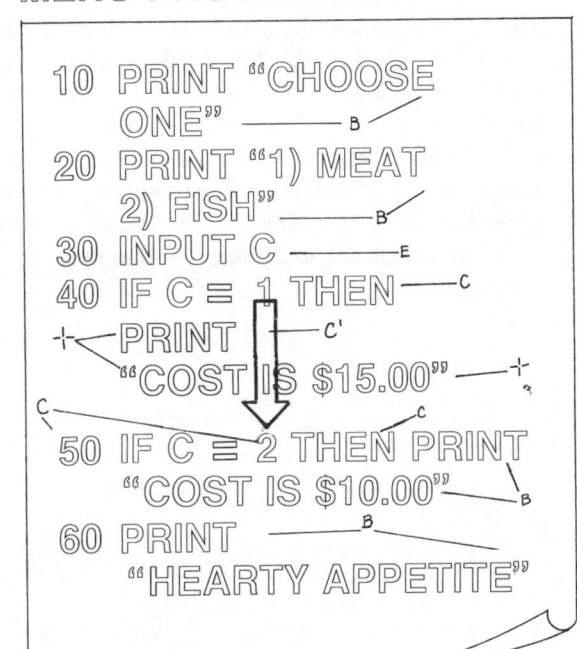

```
10 PRINT "CHOOSE
   ONE"                —B
20 PRINT "1) MEAT
   2) FISH"            —B
30 INPUT C             —E
40 IF C = 1 THEN       —C
   PRINT               —C'
   "COST IS $15.00"
50 IF C = 2 THEN PRINT —C
   "COST IS $10.00"    —B
60 PRINT               —B
   "HEARTY APPETITE"
```

INPUT INSTRUCTION_E
  DISPLAY_E'
PROMPTED INPUT/
  KEYBOARD_F
  DISPLAY_F'

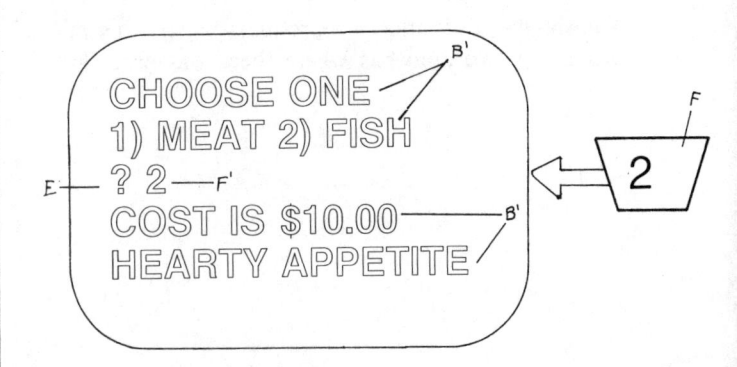

Display:
```
CHOOSE ONE              —B'
1) MEAT 2) FISH
? 2                     —F'
COST IS $10.00          —B'
HEARTY APPETITE
```
(F — keyboard with 2)

21
SAMPLE PROGRAMS: TAX TABLE AND COUNTING AMOEBAS

The instructions and techniques covered in the previous plates can be adapted for the solution of problems. The first example will show how to calculate a tax table. The second example shows how to determine the reproduction potential of one amoeba in a 24-hour period.

Color the Sales Tax Program heading, titles A through D, the Sales Tax Program, and the video display screen in the upper half of the plate.

In this program, a simple tax table is to be produced for amounts from 10 cents to 1 dollar. Assume that the tax is 6% (.06). Line 10 begins the item's price at 10 cents.

The tax is then computed using an *assignment instruction* (TAX = PRICE * .06) in line 20. Then both the price and tax are *displayed* on the screen by line 30. As in the previous plate, an assignment instruction is used to increment the value of the item by 5 cents (line 40). If this value is less than or equal to 1 dollar, line 50 directs the program flow back to line 20. The incrementing, testing, and calculation continues until the value of the item becomes more than 1 dollar. At this point, the *IF* clause statement of line 50 becomes false, the *THEN* clause instruction is ignored, the flow passes to the next line (60), and ALL DONE is printed.

Color the Counting Amoebas Program heading, titles E and F, the Counting Amoebas Program, the RAM variable value table, and the display on the lower video screen.

The single-celled amoeba reproduces by splitting in half, producing two amoebas where there was one. For our program, it is assumed that the conditions are such that the amoeba reproduces every hour, on the hour. The program is constructed to calculate the number of amoebas which will be formed at the end of each hour up to 24 hours, beginning with the lone amoeba.

Lines 10 and 20 show that the count begins at 0 hour with one amoeba. The *RAM variable values table* shows that 0 has been assigned to HOUR and 1 assigned to NUM (number of amoebas). The *PRINT instruction* of line 30 causes the display of the hour and the current number of amoebas on the screen below (0, 1). Note that without the use of quotation marks in line 30, only the values appear on the screen and not the names HOUR and NUM. The IF . . . THEN . . . instruction in line 40 tests to see if 24 hours has passed. As long as it has not, the program continues on to lines 50 and 60. At line 50, the hour is incremented by 1 and the new value is assigned to HOUR in the table at right. At line 60, the number of amoebas is multiplied by 2. The value of this product (NUM * 2) is assigned to the variable NUM. Line 70 is an unconditional branch to line 30. Line 30 causes the current values of HOUR and NUM (1, 2) to be displayed on the screen below. When the value of HOUR reaches 24, the program is halted by the STOP instruction of line 40. The final number of amoebas (1,677,216) has been displayed next to the hour 24 on the screen.

In this plate, you have seen two example programs that make use of all of the types of instructions presented in the previous plates. In addition to the syntax of the instructions, you have learned the programming technique of counting.

SAMPLE PROGRAMS.

SALES TAX PROGRAM *

TAX TABLE AND COUNTING AMOEBAS
CN 6

- A — 10 PRICE = .10
- A — 20 TAX = PRICE ✱ .06
- B — 30 PRINT PRICE, TAX
- A — 40 PRICE = PRICE + .05
- C — 50 IF PRICE <= 1.00
- C — THEN GOTO 20
- B — 60 PRINT "ALL DONE"

ASSIGNMENT INSTRUCTION_A
PRINT INSTRUCTION_B
 DISPLAY_B'
IF...THEN...INSTRUCTION_C
GOTO INSTRUCTION_D

```
.10    .006
.15    .009
 .      .
 .      .
1.00   .06
ALL DONE
```

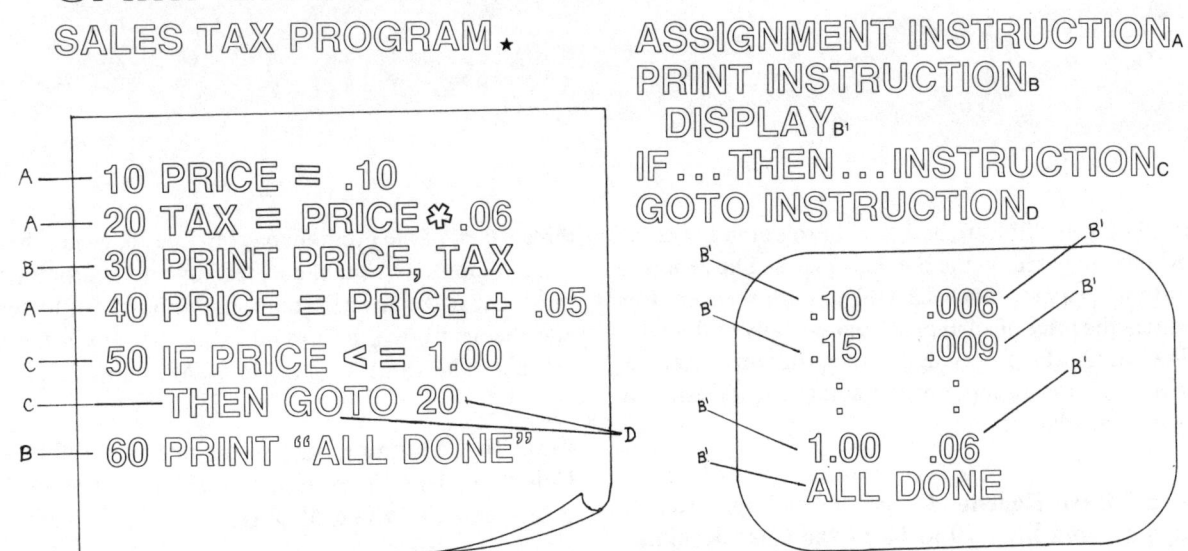

COUNTING AMOEBAS PROGRAM *

AMOEBA

RAM TABLE_E / VALUES_E'
RUN INSTRUCTION_F

- A — 10 HOUR = 0
- A — 20 NUM = 1
- B — 30 PRINT HOUR, NUM
- C — 40 IF HOUR = 24
- C — THEN STOP
- A — 50 HOUR = HOUR + 1
- A — 60 NUM = NUM ✱ 2
- D — 70 GOTO 30
- F — RUN

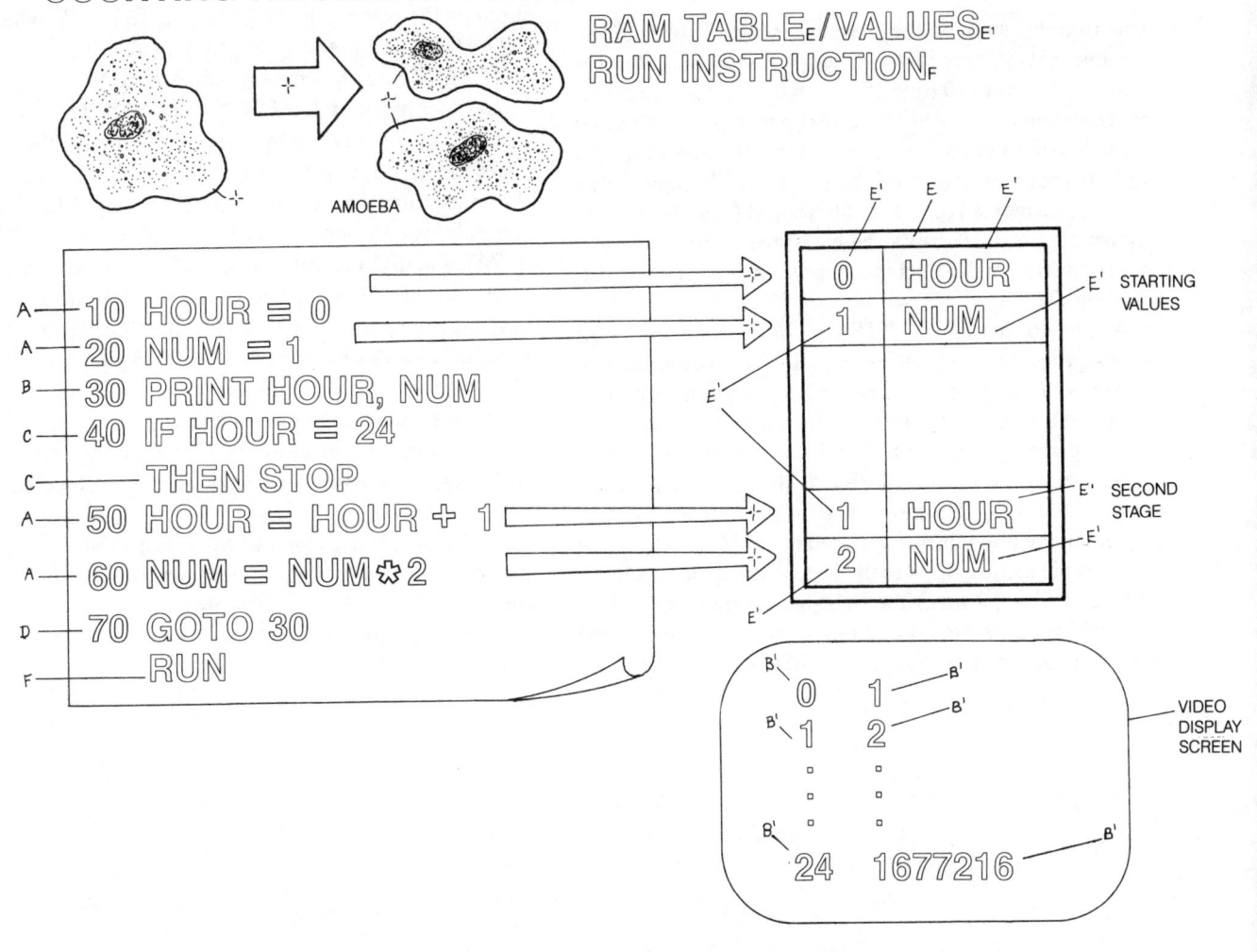

0	HOUR
1	NUM

STARTING VALUES

1	HOUR
2	NUM

SECOND STAGE

```
 0      1
 1      2
 .      .
 .      .
 .      .
24   1677216
```

VIDEO DISPLAY SCREEN

22 SAMPLE PROGRAM: CASH REGISTER

In this plate you will learn additional programming techniques that are based on the previous plates. The problem here is to have a program behave like a cash register. The user enters the price of an item. A running tally of the total cost is kept. On the proper signal, the program prints out the total, asks for an input of the amount tendered, and prints out the change.

Color the Cash Register Program heading, titles A through F[1], and lines 10 to 60 of the Cash Register Program. Color the first five lines of the representation of the variable value table in RAM and the first four lines on the video display.

The running sum of the prices is assigned to a single variable (SUM) (*assignment instruction*). Initially, the value of the sum is 0 (line 10), so that a person's previous purchases are not added to the next person's bill. The user is *prompted* to enter the price of the first item (line 20), and the program halts until the price (say, 75 cents for an ice cream cone) is typed at the keyboard (prompted input shown on the video display here). Note that the cent symbol is omitted and 75 cents is represented as the decimal fraction .75.

At line 40, the *IF* . . . *THEN* . . . *instruction,* the price is compared to a special code, -1. The special code is chosen as an impossible value for a price and is used later in the cash register operation. If the input price is not -1, the program flow passes to line 50. There the instruction is given to add the value of PRICE (0.75) to the previous value of SUM (0). The new sum (0.75) is assigned to SUM replacing the previous *value* stored in RAM (see the *RAM table* representation). Recall that in an assignment instruction (line 50 here) the right-hand expression (SUM + PRICE) is evaluated and this value is assigned to the variable appearing on the left (SUM). The next line (60) directs flow of the program back to line 20, where the next price is input, and the input, testing, and addition procedure begins again. The prompt line appears on the screen, and the next price, 1.95, is added to the sum in the same manner. The value assigned to SUM is now 2.70.

Color the remaining lines of the program (70 to 110). Color the last lines of the variable value table in RAM and the video display.

As long as -1 is not input, the cash register keeps adding to the sum a new price as entered by the cashier (user). When the cashier wants to arrive at a grand total, -1 is input as the price. The program goes to line 70 where the *PRINT instruction* causes the display of the words TOTAL IS and the current value of SUM.

Another prompt (AMOUNT TENDERED) appears (line 80) and the program halts (line 90) until the cashier types in the value of this amount (10.00 in the example). An assignment instruction (line 100) is used to calculate the value of the change (CHANGE = AMOUNT − SUM). Finally, the value of the change is shown on the video display (7.30 in the example). Of course, if this amount is negative (less than 0) the cashier should ask for more money. An IF . . . THEN . . . instruction is used to check for just such a situation (line 120). If more money has to be tendered, the program flow returns to line 80 and prompts for another amount. If the amount tendered is sufficient, the amount of change is printed together with THANK YOU.

The programmer can add features to the cash register program such as tax calculations, credit for coupons, and the printing of a receipt. The program user lets the program run until it is finished and follows instructions about what information to enter.

SAMPLE PROGRAM.
CASH REGISTER PROGRAM ★

```
A — 10  SUM = 0
B — 20  PRINT "NEXT PRICE"
C — 30  INPUT PRICE
D — 40  IF PRICE = -1
D —     THEN GOTO 70                    E
A — 50  SUM = SUM + PRICE
E — 60  GOTO 20
B — 70  PRINT "TOTAL IS"; SUM
B — 80  PRINT "AMOUNT
B —     TENDERED"
C — 90  INPUT AMOUNT
A — 100 CHANGE = AMOUNT -
A —     SUM
B — 110 PRINT "CHANGE IS";
B —     CHANGE
D — 120 IF CHANGE < 0               E
D —     THEN GOTO 80
B — 130 PRINT "THANK YOU"
```

ASSIGNMENT
  INSTRUCTION_A
PRINT INSTRUCTION_B
  DISPLAY_B1
INPUT INSTRUCTION_C
  PROMPTED INPUT_C1
IF...THEN...
  INSTRUCTION_D
GOTO INSTRUCTION_E
RAM TABLE_F
  VALUES_F1

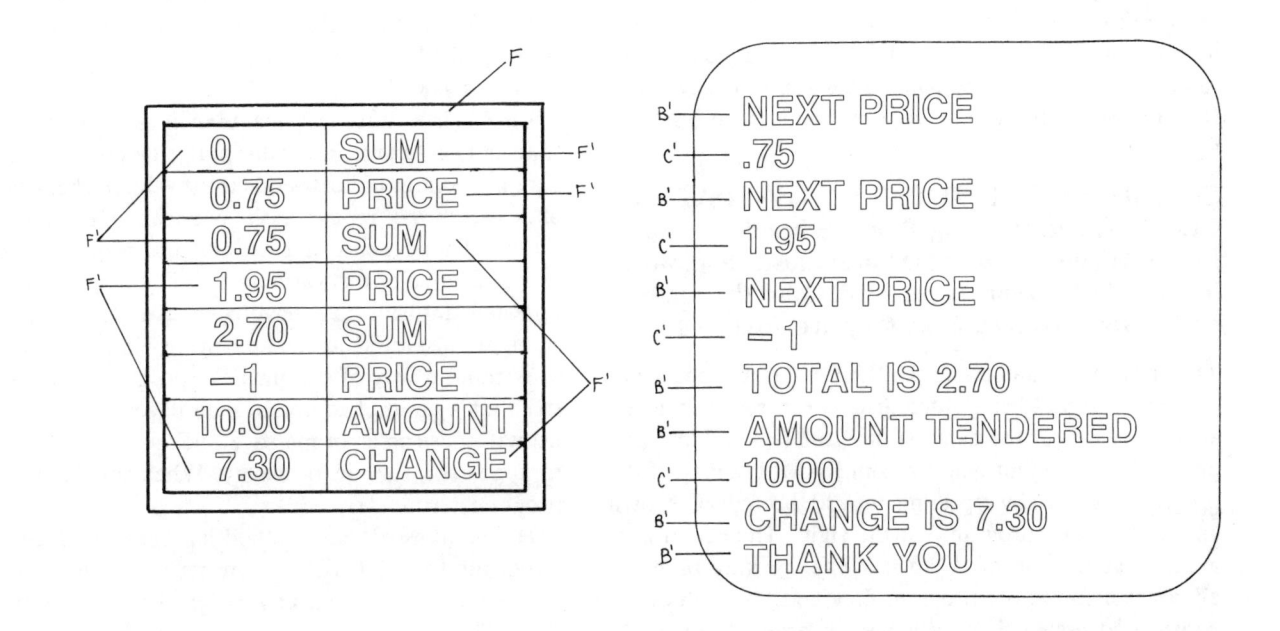

0	SUM	F'
0.75	PRICE	F'
0.75	SUM	
1.95	PRICE	
2.70	SUM	
-1	PRICE	F'
10.00	AMOUNT	
7.30	CHANGE	

(F)

B' — NEXT PRICE
C' — .75
B' — NEXT PRICE
C' — 1.95
B' — NEXT PRICE
C' — -1
B' — TOTAL IS 2.70
B' — AMOUNT TENDERED
C' — 10.00
B' — CHANGE IS 7.30
B' — THANK YOU

22
CASH REGISTER
CN 6

23
THE READ/DATA INSTRUCTIONS

Two methods of storing data values during program execution have been shown. The first method was to make the data value part of an assignment statement (Plate 17). The user supplied the data values when the program was entered at the keyboard. The second method was to use an INPUT instruction in the program and then supply the data values in response to a prompt on the screen (Plate 18). Both methods resulted in the assignment of values to variables.

In Plates 19, 20, and 22 you saw that long sets of data values can be processed by repeated use of conditional and unconditional branching. However, the user is still required to be present at execution time to supply data values. If many data values are needed, another approach is often more efficient. It employs the instructions READ and DATA.

Color the Sample Program heading, titles A through G, and the READ/DATA Sample Program at the top of the plate.

The *DATA instruction* causes the listed values of data to be stored in consecutive sections of memory (RAM). You can list several values at once after the reserved word DATA. You can place DATA instructions anywhere in your program. Usually, data instructions listing values for the same type of processing are placed in consecutive positions of a program (as in lines 10 and 20). The *READ instruction* directs the retrieval of values listed in DATA instructions in order from the first value listed in the first DATA instruction to the last value in the last DATA instruction. READ is like the INPUT instruction, except that, instead of obtaining data values from the keyboard, READ obtains the values from the data list in RAM.

Color the How READ/DATA Works, DATA Instructions, and Working Program headings, and titles H, H¹, and I. Color the lower illustration, working from left to right as you read. Color the numbers on the video screens when they are discussed.

The lines and arrows under the DATA Instructions heading represent data being stored (*store arrows*). The numerals (H¹) represent the data list in *RAM* (H) and the *read arrows* (B¹) represent reading from RAM. Looping of the program is shown by repeating lines 30 through 80, shown as the "working program" at the right. The actual program is at the top of the plate. The working program allows you to see the program flow and how values are copied and assigned to variables, in order, from RAM under the READ instruction.

Suppose that you want to add a series of paired values such as 7 and 8, and 4 and 1. Using the DATA instructions in lines 10 and 20 you can list your data values. You could list much more data than our example. First the DATA instruction's execution creates a list of values in consecutive memory locations (H). The list is built going from the values in the lowest numbered DATA instruction (line 10) to the highest numbered one (line 20) and from left to right within any one line. The values in RAM here are 7, 8, 4, 1, and 0, following their order in lines 10 and 20. A *data list pointer* (I) is set to indicate where the first value on the list is located in RAM. At this time, the data list pointer is just another location in RAM that contains the address of the first data list value. The READ instruction can only retrieve the value indicated by the data list pointer.

Referring to the working program, you can see that the first encountered READ instruction indicates that a data value is to be obtained from the data list. The location of this value is given by the data list pointer. In the example, line 30, READ A, causes the retrieval (from RAM) of the value 7 and its assignment to the variable A. Having read the data value 7 from the list, the data list pointer is changed, by the operating system, to indicate the next item on the list. Line 40 is an *IF . . . THEN . . . instruction*. The current value of A is 7. This value is not 0, so the THEN clause is ignored. Program flow passes to the next line. The next READ instruction (line 50) causes the value (8) indicated by the data list pointer to be assigned to the variable B. The pointer moves down to the next data list value. Lines 60 and 70 are then executed, causing addition of the values of A and B and the printing of the values of A, B, and SUM. They appear on the top video display screen as 7 8 15.

Line 80 is an unconditional branch back to line 30. This time, at line 30, the third value in the data list is read. (The data list pointer indicates this third value.) The new value of A becomes 4, replacing the previous value of 7. When the program reaches line 50 and the reading of B, the assigned value of this variable is 1. The looping process is repeated until all data have been used. The values and sums are *displayed* as in the bottom video display.

Without a way of stopping the program, a READ instruction's attempt to obtain data beyond the end of the list will cause an error message, such as OUT OF DATA, to appear on the video display. When this happens, the program terminates.

Here a more elegant method has been provided by the use of the IF . . . THEN . . . instruction in line 40. If the data value of 0 is read and assigned to A, the program ends. The zero value must be listed as the last data item. The last data item is sometimes called a trailer, sentinel, or break value.

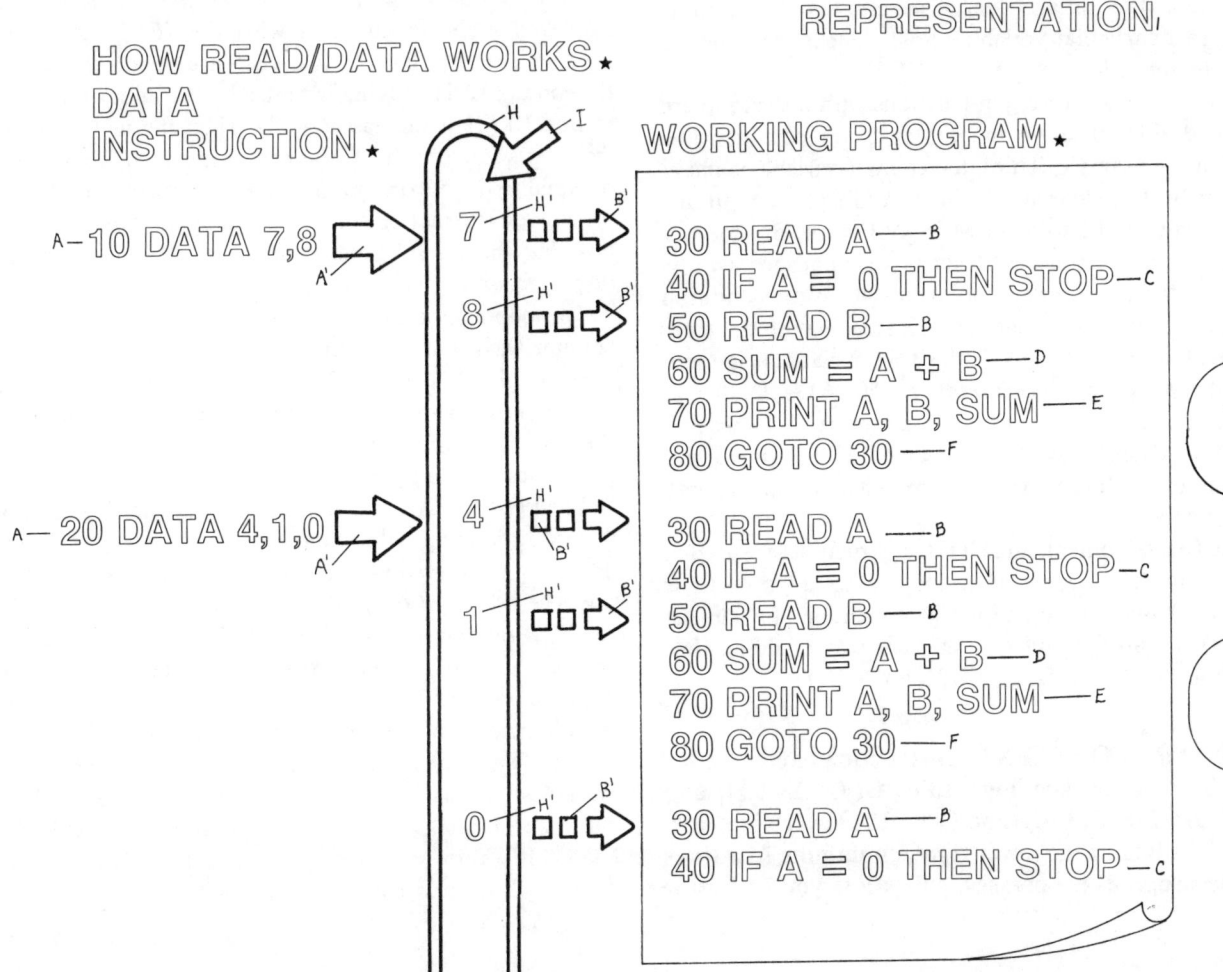

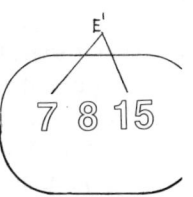

THE READ/DATA INSTRUCTIONS.

SAMPLE PROGRAM ★

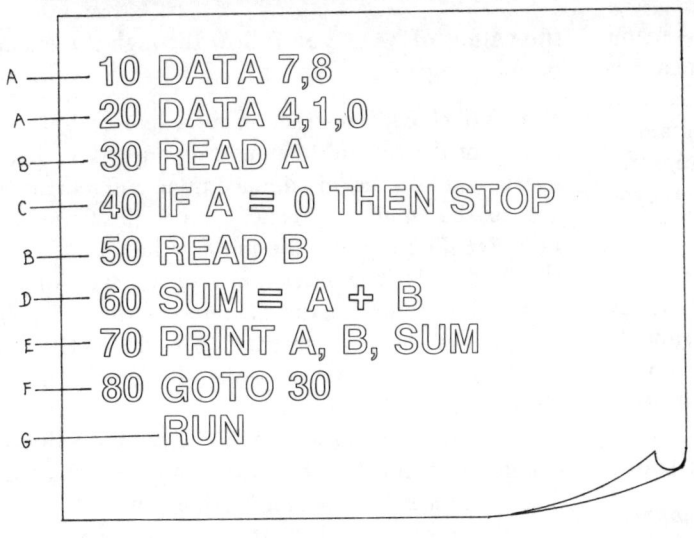

A — 10 DATA 7,8
A — 20 DATA 4,1,0
B — 30 READ A
C — 40 IF A = 0 THEN STOP
B — 50 READ B
D — 60 SUM = A + B
E — 70 PRINT A, B, SUM
F — 80 GOTO 30
G — RUN

DATA INSTRUCTION A
  STORE ARROW A'
READ INSTRUCTION B
  READ ARROW B'
IF...THEN...INSTRUCTION C
ASSIGNMENT
  INSTRUCTION D
PRINT INSTRUCTION E
  DISPLAY E'
GOTO INSTRUCTION F
RUN INSTRUCTION G
RAM TABLE H
  VALUES H'
DATA LIST POINTER
  REPRESENTATION I

HOW READ/DATA WORKS ★

DATA INSTRUCTION ★

A — 10 DATA 7,8

A — 20 DATA 4,1,0

7
8
4
1
0

WORKING PROGRAM ★

30 READ A — B
40 IF A = 0 THEN STOP — C
50 READ B — B
60 SUM = A + B — D
70 PRINT A, B, SUM — E
80 GOTO 30 — F

30 READ A — B
40 IF A = 0 THEN STOP — C
50 READ B — B
60 SUM = A + B — D
70 PRINT A, B, SUM — E
80 GOTO 30 — F

30 READ A — B
40 IF A = 0 THEN STOP — C

7 8 15

7 8 15
4 1 5

24
THE FOR/NEXT INSTRUCTIONS

The computer is often used to perform the same task many times or until a certain condition occurs. In the plate on the GOTO and IF . . . THEN . . . instructions and on sample programs you saw how a counting program is made to stop at a particular point. The same steps are performed until the required condition is met. This type of program sequence is called looping.

Color the General Looping Program heading, titles A through F, and the General Looping Program itself. Color the numerals and words on the upper video display. Note that in this plate, individual parts of the program lines are colored where indicated, so that a program line may have more than one color.

Every loop sequence has five parts. First, the *counter* (index) *variable* is set equal to an *initial* (starting) *value*. In the example, in line 10 the counter variable M is set equal to 1 (the initial value). The term counter variable refers to a particular variable whose value is incremented consistently in a loop.

Second, the processing instructions within the loop are executed: line 20 causes the *display* of the current value of M in the example. Third, the counter variable is *incremented* by a predetermined value. Adding 2 to M in line 30 increments the value of M by 2. Fourth, the counter variable's value is tested. This is accomplished by the *IF . . . THEN . . . instruction* at line 40. If the condition for ending the loop is met, the fifth step, exiting the loop, is executed. Here, if M > 7, the THEN clause is ignored and the program proceeds to line 50. ALL DONE is printed on the video display. In all, four odd integers and one ALL DONE have been displayed. If there is no program line after line 50, the program would terminate with ALL DONE.

The IF, assignment, and GOTO instructions are used to implement the sequence of the loop. When a loop is to be executed based on the uniform incrementing of a counter (index), BASIC provides an efficient way of doing this. You use two instructions, FOR and NEXT.

Color the FOR/NEXT Instruction and FOR/NEXT Program headings, titles G, G[1], and H, and the FOR/NEXT program. Color the lower video display. The box at the lower right, containing M values as the program progresses, will allow you to follow the values of M as you follow through the execution of the program.

The FOR/NEXT instruction lines replace lines 10, 30, and 40 of the general looping program above. The FOR instruction lists the initial, maximum, and increment values for the counter variable. In line 10 of the example FOR NEXT program, the initial value of M is set to 1 (FOR M = 1). The *maximum value* allowed for M is set by the value following the TO reserved word (TO 7). The last part of the FOR instruction is the STEP reserved word. After this reserved word, the increment value is given (2 in this example).

The first time the loop is executed, the value of the counter is set equal to the initial value (1 in this example) and the processing instructions that follow the FOR instruction are executed (in the example, line 20, PRINT M). You can see in the box on the far right that the first run-through uses a value of 1 for M and causes 1 to be displayed on the screen. Then, when the *NEXT instruction* is encountered in line 30, two tasks are performed. First, the counter variable is incremented by the value of the step in line 10 (M is increased by 2). Then the new value is tested, also by line 10. If the new value of M is less than or equal to the maximum (3 is less than or equal to 7), the processing instructions are executed again. Notice in the box that the second time around, line 20 causes 3 to be displayed on the video display.

The looping process continues until the new value of the counter variable is more than the maximum. Later, when the example value of M is 9, it exceeds the maximum value (7). So, the loop is said to be satisfied and the line following the NEXT instruction is executed. ALL DONE is displayed in the example.

The FOR/NEXT combination provides an elegant way of setting looping values and letting the interpreter and operating systems do the counter incrementing and testing. The user need only fill in the three values required in the FOR instruction and place a NEXT instruction at the end of the set of instructions to be repeated. If the value of the increment is 1, the STEP section is optional. The initial, maximum, and increment need not be integer constants. They can be any numbers or even variables. If variables are used, their values must be assigned in the preceding statements of the program. You will use FOR/NEXT instructions in the next few plates to perform sophisticated programming tasks.

THE FOR/NEXT INSTRUCTIONS.

COUNTER VARIABLE A
INITIAL VALUE B
PRINT INSTRUCTION C
  DISPLAY C'
INCREMENT D

IF...THEN...INSTRUCTION E
RUN INSTRUCTION F
FOR/NEXT INSTRUCTION ★
  MAXIMUM VALUE G / ARROW G'
NEXT INSTRUCTION H

GENERAL LOOPING PROGRAM ★

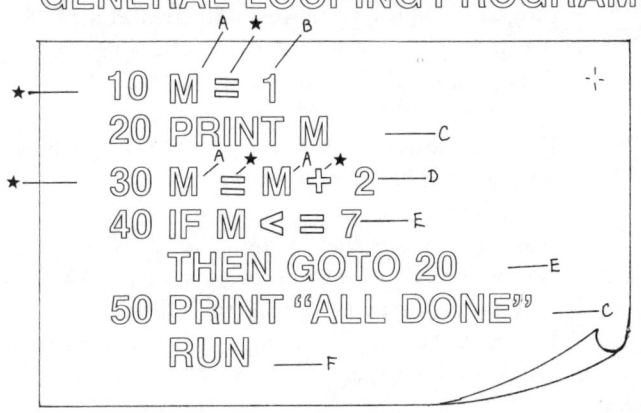

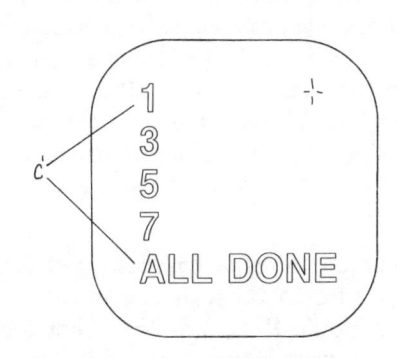

```
10 M = 1           (A ★ B)
20 PRINT M         — C
30 M = M + 2       — D  (A ★ A ★)
40 IF M <= 7       — E
   THEN GOTO 20    — E
50 PRINT "ALL DONE" — C
RUN                — F
```

Display:
```
1
3
5
7
ALL DONE
```

FOR/NEXT PROGRAM ★

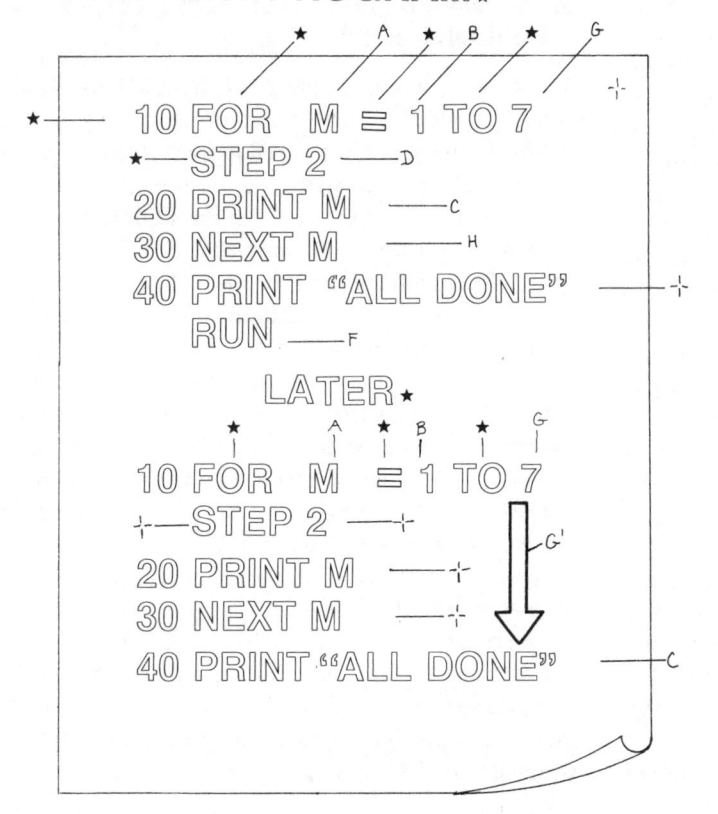

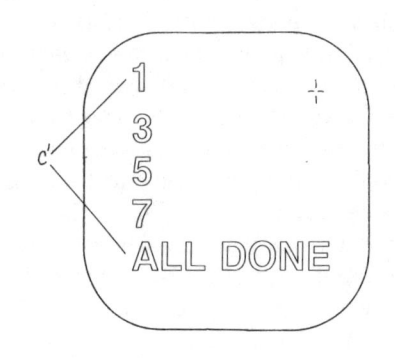

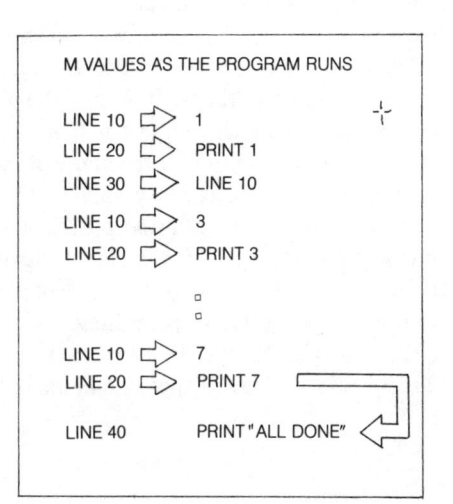

```
10 FOR M = 1 TO 7     (★ A ★ B ★ G)
   STEP 2             — D
20 PRINT M            — C
30 NEXT M             — H
40 PRINT "ALL DONE"
RUN                   — F
```

Display:
```
1
3
5
7
ALL DONE
```

LATER ★

```
10 FOR M = 1 TO 7     (★ A ★ B ★ G)
   STEP 2
20 PRINT M
30 NEXT M
40 PRINT "ALL DONE"   — C
```

M VALUES AS THE PROGRAM RUNS

LINE 10	⇨	1
LINE 20	⇨	PRINT 1
LINE 30	⇨	LINE 10
LINE 10	⇨	3
LINE 20	⇨	PRINT 3
...		
LINE 10	⇨	7
LINE 20	⇨	PRINT 7
LINE 40		PRINT "ALL DONE"

24
FOR/NEXT INSTRUCTIONS
CN 8

25
THE DIM INSTRUCTION AND SUBSCRIPTED VARIABLES

There were only a few variables used in each of the programs of the previous plates. What do you do when you want to keep a list of catalog numbers, descriptions, and prices for a large number of inventory items? You could think up thousands of numeric and string valued variables and make appropriate value assignments. If you want to look for a particular item, it could be quite tedious. In fact, some versions of BASIC do not allow you to create a thousand different variable names, due to naming restrictions (see Plate 17). However, BASIC solves this problem by the use of arrays.

Color the Sample Program and RAM Table headings, titles A through C, and lines 10 through 70 of the Sample Program. Note that individual parts of the program lines receive different colors where indicated. Color the array values (C) stored in the RAM table.

When you have several related data values (say, inventory item descriptions), instead of assigning them to separate variables, you give the list of related values a single variable name (*array name*). Here D$ is the array name for one list and P is the array name for a second, related list. Then, each data value can be named in the program by specifying the array name and its position in the list (a number called its *subscript*). The list itself is called an array. The D$ array could be catalog numbers for candies and the P array could be the price of each type of candy. So, referring to the RAM table, D$(2), P(2) indicates that the YYY candies are 4 cents each because the two subscripts in parentheses indicate the second data elements, or array values, in the D$ array and in the P array.

When an array is used, a special instruction, DIM, is required, usually at the beginning of the program (see line 10). The *DIM* (dimension) *instruction* is a way of informing the operating system of the name of the array and the number of elements or array values. The user types the reserved word DIM, followed by the name of the array and, in parentheses, the number of elements to be contained in the array (*size of array*). Note that in the DIM instruction, the value in parentheses is not the subscript. In the example, on line 10, two arrays are specified, D$ is a string valued array of three elements and P is a number valued array of three elements also. The operating system sets aside three consecutive blocks of memory in RAM for each of the arrays. (See the RAM table.)

If you want to assign a *value* to an *array* element in the program, you need only state the array name followed by the element's position in the array (the subscript). Note in lines 20 through 70 each subscript (1, 2, or 3) is written enclosed in parentheses after the array name (D$ or P). Each of the elements in the arrays D$ and P has been assigned a value in lines 20 through 70. The value of the subscript must be a nonnegative integer (0, 1, 2, 3, . . .) and must not exceed the maximum size given in the DIM instruction. Here, the maximum subscript value is 3.

A variable may be used as the subscript (for example, I in line 90) as long as its value does not violate any of the above requirements.

Color titles D through F and lines 80, 90, and 100 of the Sample Program. Color the values shown on the video display screen.

The combined use of the *FOR/NEXT instruction* and arrays provides a very useful programming technique. When the subscript is a variable (rather than a number), it can be changed to specify any array element. Here, in line 90, the counter variable I of the FOR/NEXT loop is used as the subscript. The first time through the loop the value of the counter variable I is 1 (line 80). In the next line (90) the I value, equal to a subscript value of 1, indicates that the first array element is printed. The values of the array elements D$(1) and P(1) are displayed (XXX and 3). Then NEXT (line 100) is executed causing I to be incremented by 1 (recall that if the STEP option is omitted in a FOR instruction, the increment is 1) so that I becomes 2. Two is less than or equal to 3, so the values of the second element in each array are displayed (YYY and 4). The process continues until the values of all three elements of each array are *displayed*.

The subscripted variable allows you to create, in effect, many variable names. Each can be referred to by a change of subscript. It is as if everyone in your family used the same surname but different numbers. You might call yourself JONES(18) and your sister JONES(19).

THE DIM INSTRUCTION AND SUBSCRIPTED VARIABLES.

DIM INSTRUCTION_A
  SIZE OF ARRAY_{A1}
SUBSCRIPTED VARIABLE_{B()}
  ARRAY NAME_{B1}
  SUBSCRIPT_{B2}
ARRAY VALUE_C
FOR INSTRUCTION_D
PRINT INSTRUCTION_E
  DISPLAY_{E1}
NEXT INSTRUCTION_F

SAMPLE PROGRAM ★

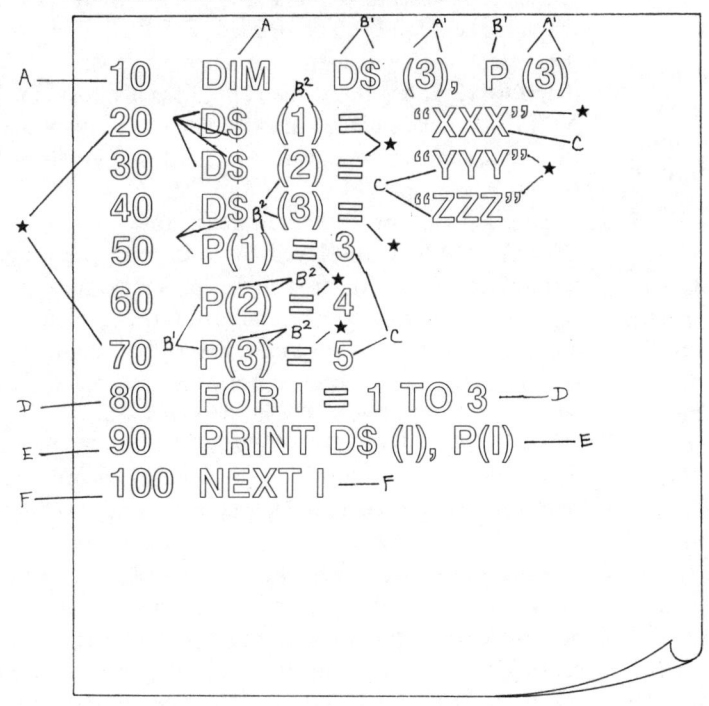

```
10   DIM  D$ (3), P (3)
20   D$ (1) = "XXX"
30   D$ (2) = "YYY"
40   D$ (3) = "ZZZ"
50   P(1) = 3
60   P(2) = 4
70   P(3) = 5
80   FOR I = 1 TO 3
90   PRINT D$ (I), P(I)
100  NEXT I
```

RAM TABLE ★

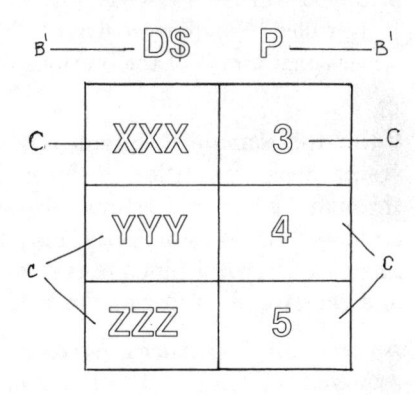

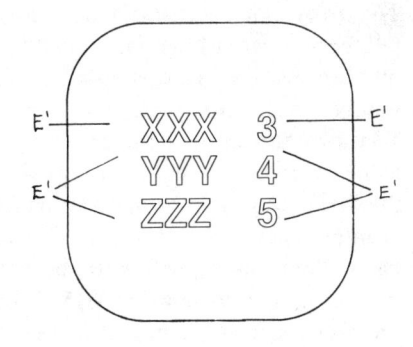

D$	P
XXX	3
YYY	4
ZZZ	5

XXX	3
YYY	4
ZZZ	5

26
TWO-DIMENSIONAL ARRAYS

In the previous plate you saw how arrays provide an efficient means of describing and referencing a large number of related values. You learned how an array can be used in a program. One array contained the inventory item's description and the other, its price. These arrays were considered as lists of values one right after the other. You referred to a particular element by specifying its position (subscript) in the list.

Suppose that you have to make a seating arrangement for a formal dinner. There are three dinner tables with six people at each. You could use an array of eighteen elements to keep track of the seating arrangements. In this plate you will learn how another form of array is used. It is called two-dimensional as opposed to the one-dimensional arrays of the previous plate.

Color the Sample Program, RAM Table, and Subscript headings, titles A through F, and lines 5 through 180 of the Sample Program. Use a light color for E. For simplicity, only pertinent program lines are shown. Color the row and column numbers and the stored values of the RAM table.

An array with two dimensions is considered as a table with rows and columns. A *DIM instruction* is used to specify the name and number of elements of the array (see line 5). The *array name* (T$ in the example) is followed by two numbers in parentheses (separated by a comma). The first number identifies the total number of *rows* and the second number the total number of *columns* in the array. Here, T$ is two-dimensional; three rows by six columns of string valued variables. You can specify a particular element of the array by giving its row and column numbers. In the example, each of the array elements is assigned a person's name. For example, in line 10, the first array element (1,1) is assigned the *array value* MIKE. Lines 10 through 180 are *assignment instructions;* lines 10 and 20 illustrate the parts of the instruction. Instead of assignment instructions, INPUT or READ/DATA instructions could be used to assign values to the variables.

You can interpret the meaning of a row and column to conform with your program needs. In the example, the row designates the dinner table number and the column designates the seat at the table. For example, you could interpret line 70 (T$(2,1) = "EILEEN") as Eileen being seated at table 2, seat 1.

Color titles G through I and the remaining lines of the Sample Program. Color the values shown on the video display as well.

Suppose that a particular row or column of the array is to be used in a program. Here, you want to display those persons seated at table 2. The instructions used to perform this task are similar to those used for one-dimensional arrays. The *FOR instruction* (line 190) initializes the value of the variable, S, to 1. Then, line 200 is executed causing the value of T$(2,1) to be printed. EILEEN is shown on the video display because the current value of S is 1, therefore (2,S) has the value (2,1), Eileen's position. The *NEXT instruction* causes the value of S to be incremented by 1 to assume the new value of 2. The value of T$(2,2), BARRY, is displayed.

The looping process continues until the value of T$(2,6), JOAN, is displayed. At this point the program terminates. Notice, the first subscript was not changed. It represents the row (dinner table) of the person whose name is stored at the second subscript position (at the table). The column (seat) subscript is changed (by using S = 1 to 6) to indicate the individual's seat.

The two-dimensional array allows the user to create lists in the form of tables. The array elements must represent the same type of data. Do not mix string and numeric values in one array. The one-dimensional array is equivalent to a table of just one column of values. Some versions of BASIC allow the user to create higher dimensional arrays. A three-dimensional array, with subscripts representing row, column, and layer, could be used to store reference to research information. The subscripts could represent author number, topic number, and publisher number. The actual value of the array element could be the reference's title. Larger dimensions may be hard to visualize, but they have applications in business, mathematics, and science.

TWO-DIMENSIONAL ARRAYS.

DIM INSTRUCTION_A
ARRAY NAME_B
  SIZE OF ARRAY_B1
SUBSCRIPT ★
  ROW_C
  COLUMN_D
ARRAY VALUE_E
ASSIGNMENT INSTRUCTION_F
FOR INSTRUCTION_G
PRINT INSTRUCTION_H
  DISPLAY_H1
NEXT INSTRUCTION_I

SAMPLE PROGRAM ★

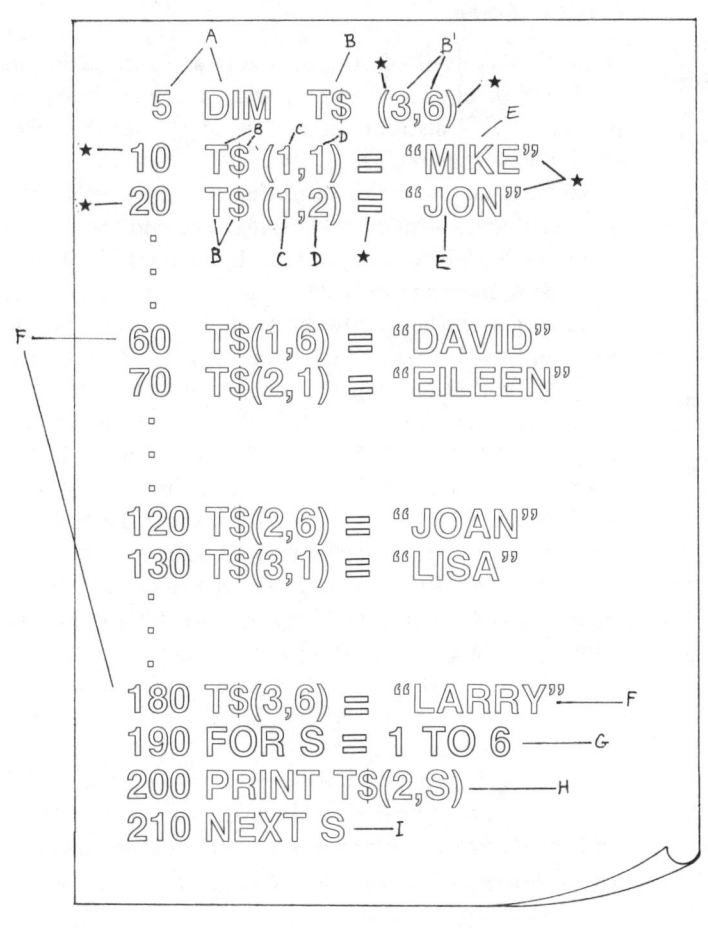

RAM TABLE ★

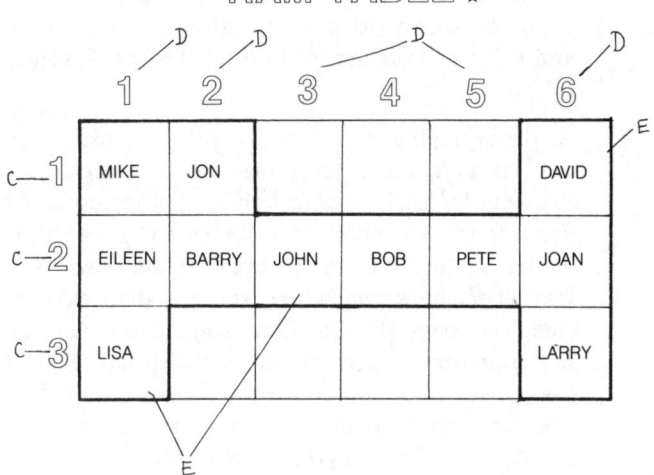

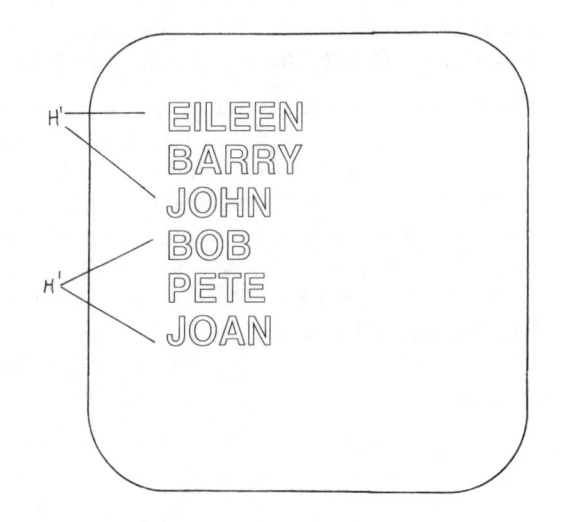

	1	2	3	4	5	6
C→1	MIKE	JON				DAVID
C→2	EILEEN	BARRY	JOHN	BOB	PETE	JOAN
C→3	LISA					LARRY

```
 5   DIM T$ (3,6)
10   T$ (1,1) = "MIKE"
20   T$ (1,2) = "JON"
  .
  .
  .
60   T$(1,6) = "DAVID"
70   T$(2,1) = "EILEEN"
  .
  .
120  T$(2,6) = "JOAN"
130  T$(3,1) = "LISA"
  .
  .
180  T$(3,6) = "LARRY"
190  FOR S = 1 TO 6
200  PRINT T$(2,S)
210  NEXT S
```

EILEEN
BARRY
JOHN
BOB
PETE
JOAN

27 SAMPLE PROGRAM: PLANE TICKET RESERVATIONS

In this plate you will learn how a plane ticket reservation program is created. Although the program is written in a simplified form, it is the basis of much larger programs used by airlines. Assume that the airline is very small. It goes from here to two cities (A and B) and has three fare groups (First Class, Business, and Tourist) whose ticket prices are fixed at $100, $50, and $25 respectively. The number of tickets available in each fare group is limited.

Color the Plane Ticket Reservation Program, Subscript, RAM Table, Tickets Available, and Price headings. Color titles A through D and the subscripts and values of the arrays in the RAM table representation.

At the beginning of each working day the user stores, in the Tickets Available array, the number of tickets that are available for each combination of destination and class (fare group). The program that is used to store this information is similar to the program of the previous plate. Instead of names, numbers are stored in the Tickets Available (TA) array. This array is two-dimensional. The first subscript (*row*) represents the ticket group (1 for First Class, 2 for Business Class, 3 for Tourist Class). The second subscript (*column*) represents the destination (1 for city A, 2 for city B). In the example, the *value* of TA(3,1) is 30, representing 30 tickets available in Tourist Class to city A.

The ticket prices are stored in the one-dimensional array, P. The values of the elements of P represent the prices $100, $50, and $25 of the tickets in each fare group.

Color the Sample Program heading, titles E through H, and lines 10 through 80 of the Sample Program. Color the first five lines on the video display screen.

The first thing that the ticket agent does is ask the customer for the destination and fare group desired. The *PRINT instructions* (lines 10 and 30) *display* a prompt describing the information to be entered. The *INPUT instructions* cause the program to halt until the ticket agent enters the responses of the customer. In the example, the customer indicates a First Class ticket is desired (C = 1) and that the destination is city B (D = 2) (see the video display screen). The program then makes use of an *IF . . . THEN . . . instruction* (line 50) to check if there are any tickets available (is the value of TA(1,2) not 0?). If the value is not 0, the program causes the value to appear together with the word AVAILABLE on the video display (line 80). In the example, there are 25 tickets available, corresponding to (1,2) of the TA table.

Airlines can run out of tickets. The program makes allowance for this possibility. If the value of TA(1,2) is 0, a NOT AVAILABLE message is displayed (line 60) and the program branches back to line 10 to allow another choice to be entered.

Color title I and the remaining lines of the program (90 through 130) and the last three lines on the video display screen.

If the number available is not 0, then the actual ticket can be shown on the video display and/or printed out on a printer. PRINT instructions are used to produce the ticket (lines 90, 100, and 110).

Before going on to the next customer, the computer is instructed to do a little bookkeeping. The number of tickets available in First Class for city B is reduced by 1 (line 120). Now there are only 24 tickets available. After the processing of the ticket information for this passenger, the program flow branches back (line 130) to allow for the entry of another passenger's requirements.

Other features that could be added to an airline ticket program include a check for wrong input data. If the ticket agent enters city 22 instead of 2, a message should be displayed indicating the data entry error. Perhaps, at the end of the day, the airline would want to know how many of each ticket type were sold and the total amount of sales. Instructions could be added to the program to display the totals when the agent types in a code number (for example, −100) for the fare group. This is similar to using the trailer in the READ/DATA program (Plate 23).

The program may ask for the customer's name and prepare a passenger seating chart. The number of cities could be increased to include several hundred destinations with possibly ten or more fare groups.

PLANE TICKET RESERVATIONS
CN 9

SAMPLE PROGRAM.

PLANE TICKET RESERVATION PROGRAM ★
ARRAY NAME_A
SUBSCRIPT ★
  ROW (CLASS)_B
  COLUMN (DESTINATION)_C
ARRAY VALUE_D
PRINT INSTRUCTION_E
  DISPLAY_{E1}
INPUT INSTRUCTION_F
  PROMPTED VALUE_{F1}
IF...THEN...INSTRUCTION_G
GOTO INSTRUCTION_H
ASSIGNMENT INSTRUCTION_I

SAMPLE PROGRAM ★

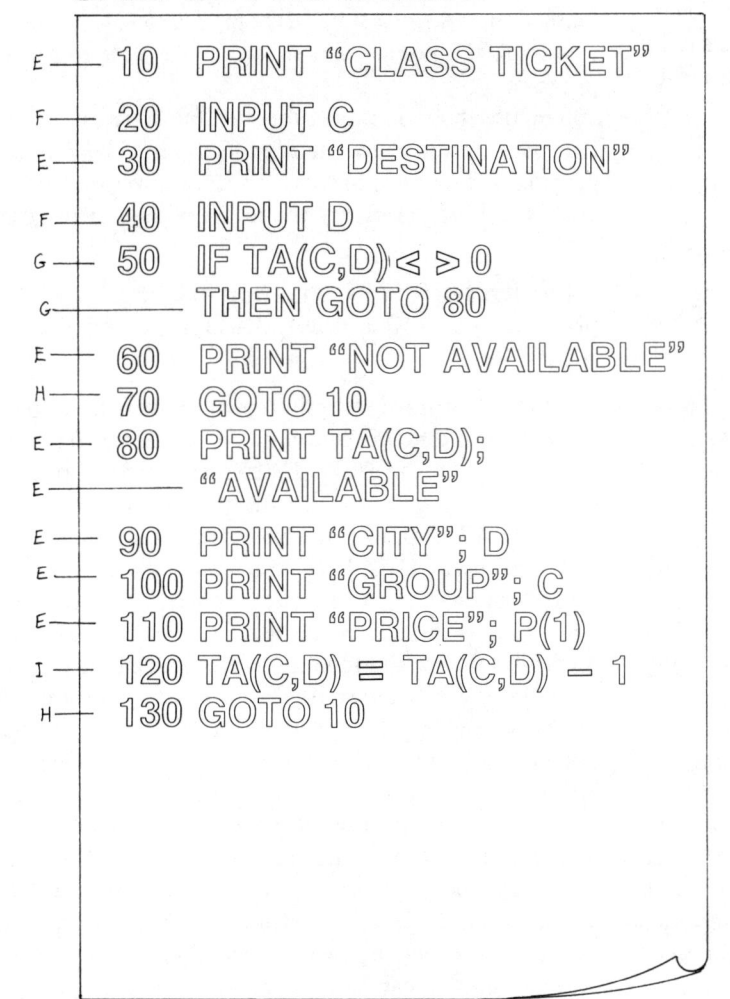

```
 10   PRINT "CLASS TICKET"
 20   INPUT C
 30   PRINT "DESTINATION"
 40   INPUT D
 50   IF TA(C,D) < > 0
      THEN GOTO 80
 60   PRINT "NOT AVAILABLE"
 70   GOTO 10
 80   PRINT TA(C,D);
      "AVAILABLE"
 90   PRINT "CITY"; D
100   PRINT "GROUP"; C
110   PRINT "PRICE"; P(1)
120   TA(C,D) = TA(C,D) − 1
130   GOTO 10
```

RAM TABLE ★

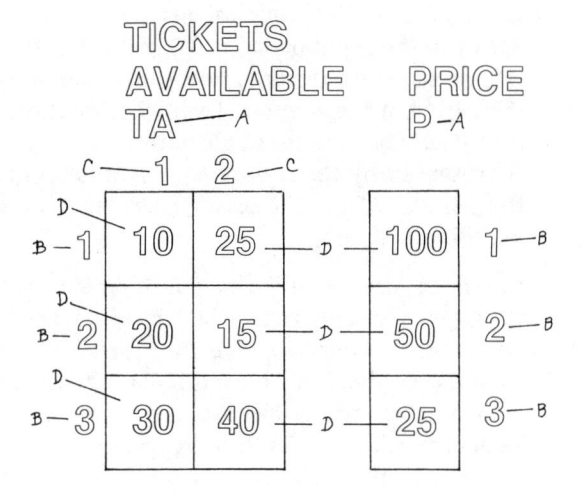

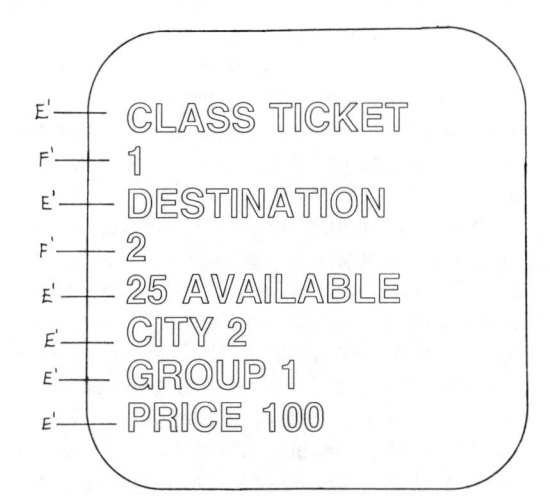

TICKETS AVAILABLE
TA — A

	1	2
1	10	25
2	20	15
3	30	40

PRICE
P — A

100	1
50	2
25	3

CLASS TICKET
1
DESTINATION
2
25 AVAILABLE
CITY 2
GROUP 1
PRICE 100

28
THE SQUARE ROOT AND INTEGER FUNCTIONS AND DEFINE FUNCTION INSTRUCTION

When you want to perform a difficult arithmetic task, such as finding the square root of a number, creating a program can be very complicated. Recall that the square root of a number is a second number that when multiplied by itself gives a product that is the original number. (For example, the square root of 16 is 4.) In BASIC, as in many computer languages, the manufacturer has supplied special programs in ROM, called function subroutines, that you use to perform such complicated tasks.

Color the Function Subroutine and SQR Function headings, titles A through G, and lines 10 and 20 of the SQR Function mainline program. Color gray the arrow to the input prompt (B[1]) and the entered value (B[2]) on the video display. Color line 30 and the arrow (F) carrying the number 16 to the function subroutine (G). The function subroutine is simplified and represented by the square root symbol contained in the box, G. Color the arrow carrying 4 back to the mainline program.

In order to use one of the manufacturer supplied subroutines, you need only know which reserved word and syntax to use in your program. In most cases, the syntax includes the *function's name* (SQR) followed by one or more numbers or variables enclosed in parentheses. These values are called the *function arguments* (or parameters). In the example, the value of N is supplied by you at the keyboard (16) in response to the question mark prompt generated by line 20. The interpreter recognizes SQR as a function subroutine name. The value of the argument, 16, is sent to that part of memory that stores the square root finding program. The *subroutine program* is executed and the square root found (4). This value is returned to the *mainline program.* In the example, the returned value is *assigned* to a variable, X.

INT(N) is another function subroutine. It returns to the mainline the largest integer less than or equal to N. That is, if N is an integer (say 3) the value returned to the mainline is the number itself (3). If N is a positive number, not an integer (say, 3.873), INT truncates (chops off) the decimal portion and returns the integer part of the number (3 in this example). Notice that this is not the same as rounding off to the nearest integer as 3.873 would round off to 4. If N is a number less than 0 (negative), the value returned is the negative integer less than N. For example, if N is −4.8, the value returned by INT(N) is −5. Negative 5 is the integer just less than negative 4.8. Let's see how such a function can be used.

Color the INT Function heading, titles H and H[1], and INT Function program lines 5 through 50. Color the arrows, the function subroutine, and the displays on the video screens.

A particular value (3.873) is assigned to the variable N (line 5). Then, in the assignment instruction following, the value of N is multiplied by 10 and the product added to .5. The resulting value is assigned to the variable K (line 10) and displayed (line 20). At this point, the INT function is called upon with the argument K. The value returned is 39 and is assigned to L (INT(39.23) is 39). A second assignment instruction causes this value of L to be divided by 10 (line 40) and assigned to another variable M. Finally, the value (3.9) of M is displayed. The net result of this program is to round off the value of N to the nearest tenth. Some versions of BASIC supply a round-off subroutine in ROM rather than requiring the user to write a program.

Suppose that you need a function but it was not one of the many supplied by the manufacturer. The rounding program is a nice one to have. BASIC allows you to create your own function subroutine to use with your program.

Color the DEF FN Instruction heading, title I, the program lines (10 and 20), the arrows, and the subroutine box.

The DEF FN (define function) instruction is used to create your own function subroutine (user defined function). First, you enter the DEF FN reserved word, followed by the name of your particular function. (Note: Some versions of BASIC allow function names of one letter only.) In the example, DEF FNR has been entered to indicate we are defining our own function, called R (for rounding). After typing the assignment symbol, "=", you type in how the value of the function is to be calculated. In the example, the rounding program from the INT example has been condensed into one formula. It is stored as a function subroutine, illustrated by the box labeled G. Now, when you need to use the function, you refer to it by name as with any other function subroutine. The only difference is that the name must be prefixed by FN. So, as in line 20, the program makes use of the function R(X) created by the DEF FN instruction. Here, the returned value (3.9) is assigned to the variable T. Your newly created function can be used anywhere in your program. Of course, when the power is turned off, the computer forgets your function, as it is not part of ROM.

SQUARE ROOT AND INTEGER FUNCTIONS AND DEFINE FUNCTION INSTRUCTION.

MAINLINE PROGRAM[A]
   INPUT INSTRUCTION[B]/ PROMPT[B1]/PROMPTED VALUE[B2]
   ASSIGNMENT INSTRUCTION[C]
FUNCTION SUBROUTINE ★
   FUNCTION NAME[D]
   FUNCTION ARGUMENT[E]
   PROCESSING ARROW[F]
   STORED FUNCTION SUBROUTINE[G]
PRINT INSTRUCTION[H]/ DISPLAY[H1]

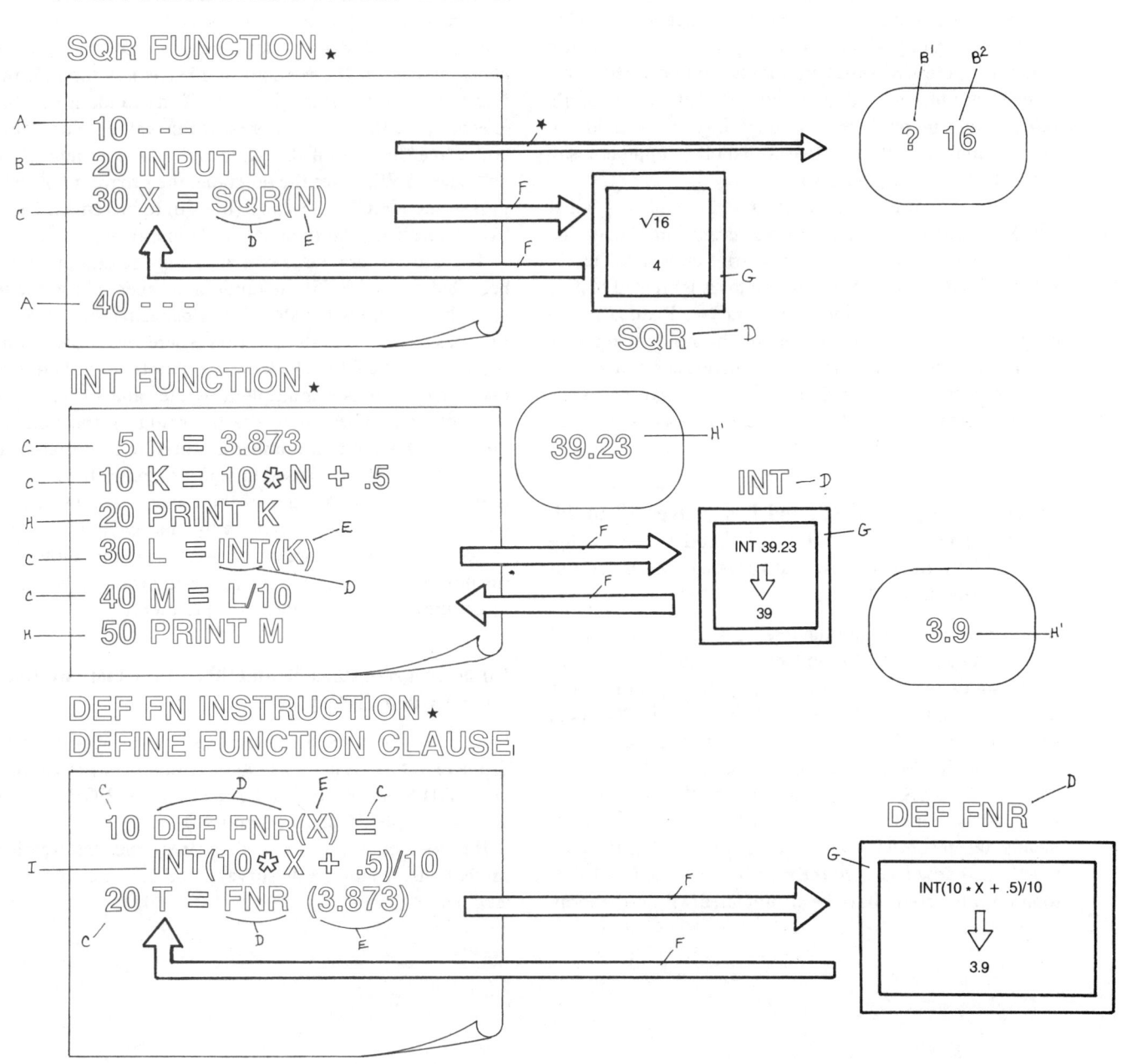

SQR FUNCTION ★

```
10 - - -
20 INPUT N
30 X = SQR(N)
40 - - -
```

?   16

√16
4

SQR

INT FUNCTION ★

```
 5 N = 3.873
10 K = 10 * N + .5
20 PRINT K
30 L = INT(K)
40 M = L/10
50 PRINT M
```

39.23

INT

INT 39.23
↓
39

3.9

DEF FN INSTRUCTION ★
DEFINE FUNCTION CLAUSE[I]

```
10 DEF FNR(X) =
   INT(10 * X + .5)/10
20 T = FNR (3.873)
```

DEF FNR

INT(10 * X + .5)/10
↓
3.9

29
THE RANDOM NUMBER INSTRUCTION

Tossing a coin is simple for humans. For the computer it is not as easy. But once you write a program to simulate tossing a coin, the computer can do it thousands of times without tiring and keep track of the results.

Color the Coin Toss Program heading, titles A, C, D, E and F, the RND Function Subroutine heading, and line 40 only of the Coin Toss Program. Then color the arrows and the box representing a random number subroutine.

A random experiment, such as a coin toss, is any experiment whose outcome cannot be predicted exactly. You can say that the coin will land with the head or tail side up, but not exactly which one will appear. The key to any random experiment simulation is the ability of the computer to produce a random number. A random number's value cannot be predicted with certainty. You could say that the number will be between two other numbers, say 0 and 1, but not its exact value.

The function used to call for a random number is called RND (*function name*). It has one *argument*, N. In the example on line 40, N was arbitrarily chosen to be 19. When RND(N) is used in a program, it is treated just as any other built-in function subroutine (see Plate 28). The program flow at line 40 passes to the random number generating subroutine (the *stored function subroutine*). A random number is created. Then the flow returns to the mainline program, line 40, where the number is assigned to X (X = the random number).

Color titles B, G, H, H¹, and I, and lines 10 to 70. Color the HEADS and TAILS listed on the video display. The dots are used to represent a longer list of HEADS and TAILS.

In addition to simulating the tossing of a coin, one would want to keep track of the numbers of "heads" and "tails." To do so, two variables (H and T) are used whose values will be the numbers of "heads" and "tails." Initially, these values are 0 (lines 10 and 20). The sequence of instructions to simulate the tossing of a coin is to be repeated 100 times. So, a FOR/NEXT loop is used (lines 30 and 70). The value of the counter variable FLIP, initially 1, is incremented by one until its value reaches 101, causing the loop to end, and flow passes to the next line (80). So in all, 100 tosses of the "coin" have been simulated within the loop.

The value generated by the random number subroutine depends on how the particular manufacturer wrote the ROM routine. There are two ways this could be done. One method gives a value of RND(N) as an integer between 0 and N (for example, RND(5) returns from the function subroutine a value 0, 1, 2, 3, or 4).

A second method, used in the example, gives a value of RND(N) as a number between 0 and 1. (In this case, the argument does not define the maximum returned value.) If the returned value is greater than .5, the program interprets this as "heads" and displays HEADS. At the same time, the counter H is incremented by 1 (line 50). The colon (:) between the *PRINT* and *assignment instruction* is a way of putting two instructions on the same line or in the same *THEN clause*. Both are executed when the *IF clause* is true. If the random number is less than .5, the interpretation is "tails" (line 60). If the random number is exactly .5, the program ignores this value. (You could add a line that says if the value is .5, the coin landed on an "edge.") Whatever the outcome, the program flow will pass to the *NEXT instruction* (line 70) to increment FLIP by 1 and repeat the tossing simulation again.

There are several ways of generating the random number. One method is for the random number subroutine to read the current value stored in a particular RAM location. Usually, this is the location where the current time is placed by the CPU clock circuit. Another method is to take a large number, multiply it by the value of N, divide by another number, and take the result as the random number. This random number is stored in a special location so that if RND is used again, it becomes the number that multiplies N. Neither of these methods gives a perfectly random number. That is why random numbers generated by a computer are called pseudorandom. However, the numbers are close enough to the real thing to be useful in creating computer random experiments.

Color program lines 80 and 90 and the last two lines on the video display screen.

Once the 100 tosses are completed, the results must be displayed. The values of H and T, numbers of HEADS and TAILS, are printed out as soon as the FOR/NEXT loop is completed (lines 80 and 90).

Random numbers are used in areas such as weather predictions, demographic surveys, and business sales projections.

RANDOM NUMBER INSTRUCTION.

ASSIGNMENT INSTRUCTION[A]
FOR INSTRUCTION[B]
RND FUNCTION SUBROUTINE ★
  FUNCTION NAME[C]
  FUNCTION ARGUMENT[D]
  PROCESSING ARROW[E]
  STORED FUNCTION SUBROUTINE[F]
IF...THEN...INSTRUCTION[G]
PRINT INSTRUCTION[H]/ DISPLAY[H']
NEXT INSTRUCTION[I]

COIN TOSS PROGRAM ★

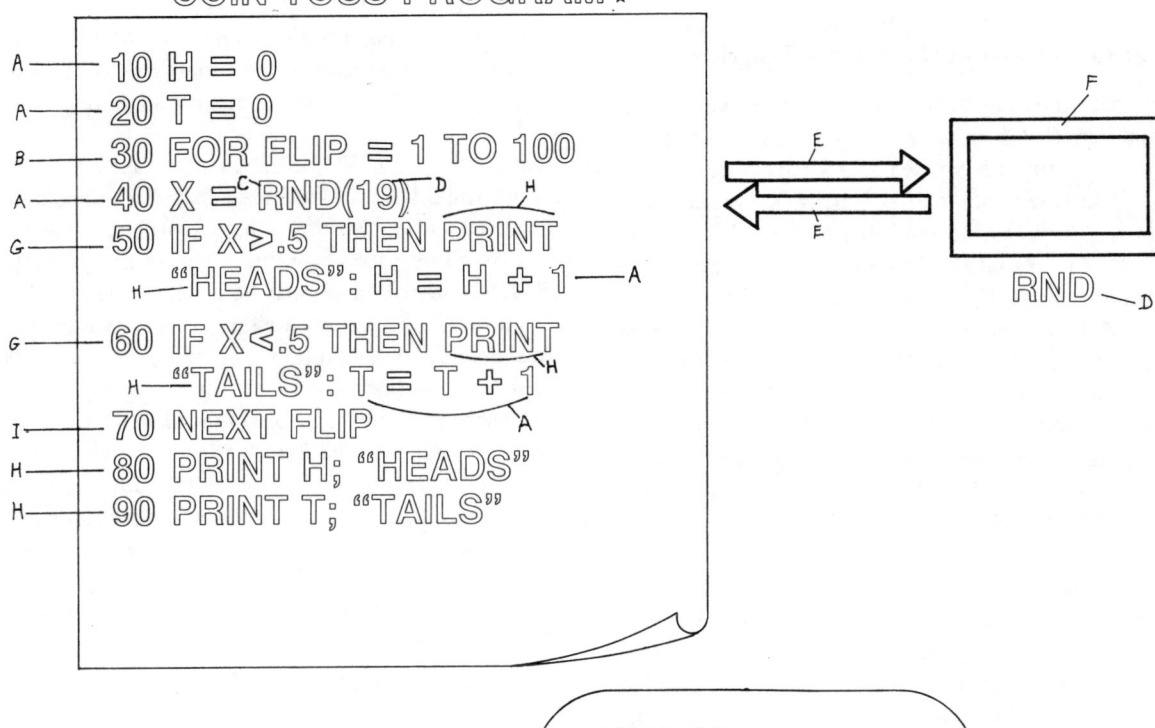

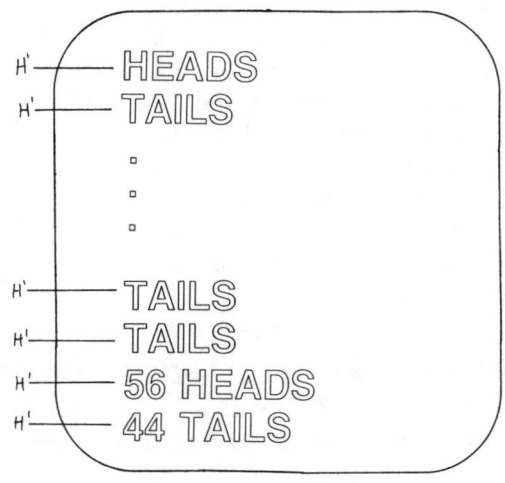

```
10 H = 0                              [A]
20 T = 0                              [A]
30 FOR FLIP = 1 TO 100                [B]
40 X = RND(19)                        [A,C,D]
50 IF X>.5 THEN PRINT                 [G]
   "HEADS": H = H + 1                 [H,A]
60 IF X<.5 THEN PRINT                 [G]
   "TAILS": T = T + 1                 [H,A]
70 NEXT FLIP                          [I]
80 PRINT H; "HEADS"                   [H]
90 PRINT T; "TAILS"                   [H]
```

RND [D]

Display output:
- HEADS
- TAILS
- .
- .
- .
- TAILS
- TAILS
- 56 HEADS
- 44 TAILS

30
THE GOSUB AND RETURN INSTRUCTIONS

In the last plates you learned that a function subroutine is used to calculate a single value (say, a square root). You use the function subroutine whenever it is needed within the mainline program. You learned how to create a function subroutine of your own by means of the DEF FN instruction (provided you could express it in one line). If you wanted to create a subroutine that could not be expressed in a single formula, your routine could require several lines. In order to create such a subroutine, you make use of GOSUB and RETURN instructions.

Color the Sample Program heading and titles A through E. Color the array values in list 1 and list 2 at the top right of the diagram. Color only lines 120 to 150 at the bottom of the Sample Program.

Suppose that you have to find the maximum value of a list of numbers (list 1 or list 2). The program *subroutine* to find this maximum is written as a separate part of the mainline. The three *values* of the array X elements are stored in memory (10, 15, and 3, for example). At the start, it is assumed that the first entry of the array is the largest number (line 120). This value is assigned to the variable MAX (*assignment instruction*). (MAX would be made equal to 10). The FOR/NEXT loop (lines 130 and 150) allows for a comparison of the second through third elements with the value of MAX. If MAX (10) is less than the value of the next entry (15), then the value of MAX is changed to reflect the larger number: IF MAX < X(I) THEN MAX = X(I) (or MAX now equals 15).

Branching to this subroutine is straightforward. One could use a GOTO that transfers control to the beginning instruction of the subroutine (line 120 in the program). However, if two different sections of the mainline are to make use of this subroutine, there will be two different GOTO instructions that branch to the first line. Lines 40 and 90 both direct the flow to line 120 (GOSUB 120). When the subroutine is finished calculating the maximum value of the array, the program must branch back to the correct position in the mainline program. There are two different places to which the program flow must return after the subroutine has completed the required task.

Color titles F through L and program lines 5 to 110 and line 160. Color the arrows to and from the subroutine box (I), including the line numbers on the top arrows (H[1]).

Line 5 of the program is a *DIM instruction,* which should be familiar from Plate 25. The assignment of values to the X array is done twice. The first time the values in list 1 are assigned to the array (lines 10 through 30). (You could use READ/DATA instructions to make the assignments also.) Next, instead of a GOTO, a *GOSUB instruction* is used. The GOSUB (line 40) behaves like a GOTO and transfers control to the first line of the subroutine. The operating system stores in RAM the line number of the next instruction after the GOSUB (indicated by arrow H[1] with line number 50 stored). This enables the flow to return to the next correct position in the mainline program (line 50) when the subroutine is done. In the example, the first time the GOSUB appears, the program branches to the subroutine that begins at line 120. At this point the instructions in the subroutine (lines 120 to 150) are executed, producing the desired maximum value assigned to MAX.

Notice the *RETURN instruction* at the end of the subroutine (line 160). It indicates that the subroutine has completed its task. At this point the program flow returns to the mainline instruction (line 50) after the GOSUB. The RETURN instruction must be at the logical end of the subroutine. The maximum value of list 1 is shown on the video display as a result of the execution of a *PRINT instruction* (line 50).

The second assignment of values to the array X is now done. The values in list 2 are assigned to the array (lines 60 to 80). Again, a GOSUB (line 90) causes a branch to the subroutine. This time, the line number following this GOSUB is stored in RAM, replacing the previous value used by the first GOSUB. The maximum value of this second array is found by the subroutine (lines 120 to 150). Then the RETURN instruction of the subroutine is executed a second time. This time, the operating system branches back to line 100. The new maximum value is displayed. The program is completed and terminates (line 110).

In addition to containing instructions for tasks that are repeated many times in a program, subroutines are used in very large programs. A large program is broken down into several subroutines. Each subroutine performs a task which is part of the large program. A typical sequence of subroutines may be to input values of a list of names, alphabetize the list, store it on a floppy disk, search for a particular name on the list, and perhaps, print out the number of entries on the list. The mainline program would then be only a series of GOSUB instructions, one to each subroutine in the required order of execution.

THE GOSUB AND RETURN INSTRUCTIONS.

ARRAY VALUES_A
ASSIGNMENT INSTRUCTION_B
FOR INSTRUCTION_C
IF...THEN...INSTRUCTION_D
NEXT INSTRUCTION_E
DIM INSTRUCTION_F
INPUT INSTRUCTION_G
GOSUB INSTRUCTION_H
  ARROW WITH LINE MEMORY_{H1}
SUBROUTINE BOX_I
RETURN INSTRUCTION_J/ARROW_{J1}
PRINT INSTRUCTION_K/ DISPLAY_{K1}
END INSTRUCTION_L

SAMPLE PROGRAM ★

LIST 1		LIST 2
10	A	4.1
15	A	2.3
3	A	6.9

```
 5  DIM X(3)
10  INPUT X(1)
20  INPUT X(2)
30  INPUT X(3)
40  GOSUB 120
50  PRINT "ARRAY 1 MAX":
    MAX
60  INPUT X(1)
70  INPUT X(2)
80  INPUT X(3)
90  GOSUB 120
100 PRINT "ARRAY 2 MAX":
    MAX
110 END
120 MAX = X(1)
130 FOR I = 2 TO 3
140 IF MAX < X(I)
    THEN MAX = X(I)
150 NEXT I
160 RETURN
```

120 – 150
ORGANIZE
ARRAY
160 RETURN

ARRAY 1 MAX 15

ARRAY 2 MAX 6.9

31
LOW-RESOLUTION GRAPHICS

In the previous plates you saw that the computer can be used for very powerful calculations and sophisticated tasks. In this plate you will learn how pictures or diagrams can be drawn by the computer to display output.

A computer has two categories of display. Text mode is used when words, numerals, or special symbols are to be displayed. (This has been the case with all of the discussion to this point.) Graphics mode is used when a diagram or picture is to be shown. Some computers allow you to combine both modes so that pictures may have captions displayed.

Color titles A through C, the Coordinates heading, and the numbers of the vertical columns and horizontal rows on the top illustration. Choose contrasting colors for A and B. Color the lighted pixel on the display screen; its coordinates, (3,0), are shown in circles. Note that all the grid boxes shown in the illustrations are much larger than an actual screen grid.

The video display screen is divided into *columns* (vertical) and *rows* (horizontal) of tiny boxes. You do not see the actual columns and rows on the screen. In the diagram there are eight columns (numbered 0, 1, 2, 3, 4, 5, 6, 7) and six rows (numbered 0, 1, 2, 3, 4, 5). Each individual box is called a *pixel* (picture element). The pixel is the smallest spot that can be referenced by a given set of graphics instructions (software).

The diagram contains forty-eight pixels which can be lighted or left dark to form a design. In the illustration, you can see that any individual pixel can be identified by first stating its *column number,* then its *row number.* These two numbers, or coordinates, allow you to locate one specific pixel. The example pixel (3,0) is found at column 3, row 0.

The computer's operating system sets aside a portion of RAM to contain the data needed for display. Usually, not more than one byte of memory is used for each pixel. The particular code number determines how the operating system will direct the video display control circuits to light up the corresponding pixel. The pixel may be lighted with varying intensities of light. If you have a color video display, some computer operating systems allow the pixel to be lighted in a user-specified color. In order to instruct the computer to light up a pixel, special graphics instructions are supplied. Although the instructions vary among computers, they are used in programs just like any BASIC instruction.

Color the column and row numbers of the lower video display screen. Color the Plotting Coordinates and Plotting Program headings, title D, and the plotting instruction for the column and row coordinates of the first pixel (PLOT (0,5)). Then find and color the corresponding pixel that would be lighted on the display; it is indicated for you. Color all of the plotting instructions and corresponding pixels.

The microcomputer graphics instructions use the format PLOT (X,Y), (or SET (X,Y) or DRAW (X,Y)), as part of the program. In order to plot the shape in the illustration, a program would include the listed sequence of *plotting instructions.*

Plotting instructions are interpreted by the operating system, and a code number is stored at the RAM location for each pixel whose coordinates are given. Then, the video display circuits are instructed by the operating system to light up the designated pixels. In the diagram, the instruction to light up the pixel whose coordinates are (0,5), (column 0, row 5) would be of the form PLOT (0,5), resulting in the pixel in the upper left being lighted. If you located the pixels on the screen correctly, the display shows a square "O" in the top left corner. You may wish to list the coordinates of the pixels that, when lighted, display your initial.

Our sample screen consists of only forty-eight pixels. This number limits the screen graphics to very simple designs (low resolution). Most computers have a larger number of columns and rows for screen graphic displays, usually on the order of forty columns by forty rows.

Increasing the number of pixels to a much larger density (say four hundred columns by four hundred rows) affords a much more detailed display (high resolution). This results in the pixel size being much smaller. One hundred high-resolution pixels would fit in a screen location held by only one pixel in low resolution. See Plate 33 for a discussion of high-resolution graphics.

LOW-RESOLUTION GRAPHICS.

COLUMNS_A
ROWS_B
COORDINATES ★
    COLUMN NUMBER_{A'}
    ROW NUMBER_{B'}
LIGHTED PIXEL_C

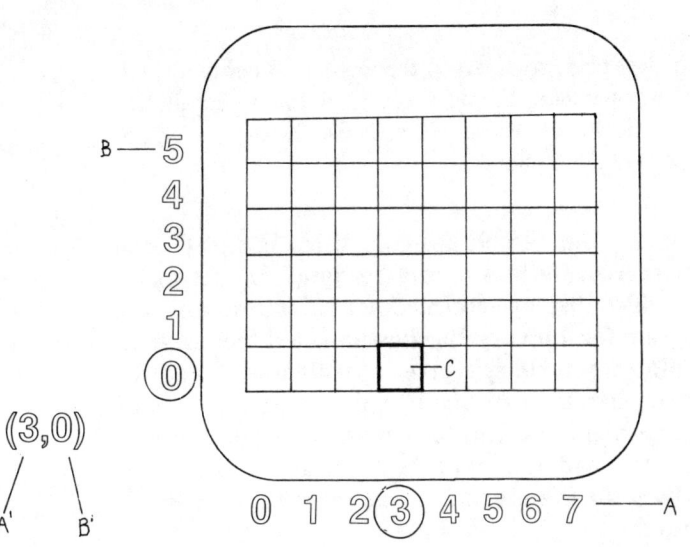

(3,0)

PLOTTING COORDINATES ★
PLOTTING INSTRUCTION_D

PLOTTING PROGRAM ★

```
10 PLOT (0,5)
20 PLOT (0,4)
30 PLOT (0,3)
40 PLOT (1,5)
50 PLOT (1,3)
60 PLOT (2,5)
70 PLOT (2,4)
80 PLOT (2,3)
```

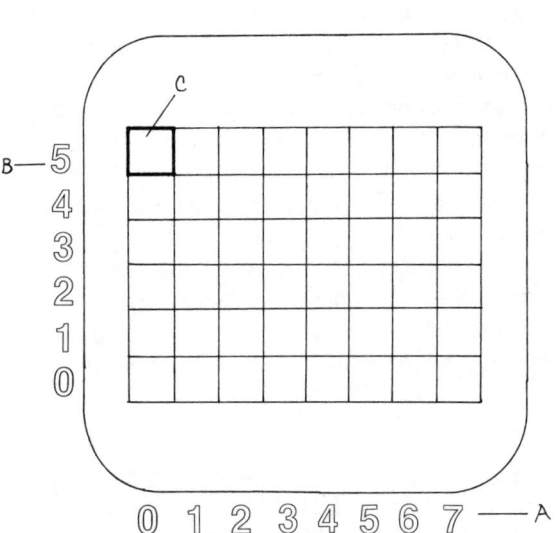

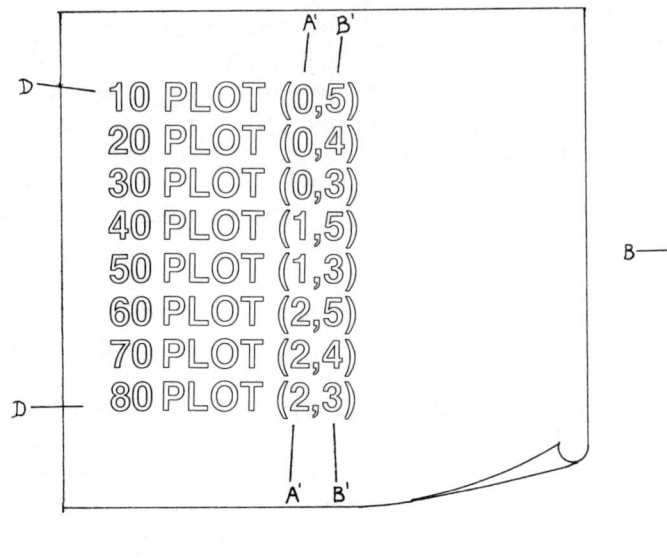

32 LOW-RESOLUTION GRAPHICS AT WORK

In the last plate you learned the method of lighting (plotting) a particular graphics pixel on the video display screen. In this plate you will see how the display can be made to show a chart.

Color the Bar Graph heading, titles B and C, and their representations on the bar graph on the upper right video display screen. Color titles A and D, the Program for January Bar heading, and the program for plotting January's pixel coordinates. Color the January bar, pixel by pixel, on the graph as you color the program lines. Use the column and row numbers at the side and bottom of the graph as a guide. Color the bars for the other three months (F, M, and A). Use light colors for A and C.

A bar graph consists of parallel *bars* whose lengths represent certain quantities. A larger quantity will have a longer bar than a smaller quantity. In the diagram each vertical bar represents the numer of sales in a particular month. For example, in January there were four sales. Each *pixel* represents one sale, so that the vertical bar for January is four pixels high. The vertical bar for February is seven pixels high, representing seven sales. If you want to add titles or *legends* to the vertical and horizontal lines (axes), some computers allow you to do so by means of PRINT instructions.

Let's see how the graphics instructions are used to display this bar chart on the screen. One method of plotting a bar graph is to plot the pixels of the bar one at a time. To do this, an instruction such as PLOT is used for each pixel. For January, four *plot instructions* are used in the program. For February, you would need seven instructions. You are plotting a bar (line segment) pixel by pixel. Most microcomputer graphic systems have additional instructions that relieve you of the tedium of plotting pixel by pixel. An example of this type of instruction is VERT LINE.

Color the Program for Bar Graph heading, titles E and F, and the first VERT LINE program instruction. After you color this instruction, go to the lower video display screen, color all the pixels from the first pixel in the instruction (1,1) to the last pixel (1,4) going in a vertical line. The first one is outlined for you. Do the others on your own, coloring the program lines and columns of pixels indicated. When you color the last program instruction, color the bottom horizontal line of the display. When you finish, you will have reproduced the top bar chart, only more efficiently than by the PLOT instruction.

The *VERT LINE instruction* tells the computer to display a vertical line segment from the given starting coordinates to the given ending coordinates. A similar *HOR LINE instruction* is used to draw the horizontal line at the bottom of the display screen.

Let's see how a "bug" can be made to move across the display screen. This technique is one method that you can use for screen animation.

Color the Program for Bug heading and titles G and H. Color the Row 3 on the Screen heading and the three related diagrams, coloring only the indicated pixel. Each diagram represents the display of row 3 at a different time. Color the time period numbers.

The method of programming the simulated movement of a pixel ("bug") across a screen is straightforward. The first instruction (line 10) plots the initial position (0,3). The next instruction (line 20) *erases* the plotted pixel. (Some computers use an instruction like RESET (0,3) or change the plotting color and then plot the pixel again.) The third instruction (line 30) plots the pixel in the next position (1,3). This procedure of erasing and then plotting the pixel at the new position is continued until termination. A program such as this may contain many plotting and erasing instructions. The computer executes the instructions so fast that the eye cannot see the individual plotting and erasing activity; rather, one sees a pixel moving rapidly across the screen at row 3. This method can be used to show the flow of electric current around a circuit or, as in Plate 43, a creature running around an obstacle course.

There are two disadvantages to the use of low-resolution graphics. The first is that the number of pixels that can be referenced (lighted) is very small. That is, some computers have a display that is forty columns by forty rows, or thirty-two columns by twenty-four rows. For large charts, such as bar graphs or very detailed diagrams, these dimensions prove a problem. You could not fit more than forty sales on a bar graph unless you assigned multiple sales to each pixel. A second disadvantage is that if a line is not vertical or horizontal, then it will appear as a series of steps rather than a smooth graph. Imagine plotting a line segment from the lower left to the upper right of a low-resolution display. The best you can do is create a stairway. For better detail and finer line segments, high-resolution graphic displays are used. They are discussed in the next plate.

LOW-RESOLUTION GRAPHICS AT WORK.

BAR GRAPH ★
   BAR/LIGHTED PIXELS A
   LEGEND B
   ROW 0 C
   PLOTTING INSTRUCTION D

PROGRAM FOR JANUARY BAR ★

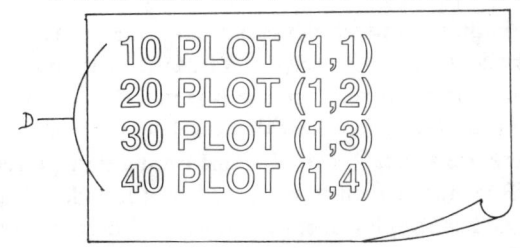

```
10 PLOT (1,1)
20 PLOT (1,2)
30 PLOT (1,3)
40 PLOT (1,4)
```
D

PROGRAM FOR BAR GRAPH ★
VERTICAL LINE INSTRUCTION E
HORIZONTAL LINE INSTRUCTION F

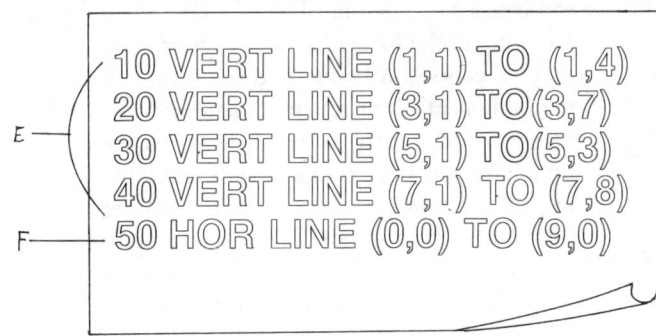

```
10 VERT LINE (1,1) TO (1,4)
20 VERT LINE (3,1) TO (3,7)
30 VERT LINE (5,1) TO (5,3)
40 VERT LINE (7,1) TO (7,8)
50 HOR LINE (0,0) TO (9,0)
```
E, F

PROGRAM FOR BUG ★
ERASE INSTRUCTION G
TIME H

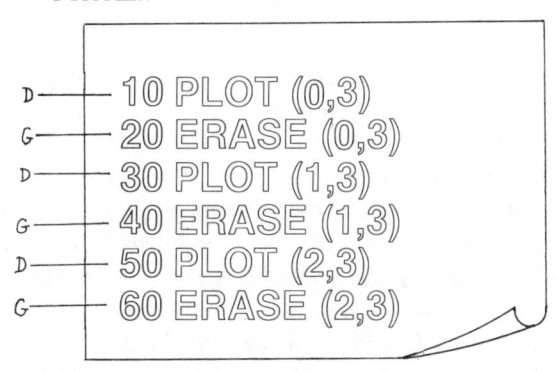

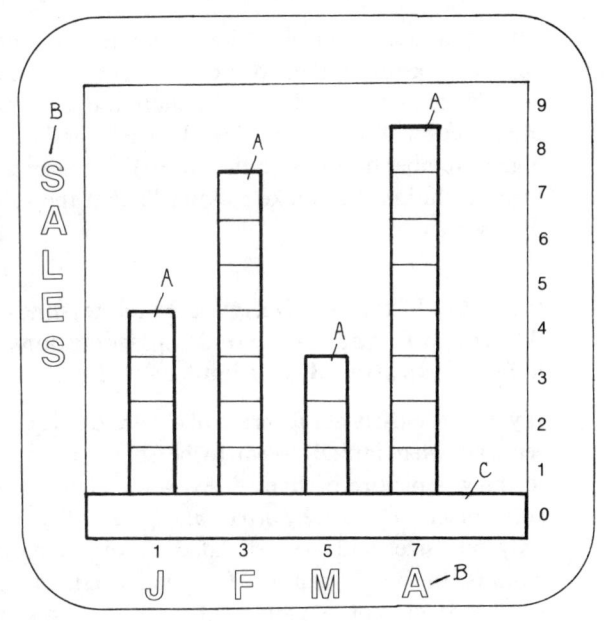

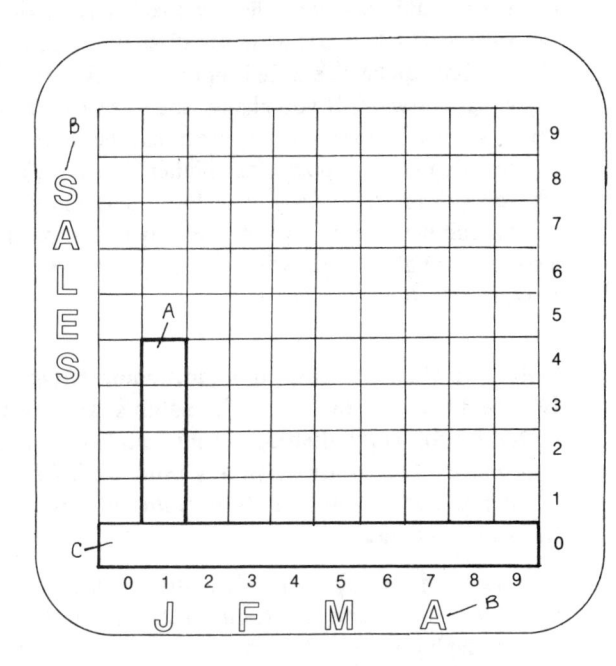

```
10 PLOT (0,3)
20 ERASE (0,3)
30 PLOT (1,3)
40 ERASE (1,3)
50 PLOT (2,3)
60 ERASE (2,3)
```

ROW 3 ON THE SCREEN ★

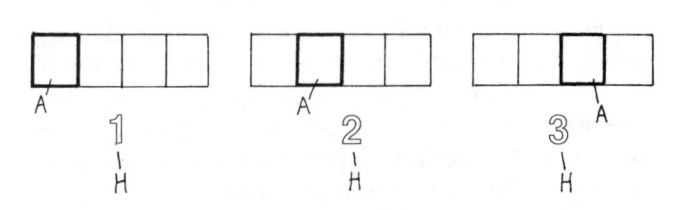

33
VIDEO DISPLAY GRAPHICS IN FINER DETAIL

When you use the pixels of low-resolution graphics they appear as boxes on the video display. More detailed and complicated charts and graphs require use of a finer type of resolution. You have read (in Plates 31 and 32) how a higher number of pixels on the video display can give this finer resolution. Let's take a closer look at the video display screen.

Color the Pixels and Software Pixel headings, titles A through C, and the related representations in the upper illustration. Use a light color for A.

If you look closely at the screen of a video display, you will see that what initially seem to be solid shapes of light forming a picture or line of text are composed of very small pixels. These are *video display pixels*. They come in only one size, and are generated by the video display circuits. In the diagram of H at the far left, the letter is composed of representations of activated video display pixels. Here a distinction must be made between the software pixel and the video display pixel. Recall that the software pixel (Plate 31) is the smallest spot on the video display that can be referenced (lighted or left dark) by the particular software. If you change the software, the number of software pixels on the screen can be increased up to the video display pixel size (higher resolution) or decreased (lower resolution). The low-resolution software pixel is composed of many video display pixels, producing a solid rectangle of light which then operates as one *low-resolution picture element* (C).

Color the Raster Scanning heading and titles D and D¹. Begin at the left of each raster scan line illustrated on the video display screen and follow it to its end, coloring only those pixels indicated. For illustrative purposes, only a few enlarged raster scan lines are shown.

The electronic circuitry in a video display causes an electron beam to traverse a pattern on the inside of the face of the display screen. This pattern is called a *raster*. A typical pattern consists of 525 horizontal *raster scan lines* repeated 30 times a second from the top of the screen to the bottom. The screen is coated with a compound (phosphor). The electron beam moves across the screen, synchronized by the video display circuitry with the timing circuits of the computer, to light or leave dark the video display pixels. The energy of the beam is controlled so as to vary the intensity of the light output.

The light output of the video display falls off rapidly after the electron beam has passed by. A steady picture is maintained by repeating the scanning pattern 30 times per second. The process is called video refresh.

Color the Video Refreshing and Bit Mapping headings, titles E, F, and G, and the related representations.

The computer's operating system sets aside enough memory (*video refresh memory,* or VRM) to store all of the data that is to appear on the screen. This memory is referenced every time the video display is refreshed.

There are several ways of transforming data stored in the VRM into a picture produced by the video display circuits. The simplest method, illustrated here, is to take the data just as it is read from the VRM and transmit it to the display circuits that control the electron beam. Each 1 bit appears as a lighted video display pixel and each 0 bit as darkness on the screen. For each screen pixel, one bit of VRM is assigned. In the example, the VRM bits give the top raster scanning line of video display pixels contributing to the formation of the letter H. Such an assignment is called a *bit map,* and the technique of using this method is called bit mapping display. This method gives very fine detail on the screen. You have a choice of lighting up a large rectangle (consisting of many screen pixels), as in low-resolution graphics, or just one screen pixel to give finer details. The amount of memory required for bit mapping is quite high. For example, a pattern of 400 pixels across by 400 high requires 160,000 bits or 20,000 bytes of memory (8 bits = 1 byte).

Most versions of BASIC have instructions that enable you to make use of the finer video display pixel for graphing.

Color the Character Generator heading, titles H through K, and the related representations. Use a light color for I.

A more efficient approach to displaying text (letters, numerals, punctuation, or special symbols) is available. This method makes use of a special hardware circuit (*character generator*) to produce the display. Each *character* to be displayed is encoded in a single byte (8-bit) code in *ROM*. The byte *code* for the character is converted into a suitable pixel pattern by the character generator for the video display. The conversion process uses a table in ROM to look up the particular pixel pattern. In the example, the binary character generator code is converted into the display pixel pattern for the letter H.

VIDEO DISPLAY GRAPHICS.

PIXELS ★
VIDEO DISPLAY PIXEL A
SOFTWARE PIXEL ★
   HIGH-RESOLUTION B
   LOW-RESOLUTION C

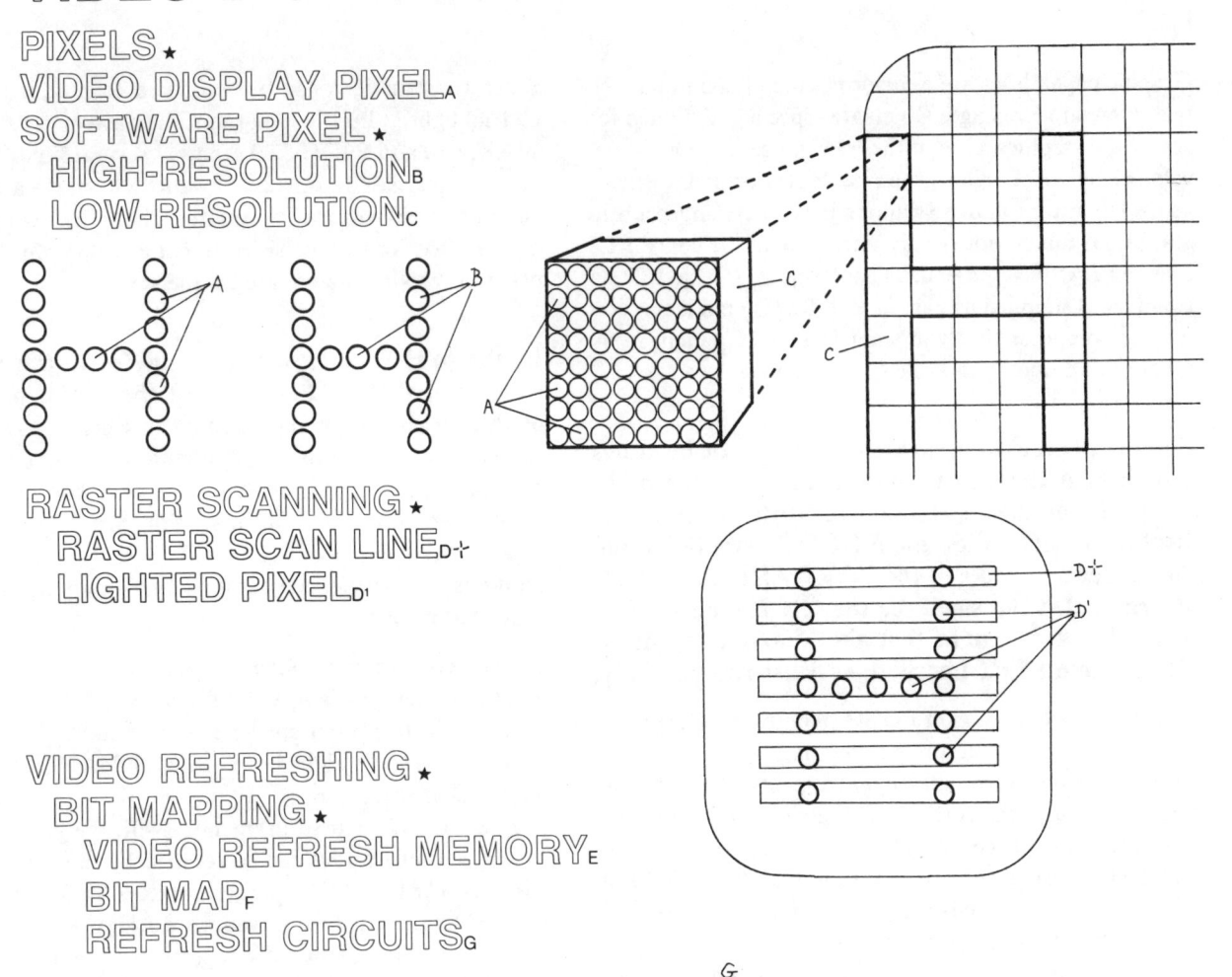

RASTER SCANNING ★
   RASTER SCAN LINE D
   LIGHTED PIXEL D'

VIDEO REFRESHING ★
   BIT MAPPING ★
     VIDEO REFRESH MEMORY E
     BIT MAP F
     REFRESH CIRCUITS G

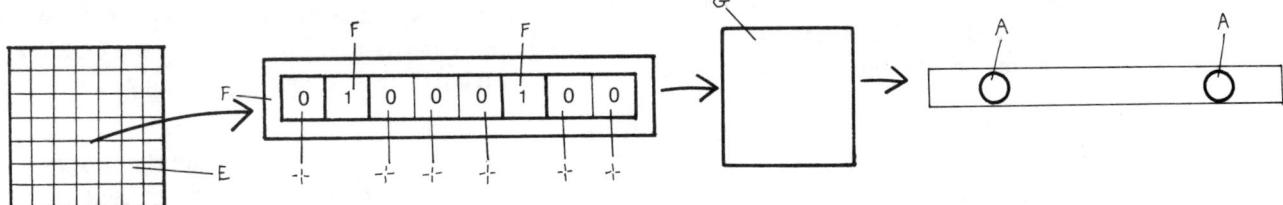

CHARACTER GENERATOR ★
   ROM H
   CHARACTER CODE I
   CHARACTER GENERATOR J
   CHARACTER (H) K

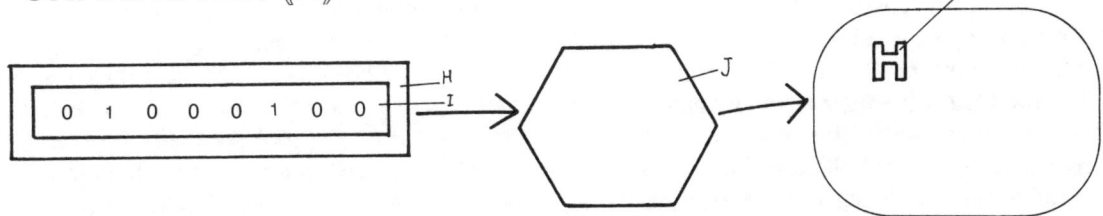

34
TURTLE GRAPHICS: LOGO

Graphic capabilities are a major feature of computers. In fact, there are languages which are especially designed for computer graphics. One of these languages is LOGO, developed by the LOGO group of MIT's artificial intelligence laboratory under Seymour Papert. Its approach to graphics is much more easily learned than the coordinate oriented BASIC approach. The interpreter for the LOGO language is supplied as part of ROM or is on a disk. You tell the computer that you want to use this language by typing in an operating system command.

Color the Direction Instructions and Turtle headings and titles A through D[1]. Use light colors for A, B, and C. Color the representative turtle on the video display screen. Color the LOGO instructions and the turtles and trails of the FORWARD and BACK diagrams. Do the same for the RIGHT and LEFT instructions, but note that they have no trails as RIGHT and LEFT instructions cause rotation only.

The graphic capabilities of LOGO stem from turtle graphics. Turtle graphics require you to imagine that you have a little creature called a turtle that appears on the display screen. Initially, the turtle is at the center of the screen "looking" toward the top. The turtle will respond to several *LOGO instructions*. If you type FORWARD 10 on your keyboard, this tells the turtle to move ten spaces in the direction that its *eye* is pointing. Normally, when the turtle moves it leaves a *trail* that appears as a high-resolution line on the screen. BACK 10 causes the turtle to go back ten spaces in the direction opposite to where it is looking.

Typing RIGHT 90 causes the turtle to turn 90 degrees to the right. It does not move away from its initial position but only turns on the spot. (Recall that one complete revolution measures 360 degrees. So a turn of 90 degrees represents a one-quarter turn.) LEFT 180 causes the turtle to turn 180 degrees to the left.

Note that by switching to LOGO, you eliminate having to calculate coordinates of the turtle positions.

Color the Combined Instructions and Square headings. Color the initial position (C) and the turtle at the starting point in the SQUARE diagram. Color the first instruction of the LOGO program, TO SQUARE, and follow the instruction by coloring the 10 unit path above the initial position. Color the second instruction, RIGHT 90, and follow it by coloring the turtle turned 90 degrees to the right. Color and follow each of the remaining instructions, coloring in the trail and turned turtle as required.

Several instructions can be combined to produce a geometric figure. In the diagram, the instructions FORWARD 10 and RIGHT 90 are used several times to produce a square. You instruct the turtle to move a certain amount and then turn. No matter where the turtle starts on the screen or in which direction it is facing, this LOGO program produces a square on the screen.

In the WHAT diagram, pretend to be the turtle. Color the WHAT heading and the initial position of the turtle. Color and follow the FORWARD and RIGHT instructions by drawing the correct path and then turning the turtle. The first one has been illustrated for you. Repeat the procedure three times and color the REPEAT 3 instruction. (Remember, a 120-degree turn is one-third of a complete rotation.)

If you have correctly followed the LOGO program, then you have drawn a triangle. All LOGO programs are given a name. The two programs here are named SQUARE and WHAT (WHAT might be renamed TRIANGLE). The word TO preceding the program name designates that the program is to be stored in memory with the given name. Just as variable values can be recalled by referring to the name in BASIC, LOGO programs stored in RAM can be recalled by name. The reserved word REPEAT causes the instructions that follow to be repeated the indicated number of times. Using REPEAT 3 enabled the WHAT program to draw a triangle using only one FORWARD and one RIGHT instruction repeated three times.

Color the HOUSE heading and the program instructions of the HOUSE diagram. Execute each line as before, drawing the correct trail and making the correct turtle turns. Whenever you see the name of one of the previous programs, go to that program and draw the required result in the HOUSE diagram. The dotted lines serve as a check on your execution of the proper instructions.

You can make use of a RAM stored LOGO program in another program by typing in the name of the program. In the HOUSE program, using the name SQUARE causes a square to be drawn. The next two instructions are needed to make sure the turtle is positioned so the WHAT program draws the roof properly.

LOGO is used when a simple high-level language is desired for graphic display. Children as young as five years have mastered turtle commands and can produce very complicated designs.

TURTLE GRAPHICS: LOGO.

DIRECTION INSTRUCTIONS★
   TURTLE★
      BODY_A
      EYE_B
      INITIAL POSITION_C
   LOGO INSTRUCTION_D
   TRAIL_D'

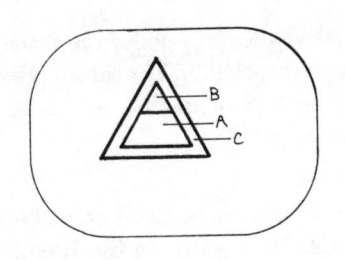

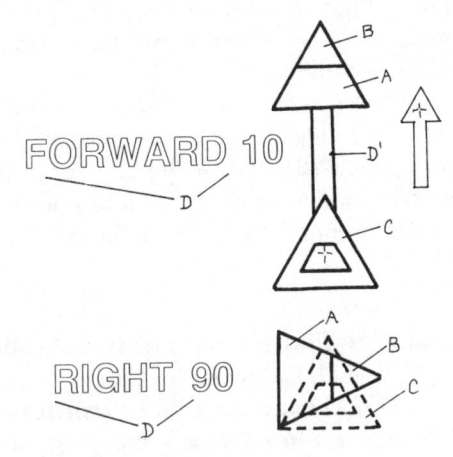

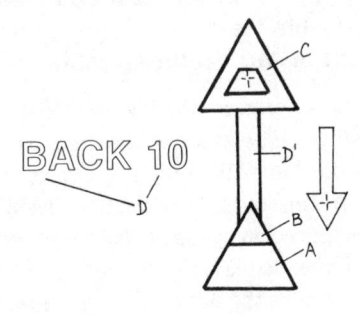

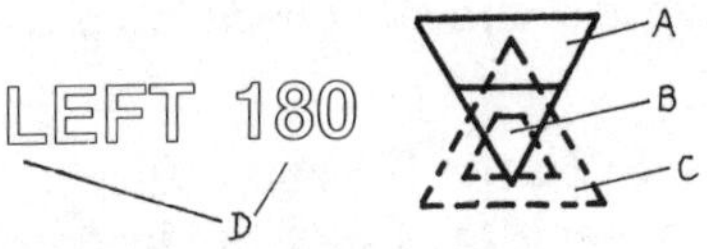

FORWARD 10_D

BACK 10_D

RIGHT 90_D

LEFT 180_D

COMBINED INSTRUCTIONS★
SQUARE★

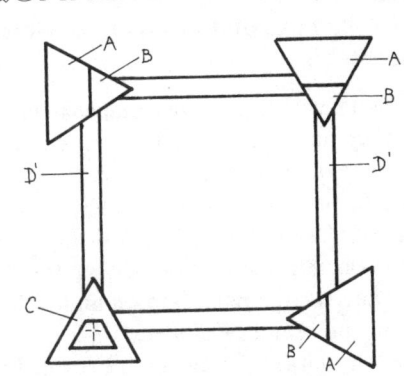

WHAT★

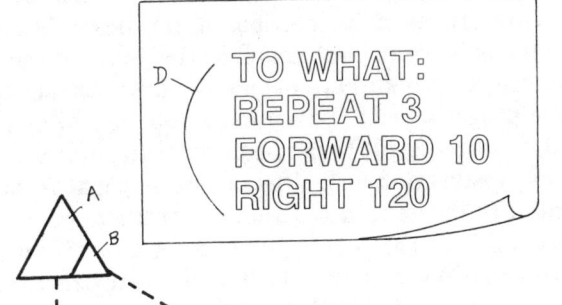

TO WHAT:
REPEAT 3
FORWARD 10
RIGHT 120

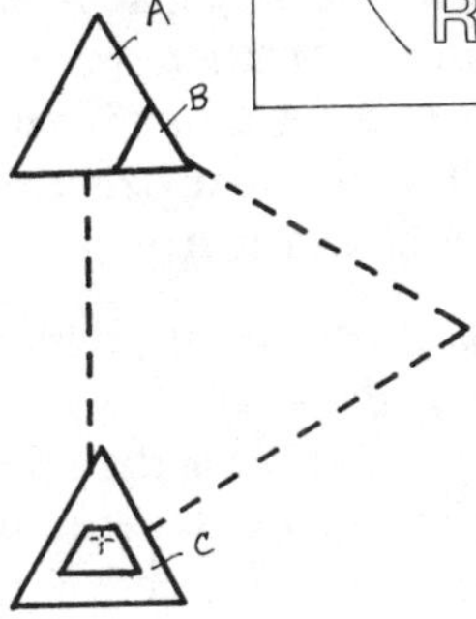

TO SQUARE:
FORWARD 10
RIGHT 90
FORWARD 10
RIGHT 90
FORWARD 10
RIGHT 90
FORWARD 10
RIGHT 90

HOUSE★

TO HOUSE:
SQUARE
FORWARD 10
RIGHT 30
WHAT

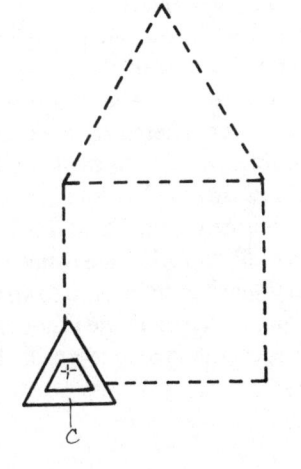

35
VECTOR GRAPHICS AND PLOTTERS

In Plate 33 you learned about the raster scan method of displaying a diagram on the screen. Here you will learn about another type of graphics display method. It is called vector graphics.

Color the Raster Scan and Vector Graphics headings and titles A, A[1], and B. In the Raster Scan diagram, follow each scan line and color only the indicated pixel. Color the vector line as one continuous line segment in the Vector Graphics diagram.

If the raster scan method is used to draw a diagonal line, the result resembles a staircase pattern, no matter how fine the resolution. The vector graphics method overcomes this problem because the electron beam does not trace out closely spaced *raster scan lines*. Instead, the circuits that control the display move the electron beam so that it directly draws the desired image on the video screen. The beam can move in any direction on the screen.

Color the Vector Graphics Display heading and titles C through D[2]. Color the instructions of the simplified vector graphics program. You will follow the program instructions to color a pattern on the screen. In each instruction, if the beam intensity entry is 0, place your pencil at the point on the grid whose coordinates are listed. The first instruction of the program tells you to place your pencil at point (0,0) on the grid. If the beam intensity entry of the next instruction is 1, draw a line segment from the point to the next instruction's coordinate point. The second instruction tells you to draw a line from (0,0) to (4,5). Continue by following all the instructions of the program. You will have drawn a triangle.

Each point of the vector graphics display is given a pair of *coordinates* (column, row) as in raster scan graphics. The computer sends pairs of coordinates and a *beam intensity code* to the video display circuits as result of the program *instruction*. If the beam intensity code is 0, the beam is simply moved to a new point without drawing a *line segment*. Therefore, the drawing begins at (0,0) without a line segment to it. If the intensity code is not 0 (1 in this illustration), a line is drawn from the point to the indicated new point. You drew a line from (0,0) to (4,5), from (4,5) to (6,2), and from (6,2) to (0,0) because the beam intensities in lines 20 to 40 were 1. Unlike raster scan graphics, a diagonal line is not composed of separate steps but appears as one smooth, high-resolution graph.

Since the video image lasts for only a fraction of a second, the computer continually sends the current list of points and intensities to the video display circuits. Although the same type of video display tube is used, raster scan and vector graphics use different display circuits and instructions. The advantage of vector graphics, aside from the improved image, is greater speed. You do not have to wait for a scan line to complete its horizontal path before the next position of the line segment is drawn. A computer system will come with one of these two methods as part of its operating system.

At this point you have learned about the various methods of creating diagrams on a video display. Some operating systems allow you to preserve the picture on auxiliary storage (disk or tape) or send it to a printer for hard copy. A device especially designed for graphic hard copy is a plotter.

Color the Plotters and Positions headings and titles E, F, and G. Color the first down position, (1), of the pen, (F). Then, draw a line segment to the next position, (2). Follow through the positions in order and, if the pen is down at a position, keep your pen on the paper and draw a line segment to the next position. If the indicated pen holder is up, (G), lift your pencil and go to the next plotter position without drawing a line segment.

A plotter is a mechanical device that enables the computer to draw graphic images on paper. It is not restricted to drawing dots (as is a dot matrix printer) or preformed characters (as is a daisy wheel printer). The drawing pen is held in a *holder* (trolley) that is sitting on a track (like a train car on railroad tracks). Either the trolley moves over the paper or the paper moves under the trolley, depending on the brand of plotter.

The plotter works by drawing line segments. Most plotters can draw line segments in eight directions (up, down, right, left, and four 45-degree or quarter-turn diagonals). Depending on the smallest step size, the plotter may draw smooth diagrams, almost eliminating a staircase-type design. An instruction may be given to lift the pen from the paper and move it to another position without drawing a line segment. Colors are used in a drawing by having the pens change. In the diagram, if you followed the instructions correctly, you have drawn the letter N followed by the letter I. Some plotters come equipped with built-in circuits that allow you to give instructions within the program to draw letters or special symbols.

VECTOR GRAPHICS AND PLOTTERS.

RASTER SCAN GRAPHICS ★
RASTER SCAN LINE_A┼
LIGHTED PIXEL_A'

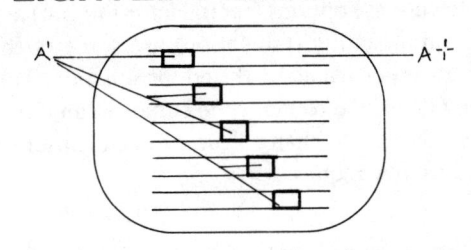

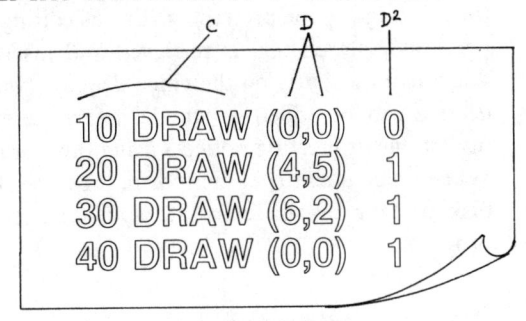

VECTOR GRAPHICS ★
VECTOR LINE_B

VECTOR GRAPHICS DISPLAY ★
DRAW INSTRUCTION_C
COORDINATES_D
POINT_D'
BEAM INTENSITY CODE_D²

```
10 DRAW (0,0)  0
20 DRAW (4,5)  1
30 DRAW (6,2)  1
40 DRAW (0,0)  1
```

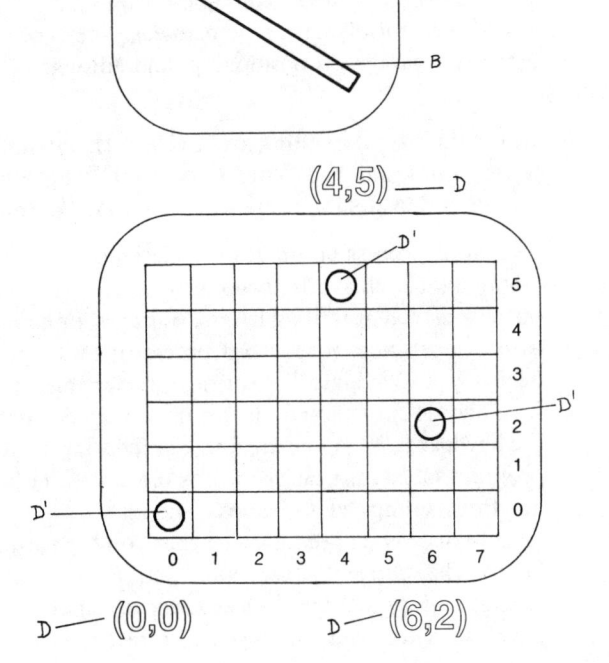

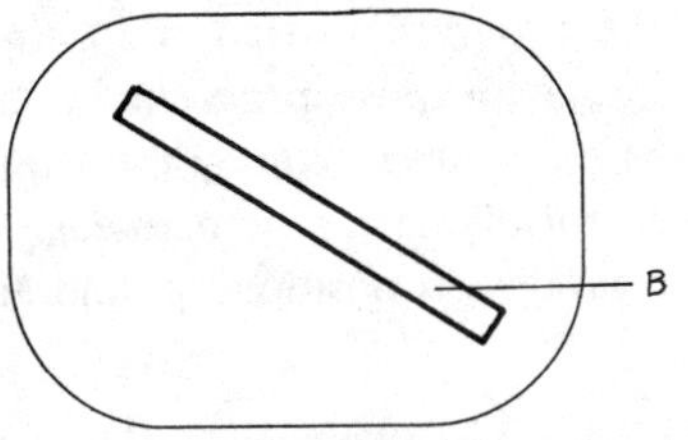

(4,5) — D
D — (0,0)   D — (6,2)

PLOTTERS ★
2★ 4★ 5★
1★ 3★ 6★

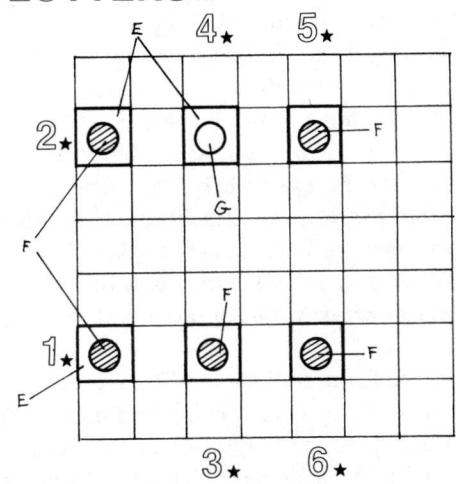

HOLDER_E
PEN DOWN_F
PEN UP_G
POSITIONS ★
  1, 2, 3, 4, 5, 6 ★

36 WORD PROCESSING PROGRAMS

It is possible to have your computer print out a business or personal letter using a BASIC program. You place each of the sentences between quotes in a PRINT instruction and run the program so that the output is sent to the printer. Special purpose programs, called word processors, have been written to simplify printing and combine it with control of margin adjustment, line spacing, sentence and paragraph positioning, and editing.

Color the Menu heading and titles A through C using light colors, and the Word Processor Program menu on the video display screen (words A, B, and C).

The word processing program is designed to handle the manipulation of words to serve written communication purposes (such as writing letters, speeches, or books). For ease of operation, most word processor (WP) programs begin by displaying a list (menu) of available functions. You choose the function by typing a number or letter at the keyboard. What you are doing is choosing a particular program subroutine that performs the desired task. There are three groups of functions. The *editor functions* are used to display and modify text that you type at the keyboard. The *storage functions* store and retrieve text to and from auxiliary storage devices (disk or tape). The *print formatting functions* allow you to direct the form of the printed output.

Color the Text Lines heading and, using contrasting colors, titles D through G. Color the editor function arrow (A) from the menu, through the keyboard, to the editor functions (insert, move, and delete). Color the editor functions and the representative text lines on the video displays. It is important to follow the labeling carefully when coloring the text lines.

The text of the document is typed at the keyboard. The editor function allows you to manipulate the text. If the text has to be modified by the insertion or deletion of a word or an entire paragraph, the editor function allows you to do so by typing a special instruction (usually with a control key and an alphabet key on the keyboard). In the diagram, the *insert* instruction allows the addition of *line 4* to the document. A *move* instruction allows you to move a word, sentence, or paragraph to another location. In the diagram, *line 2* is interchanged with *line 3* on the screen. When the *delete* instruction is typed, *line 1* is removed, leaving only lines 3, 2, and 4.

Some word processing programs have the added feature of automatically taking a word that would be split at the end of a line (hyphenated) and placing it at the beginning of the next line. This feature is called word wrap. Uppercase or lower-case options (capital letters or not) and automatic column setting (tabulation) are some of the additional features provided by the editor function. The editor function allows you to move the cursor to any line on the screen so that these changes, deletions, or insertions can be made as you require.

Color the storage function arrow (B), the functions (store and retrieve), and the arrows to and from auxiliary storage.

The storage functions of the WP program are used when the document is typed and edited to your satisfaction. A previously *stored* document (on disk or tape) may be *retrieved* from storage so that it appears on the screen ready for printing (by the printer) or further editing. Sometimes previously stored text is retrieved and inserted into the document currently on the video display. Names and addresses can be added to standard form letters (such as invitations or meeting notices) using the storage function. When a document is in final form, it can be stored on the disk or tape by using the storage function of the WP program.

Color the print function arrow (C) to the print format instructions and color them as well. At each instruction, color the representative text lines that appear on the video display or paper.

The WP print subroutine allows you to adjust the format of the printed document before it is printed in hard-copy form by the printer. You set the *margin* to any desired width. For example, you could specify sixty characters to a line to begin in column 10 of the printed page. The character *font* (for example, **boldface** or *italics*), the number of *lines per page,* and inclusion of footnotes can be specified. Most WP programs display the page on the video screen exactly as it is to appear on the hard copy so that you can preview the appearance of the printed document.

Advanced features of some WP programs allow you to ask for a check on your spelling and punctuation before printing the document. Word processing programs are so specialized that sometimes an entire computer's only job is this function. In that case, the term "word processor" is used to refer to the entire computer system, including the printer, auxiliary storage, and video display.

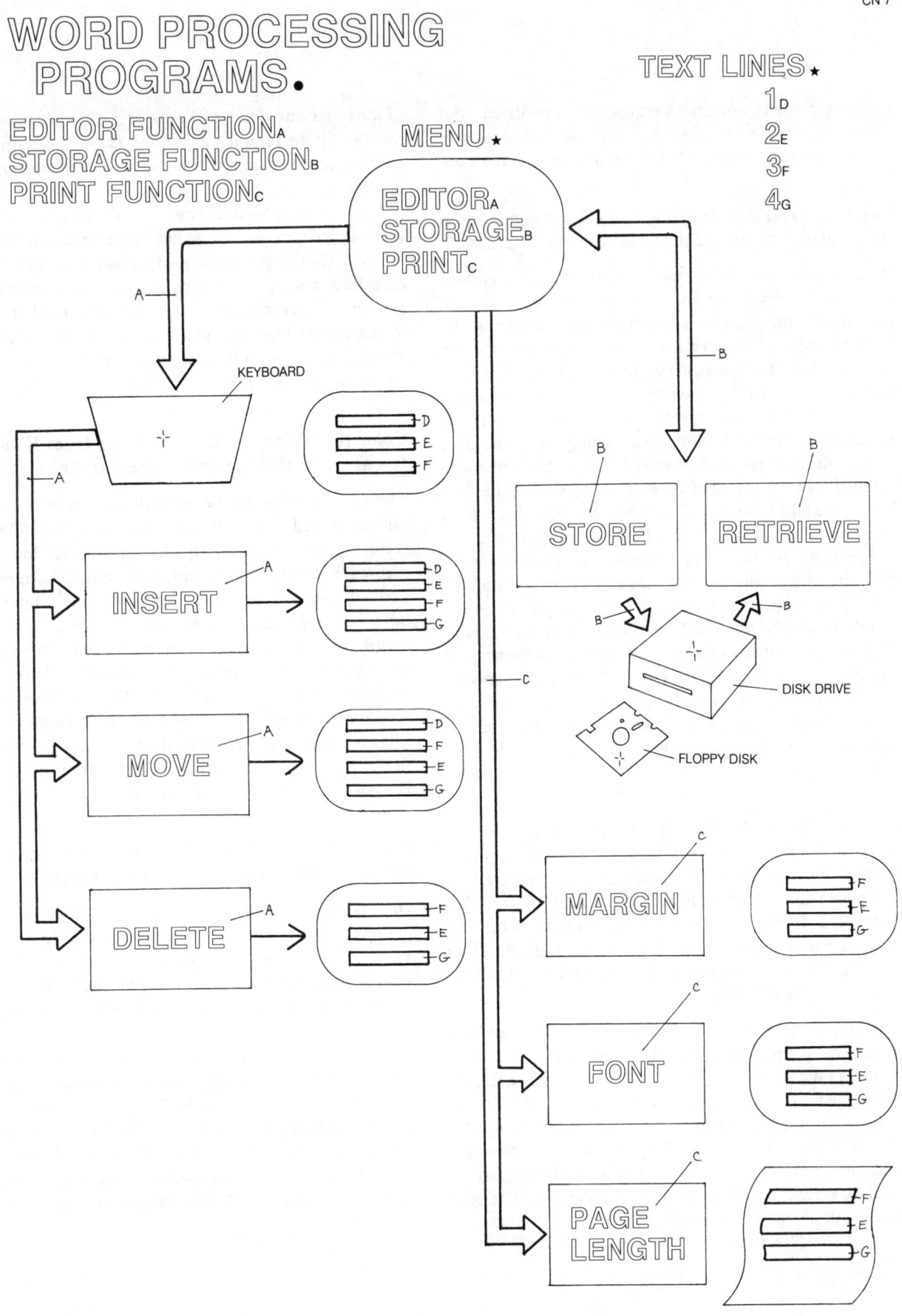

WORD PROCESSING PROGRAMS.

EDITOR FUNCTION A
STORAGE FUNCTION B
PRINT FUNCTION C

MENU ★

EDITOR A
STORAGE B
PRINT C

TEXT LINES ★
1 D
2 E
3 F
4 G

KEYBOARD

INSERT

MOVE

DELETE

STORE

RETRIEVE

DISK DRIVE

FLOPPY DISK

MARGIN

FONT

PAGE LENGTH

37 DATA BASE MANAGEMENT PROGRAMS

Data base management programs are specialized programs that have been created to organize information in a format that corresponds to the requirements of the user.

Color the Overview heading, titles A through D, and their related representations in the top diagram.

Data base management program functions include gathering data, manipulating and evaluating the data so that meaningful information is produced, and managing the output results. Data is gathered from keyboard *input* or from another machine-readable form (such as a specially printed document). The data base is *processed* by program segments that provide classification, sorting, calculating, and summarizing of information. Sorting aligns the data in ascending or descending order based on the alphabetical or numerical values of a particular section of the data (see Appendix Plate 7). Classifying the data places it in appropriate sections of a data base management file.

The management of *output* includes storage and retrieval of the data in auxiliary storage and the preparation of reports for video or printer display. The output may be as simple as a list of selected data items, or it may be a more elaborate presentation including a statistical summary or subtotals of particular data sections. Mailing lists, checks, purchase orders, and invoices are also typical output reports. The user defines the type of report required by entering special instructions when prompted by the data base management program.

Color the Using the Data Base File heading, title E, and the related representation. Color the Applications Programs/Results heading gray. There are five programs and results illustrated. Color their titles (numbers 1 through 5) with light colors and the related representations in the middle diagram. The data base file is represented as a cylinder, indicating large storage capacity.

The data gathered and output produced by the data base management program is called a *data base file*. It may consist of many items (fields) of information for each particular record. A data base file may consist of a list of names, addresses and phone numbers, for example. This data base file, once composed by the data base management program, is stored (usually on a disk) and may be used by several different *applications programs*. The data base items are stored together in a file that is independent of the programs which make use of it. One program might use the file to produce a *mailing list,* for example, and another program might use the file to conduct a demographic *survey*.

Many of the new data base files are constructed so that they are independent of the hardware on which they were created. That is, you store the data base file created by one data base management program on one computer disk system and then are able to access it using another system. When a data base is organized and stored on auxiliary storage, the application program references it independently of how the data is originally organized.

Color the Managing Data heading, titles K through Q only, and their related representations.

The data base file may be divided into *records,* each containing related information about a particular individual, company, or other category. A data base file for student records is shown here. Each record contains a *name field* and a *grade field.* In the example, the data is input to the *data base management program* by means of the *keyboard.* The user is prompted by the data base management program to enter the appropriate data value. Three names and grades are entered at this time. The data base management program processes (*processor unit*) the data so that it is *stored* in name alphabetical order on auxiliary storage (a *disk system* in this example). The program can also sort the data according to a user-specified order.

Color titles R, S, and T, their related representations, and the lower keyboard representation.

Once the data base file is created, you can *use* the processing programs to scan the *file* and print out desired information. Here, the record of Jones is *displayed* on the screen. Another requirement may be that you may want to see a list of all students who received a grade of 90 or better.

In order to provide quick access to a data base file, special very high-level languages have been created. These are called "query" languages. They allow you to specify your information requirement without having to write a special program. You could say "Show me all who passed math," and the query language interprets the command to display the names of all those people who fit the required description.

DATA BASE MANAGEMENT PROGRAMS.

OVERVIEW ★
DATA BASE MANAGEMENT PROGRAM_A
 INPUT_B   PROCESSING_C   OUTPUT_D

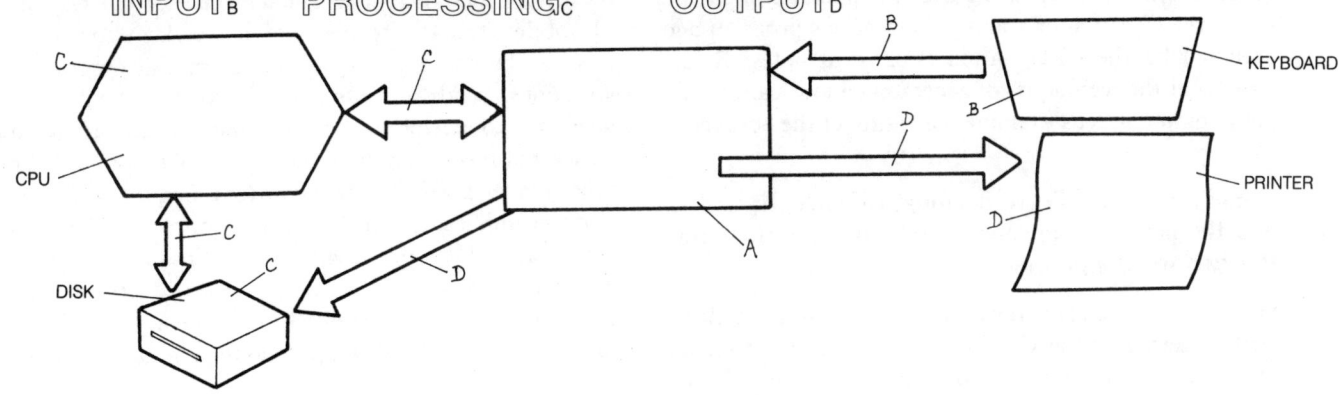

USING THE DATA BASE FILE ★
DATA BASE FILE_E
APPLICATION
  PROGRAM/RESULT ★
  1_{F/F¹}
  2_{G/G¹}
  3_{H/H¹}
  4_{I/I¹}
  5_{J/J¹}

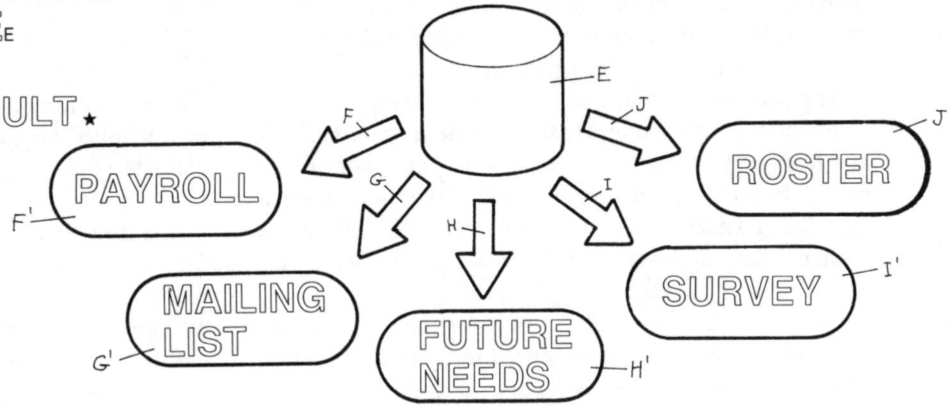

MANAGING DATA ★
  CREATING THE FILE_K
  INPUT RECORD_L
    NAME FIELD_{L¹}
    GRADE FIELD_{L²}
  KEYBOARD_M
  PROCESSOR UNIT_N
  DATA BASE MANAGEMENT
    PROGRAM_O

DISK SYSTEM_P
STORED RECORD_Q
USING THE FILE_R
INSTRUCTION_S
DISPLAY_T

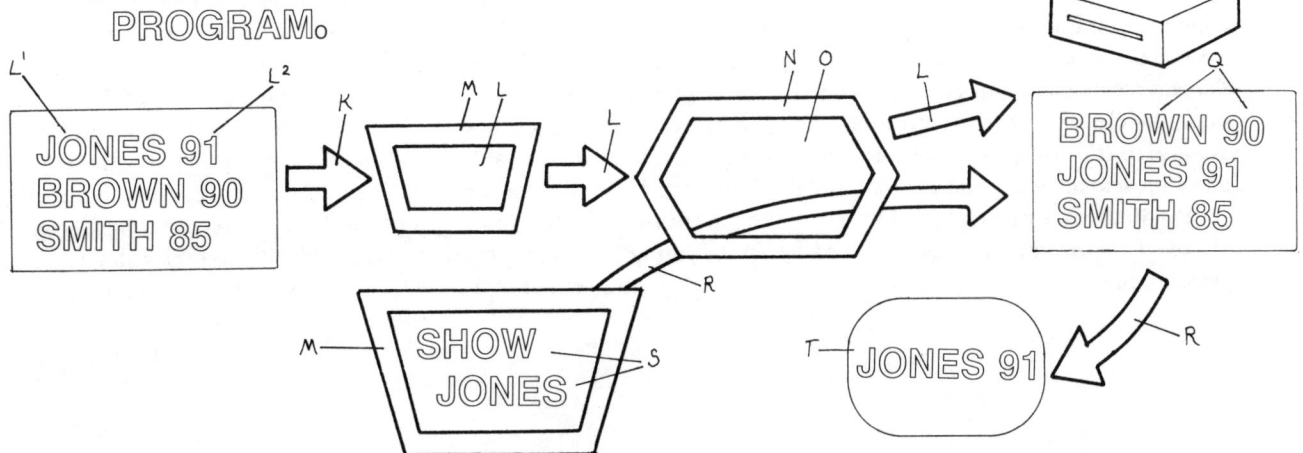

38
MUSIC SYNTHESIS

There is a type of music generating system for every microcomputer. Usually, a piece of peripheral equipment, under the direction of a music applications program and executed by the CPU, produces musical notes. Before looking at the techniques of generating a musical note on your computer, let's examine the nature of the note itself.

Color the Sound Wave heading, titles A, B, and C, and the parts of the sound wave diagram, including the two word equations.

Sound waves are created by an object vibrating. A drum beat is caused by the vibration of a membrane stretched over a frame. The sound of your voice is caused by vibration of a part of the throat called the larynx ("voice box") under the control of the speech center of your brain. To produce music, the computer makes something move according to a predetermined pattern.

The two characteristics of sound that you need to know to understand computer sound generation are *amplitude* and *frequency*. Amplitude is the loudness or volume of the sound. In the diagram the amplitude of the sound wave is given as 1 (maximum value above the 0 base line). A higher volume wave would have an amplitude larger than 1.

The frequency of sound waves is the number of *cycles* or vibrations *per second*, measured in units called hertz. The frequency illustrated is 1 hertz, as there is one complete cycle in 1 second. The range of human hearing is about 15 to 20,000 hertz. Low-frequency waves produce a low sound like a drum. High-frequency waves produce a high sound like a whistle.

Color the Tone Generator heading, titles D through G^1, and their related structures in the middle diagram. Use light colors for E and G. The tone generating program instruction is represented inside the CPU.

A sound is produced electronically by sending a signal to a special device called a *speaker*. A simple speaker consists of an *electromagnet* connected to a *cone* of cloth or paper. When the electromagnet is activated, the cone moves in response to the strength of the electronic signal. It is the cone's movement that produces the sound. If the cone is moved 440 times per second (= 440 hertz), then the musical *note* A above middle C is produced by the vibrating speaker cone.

The simplest approach to controlling the speaker is by means of a *tone generator*. The tone generator is responsible for directing the frequency of the speaker's cone movements. The computer, by means of special program instructions, sends a *control signal* to a particular tone generator to activate a note. The form of the instruction varies, but it is generally of the type: TONE 440,1,.5. The first number gives the particular tone frequency, the second the amplitude, and the third the duration of the note (.5 second). The operating system subroutine that is designed to recognize and implement the instruction causes the 440 hertz tone generator to produce a preset desired *tone signal* of one unit amplitude for one half second.

Color the Sound Synthesizer heading, titles H through K, and their related representations in the lower diagram.

The most commonly used method of producing a computer-controlled note is the sound synthesizer. A synthesizer consists of a program-controlled power supply used to produce many sounds. *Output* of a *voltage*, from a *converter*, directly proportional to a numerical value received from the processor unit, controls the sound produced by the speaker. When the music applications program changes the numerical value sent to the converter, the output voltage changes to reflect this new value. The changing voltage is sent into an audio *amplifier* that takes a small *signal* and makes its amplitude as large as indicated in the associated program instruction. The cone of the speaker is moved so that the pattern of movement reproduces the waveform. The waveform (and thus the sound) is given by the distance of the wave crest above or below the base line at a particular instant in time.

The real problem for the computer is to be able to compute this distance (wave shape) at each point in time. If the computer has to compute coordinates for each point on the wave with each note, the time required would be so large as to impair the sound quality. A much simpler method is used. A *waveform table* is created and supplied with the computer in ROM or an auxiliary storage device to be read into RAM. The table consists of the coordinate values of a *digital signal* needed to produce the required note. Table "look up" for a computer is extremely rapid. To send a particular set of signals, the computer need only reference the proper table for the required signal code. The actual program that details which tables should be referenced and in what order is written by the user.

MUSIC SYNTHESIS.

SOUND WAVE ★
AMPLITUDE_A
ONE CYCLE_B
ONE SECOND_C

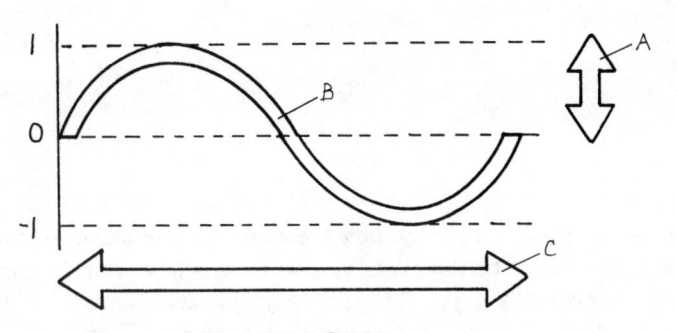

CYCLES/ SECOND = FREQUENCY ★
1 CYCLE/1 SECOND = 1 HERTZ ★

TONE GENERATOR ★
NOTE_D
SPEAKER_E()
  CONE_E1
  ELECTROMAGNET_E2

TONE GENERATOR_F
TONE SIGNAL_F1
CPU_G
  CONTROL SIGNAL_G1

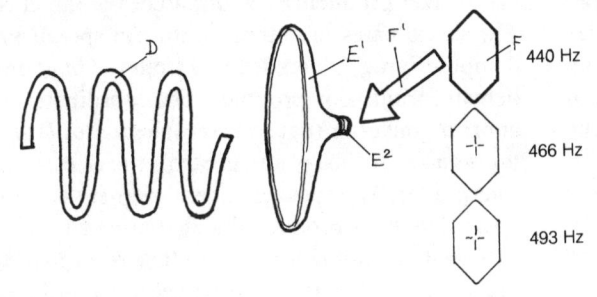

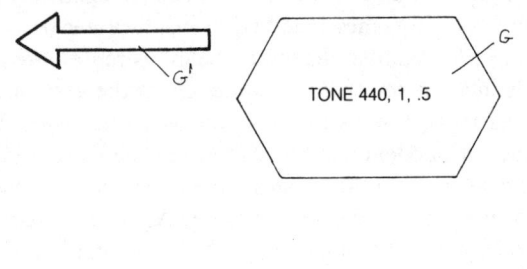

440 Hz
466 Hz
493 Hz

TONE 440, 1, .5

SOUND SYNTHESIZER ★
AMPLIFIER_H/SIGNAL_H1
CONVERTER_I
  OUTPUT VOLTAGE_I1

DIGITAL SIGNAL_J
WAVE FORM TABLE_K

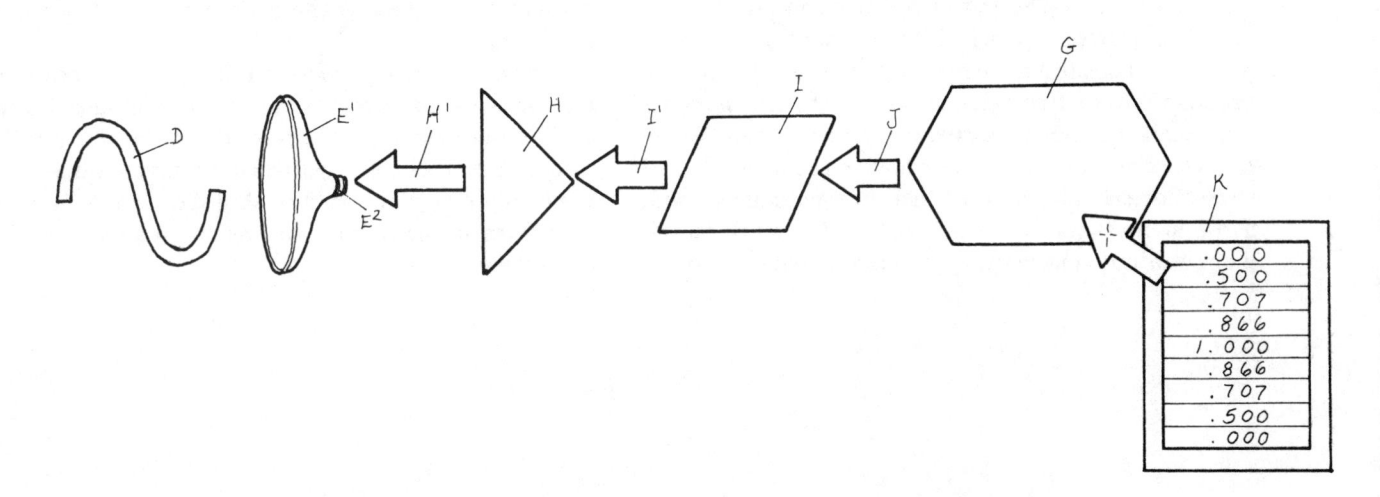

.000
.500
.707
.866
1.000
.866
.707
.500
.000

39 VOICE SYNTHESIS

In the last plate you learned how the computer can make beautiful music. In this plate you will learn how your computer can talk to you. The speech synthesizer is hardware controlled by the computer to produce speech. There are several techniques presently used to allow computers to speak.

Color the Phoneme Voice Synthesis heading, titles A through E, and their related representations in the top diagram. Use a light color for B.

All the words of the English language can be spelled using only 26 characters. However, the language contains about 64 distinct sounds called *phonemes*. The phonemes can be thought of as an alphabet of speech. You string the proper sequence of phonemes together to produce a particular word. In the example, the word "hello" is represented by five distinct sounds (*h* as in *home*, *eh* as the *e* sound in *leg*, *l* as in *ball*, *o* as in *boat*, and *w* as in *why*). The sequence of phonemes is typed in at the keyboard and an *applications program* translates these phonemes into *codes* (shown here in hexadecimal code; see Appendix Plate 2). The codes are sent to a *speech synthesizer microchip*. Here the microchip circuits receive the code and produce a string of signals, similar to tone generation signals, that are sent to the *speaker*. The sound produced by the speaker mimics human speech.

The program adds to the synthesizer chip signal additional instructions to allow the resulting sound to appear as speech. For example, rules of stringing the phonemes are incorporated. The end of one phoneme sound may have to be slurred together with the beginning of the next phoneme to create a more natural sound. In addition, the program adds to the original data string of phoneme codes such characteristics as pauses, tones, and accents. Sometimes special codes have to be added to produce a desired stress. For example, the word "hello?" is pronounced with a rise in stress (pitch) on the final *o*. The word "hello" without a question mark is pronounced with a drop in stress at the end. You have to specify the proper phonemes, stress, and amplitude so that you hear the word "hello" exactly as you desire.

Color the Waveform Digitization heading, titles F through I, and their related representations in the lower diagram.

A second method of producing computerized speech is called waveform digitization. To begin the process, a human (you or a manufacturer) speaks a particular *word* ("hello" in this case). The *converter* changes the sound waves into digital signals representing the coordinates of points along the sound wave. This is the same as the music synthesizer producing the amplitudes of the musical tone. The coordinates are stored until the speech synthesizer computer program reads them from the main memory on demand from your program. The coordinates are sent to another converter that reverses the process. The converter takes the coordinates and controls the electronic signal to the speaker. The speaker cone movement is controlled by these signals to produce the chosen word.

Since the word is similar to a tape recording, the resulting sound retains the original accents and inflections. A word such as "hello" retains the stresses of the original speaker. You choose a desired word by entering a code number representing the location of the particular word in main memory. The code number would be supplied by the manufacturer or noted by you when you created the voice memory. Of course, this method does not allow the large vocabulary afforded by the phoneme method of speech generation.

Speech synthesis provides a form of computer output that can act as an alternative to the video display or printer. The user need not read a printed line of text, but is able to hear the result of a particular operation while doing something else. You could wash dishes and at the same time listen to the results of a complicated mathematical calculation.

VOICE SYNTHESIS.

PHONEME VOICE SYNTHESIS ★
PHONEME_A
APPLICATION PROGRAM_B/ CODE_{B¹}
SYNTHESIZER MICROCHIP_C
SPEAKER_D
AUDIBLE WORD_E

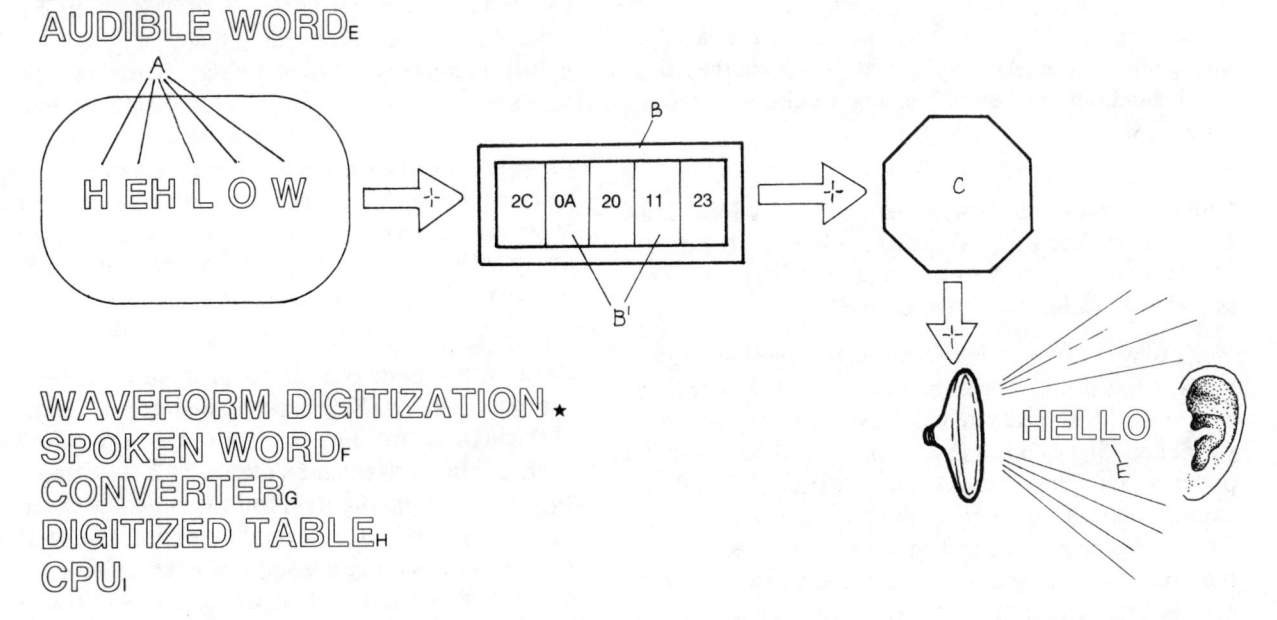

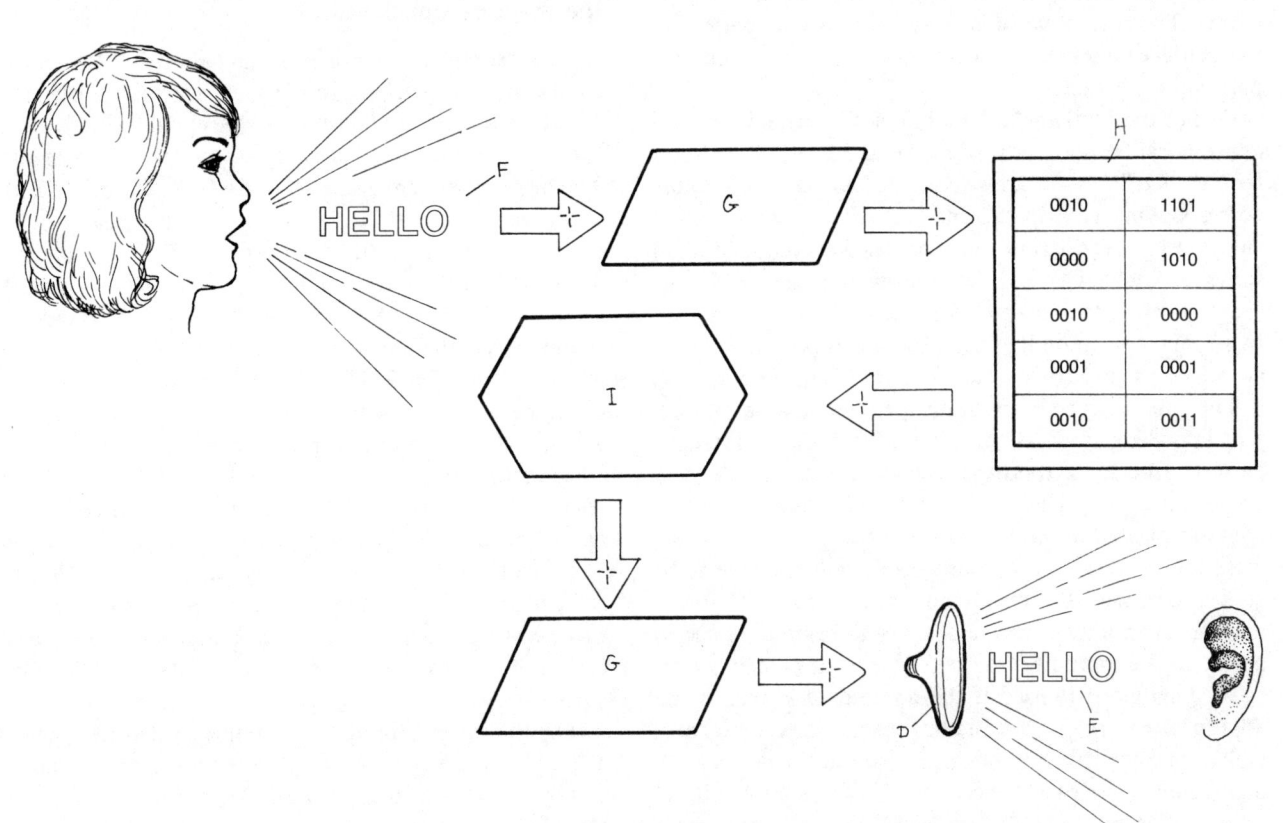

WAVEFORM DIGITIZATION ★
SPOKEN WORD_F
CONVERTER_G
DIGITIZED TABLE_H
CPU_I

40
A SYSTEM FOR ARTIFICIAL INTELLIGENCE

The high-speed calculation, large memory storage facility, and data processing ability of the modern computer allow the user to create programs that attempt to emulate the human thinking process. Computer simulation of the human capabilities of reasoning and learning is called artificial intelligence (AI). In this plate you learn the principles behind one method of creating programs for AI applications.

Color the Example Sentences and Rules Headings. Color titles A and B, using light colors. In the example, color with gray the one sentence of the three that is correct. Color the rules as well.

You rarely solve everyday problems by conscious reasoning based on primary principles of logical deduction, such as spelling rules. Rather, you solve them by relying on your knowledge and recognizing one of the many familiar patterns that apply to the current situation. You subconciously recall the appropriate thing to do when a particular pattern occurs. You picked the sentence that contains the word "two" as being correct. You were aware that the correct sentence is the one containing all the correct words. The correct word is "two" because the pattern of the sentence required a word meaning a number at a particular position.

One of the fundamental approaches to artificial intelligence is called the Knowledge Based Expert (KBE) system. A KBE system consists of a data base containing corresponding *consequent* and *antecedent* arrays and a rule interpreter program which are used in combination to simulate knowledge and decision-making ability. In the example rules, the correct consequent component is "use two." The corresponding antecedent component is "if an adjective is needed" (instead of an adverb or preposition).

The rule interpreter program uses the data base of expert knowledge by first choosing, after some preliminary pattern processing (perhaps even a random process), a consequent entry. Then, the corresponding antecedent entries are located in memory. In order to prove the consequent entry to be true, the antecedent entries have to be shown to be true. If these are not true, the rule interpreter goes on to another consequent entry to begin the process again. In the example, the first consequent choice is "use too." This word is used if the antecedent entry, "if an adverb is needed," is true. In this case the antecedent entry is false and the rule interpreter goes on to the next consequent entry, "use two." The corresponding antecedent, "if an adjective is needed," is true. So the rule interpreter program uses this rule and picks the correct sentence, just as you did.

Most KBE systems contain hundreds of rules obtained by interviewing human experts in the subject. In the above example, English grammar experts might have been polled to create the "rules" or data base. Once the data base is created, the user enters a set of data values (above, the example sentences) for a particular problem and runs the rule interpreter program. The program picks the elements of the consequent array and attempts to prove each. When one or more is found to be correct, it is displayed as the answer to the particular problem. Let's take a look at a more complicated example.

Color the Quadrilateral KBE System heading and the statement, ABCD is a Quadrilateral. Color titles C through E and the quadrilateral at the side. Color each of the consequent entries, (A). Starting at the square consequent entry, follow and color the arrows back to each of the antecedent entries, (B), that have a path to the square consequent entry. Color the And circle and the antecedent entries. Leave the rest of the diagram uncolored.

In the example, the preprocessing of the KBE system shows that a given polygon is four sided (*quadrilateral*). The problem is to determine if the quadrilateral is of a special type (square, rectangle, rhombus, or trapezoid). The first consequent entry, SQUARE, is chosen. In order to prove the quadrilateral to be a square, each of the corresponding antecedents must be shown to be true. They are "all sides of equal length," "two pairs of parallel sides," and "contains a right angle." The last antecedent requires that the antecedent "measure of angle is 90 degrees" be true. The KBE system follows the pattern of first choosing a consequent entry (square in the example). Then, each path from it is followed to the last antecedent. The antecedent is proved true or false. If it is true, the next level is proved true or false. The process continues until all antecedents are proved true so that the corresponding consequent is proven true. If any antecedent is false, the system moves on to the next consequent to repeat the process. In the example, the quadrilateral is proved to be a square because all of the antecedents are true for a square.

The example, although it is simple in nature, provides a sample of the type of program planning and execution of highly sophisticated AI Knowledge Based Expert systems.

ARTIFICIAL INTELLIGENCE.

CONSEQUENT_A
ANTECEDENT_B

EXAMPLE SENTENCES ★

JOHN HAS TOO HOUSES.
JOHN HAS TWO HOUSES.
JOHN HAS TO HOUSES.

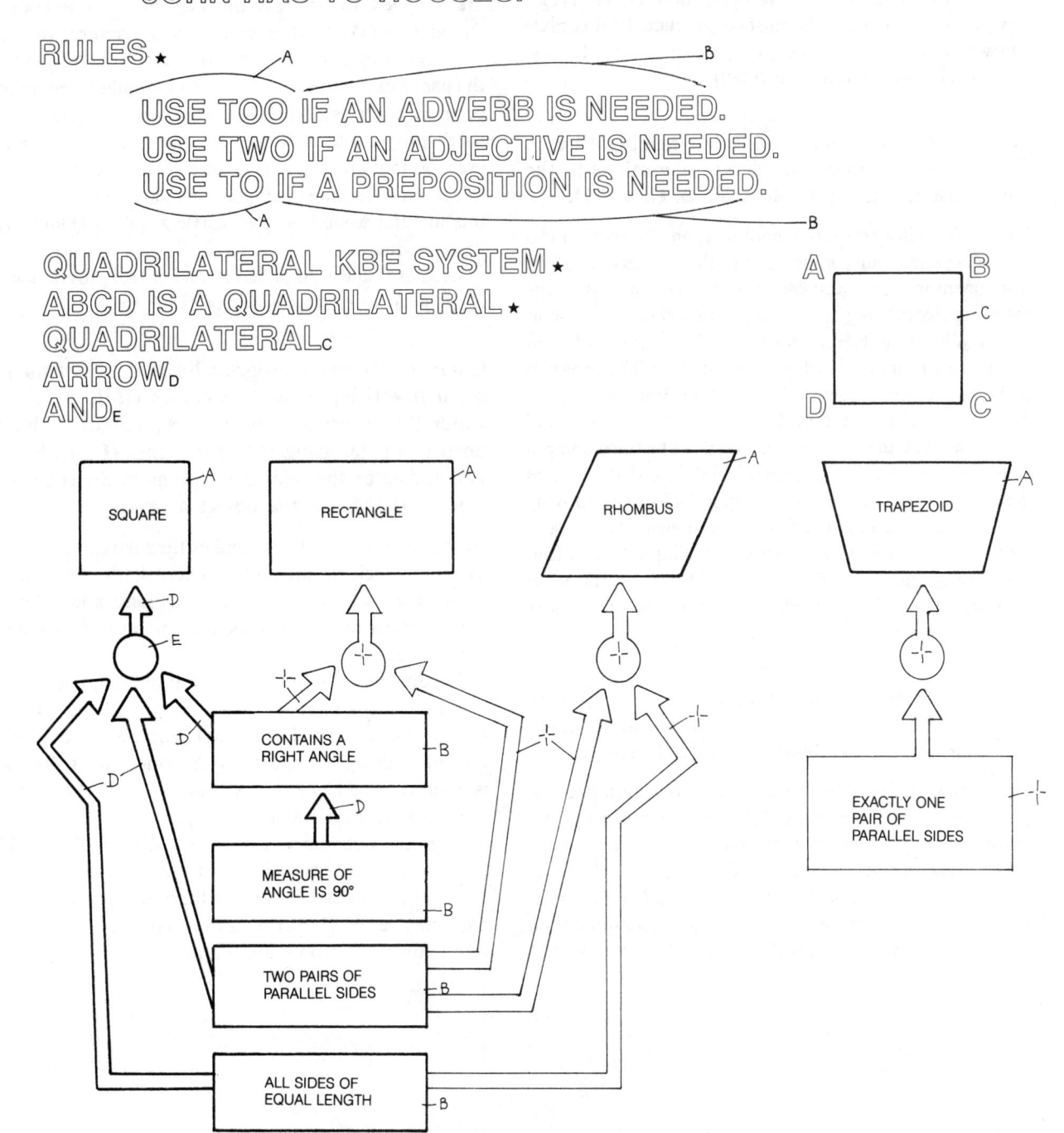

RULES ★

USE TOO IF AN ADVERB IS NEEDED.
USE TWO IF AN ADJECTIVE IS NEEDED.
USE TO IF A PREPOSITION IS NEEDED.

QUADRILATERAL KBE SYSTEM ★

ABCD IS A QUADRILATERAL ★
QUADRILATERAL_C
ARROW_D
AND_E

SQUARE   RECTANGLE   RHOMBUS   TRAPEZOID

CONTAINS A RIGHT ANGLE

MEASURE OF ANGLE IS 90°

TWO PAIRS OF PARALLEL SIDES

ALL SIDES OF EQUAL LENGTH

EXACTLY ONE PAIR OF PARALLEL SIDES

41
INTRODUCTION TO ROBOTICS

Robotics is the use of machines to handle multiple, relatively complex manufacturing or manipulation operations continuously and automatically. Many aspects of artificial intelligence have applications in robotics. The mechanical device (robot) must interact with the environment to perform a particular function. The robot may be as simple as a mechanical arm used to manipulate objects, or it may be as complex as an entire machine that produces a particular item from raw material to finished product. In this plate you will learn the fundamental operating principles and the place of the computer in robotics.

Color the Human Controlled Robot heading, titles A through D, and their related representations in the top diagram. Use light colors for B, C, and D.

The example illustrates the manipulation of a mechanical arm. There are four components to this process. The first component is the *human operator*. The person acts as the controller by moving a lever to position the robot arm at a desired location. Here, *rotation* and *horizontal* and *vertical movement* are directed by the controller. The program is the second component of the system. For the human, the "program" is stored in the brain as the knowledge of how to activate the robot arm correctly. The third component is the *robot arm,* a mechanical device that executes the desired task such as picking up an object and moving it to another position. The fourth component is *input* and *feedback;* the human controller receives input by continuously watching the results of the robot arm operation. If the goal is not being achieved, the human controller modifies the setting of the mechanical controls.

Color the Computer Controlled Robot heading, titles E through H, and their related representations in the middle diagram. Use light colors for F and G.

The human can be replaced by a *computer* acting as the *controller.* Signals from the CPU of the computer activate the desired *mechanical function* (rotate, move horizontal or vertical) through electronic signals carried by data buses. This is not unlike the CPU's activation of the printer in a microcomputer system. Between the computer and the robot arm there is an *interface unit.* This unit converts the electronic signals from the computer into special control signals understood by the servo (motion) motors of the arm.

In order to create the program, the machine (the robot arm in the example) can be guided by a human, step by step, through the positions required for operation. A program stores, in memory, the sequence of commands that are supplied to perform the task. The commands are stored in ROM (at the time of manufacture) or on an auxiliary storage device (disk or tape) to be retrieved by the user's execution program. The manufacturer supplied program controls all motions of the robot's capability. The user's program then directs the specific sequence and degree of motion required to meet the user's particular needs. In a simple sense, you have controlled a robot by this method when you used turtle graphics (Plate 34) to draw a square.

Let's examine a simplified robot control program which is designed to control grasping an object.

Color the Robotics Program heading. Color the program line title, using four colors (I, J, K, and L). Color the program lines (I, J, K, and L). Color the positions title, using the four colors (I^1, J^1, K^1, and L^1), and color the related positions of the robot arm. Color title M and the object as well.

In the example, the user supplies the instructions to have the robot pick up an object. The robot's servo motors respond exactly to the program's commands. The sequence of instructions causes the robot arm to pick up the given object.

In addition to simple mechanical motion, many robots contain sensors to supply *feedback* (middle diagram) to the control program. For example, the amount of pressure needed to grasp an object may be detected. If the object is a tomato, light pressure is required. A steel object may require a stronger robot arm grip.

Heat and light sensors may be added to allow a robot to move around a hot object or distinguish between different colored objects. Voice synthesis and recognition circuits may be added to provide means of audio communication between the robot and human.

INTRODUCTION TO ROBOTICS.

HUMAN CONTROLLED ROBOT ★
HUMAN OPERATOR A
OUTPUT FUNCTIONS B
   ROTATION B^1
   HORIZONTAL B^2
   VERTICAL B^3
ROBOT ARM C
INPUT D
FEEDBACK PATH D^1

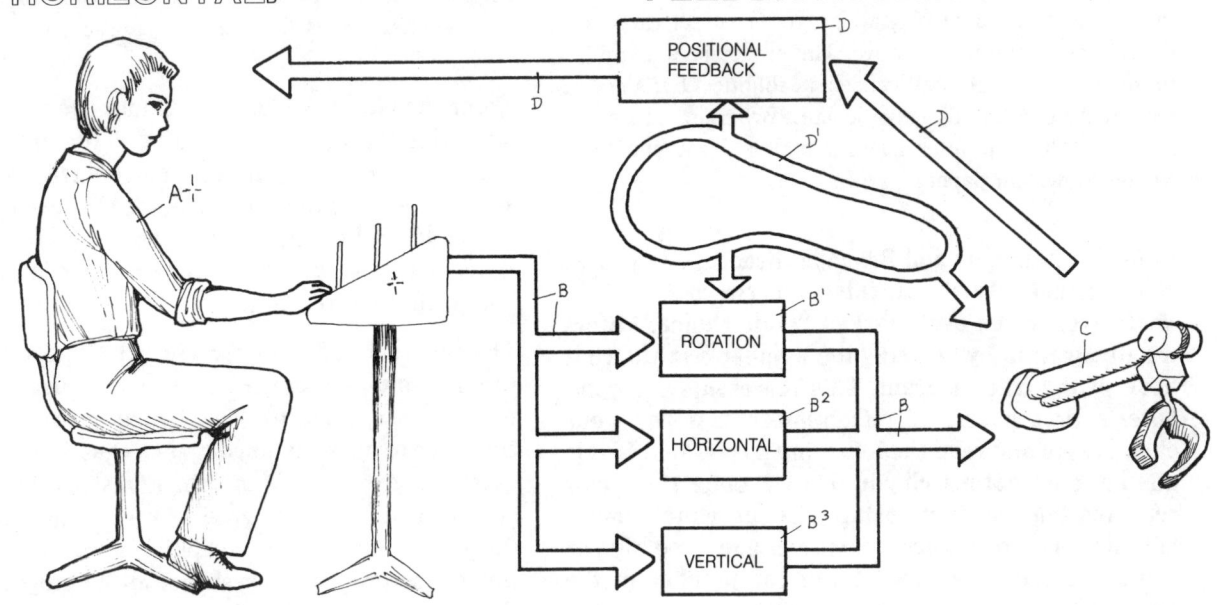

COMPUTER CONTROLLED ROBOT ★
COMPUTER CONTROLLER E
INTERFACE UNIT F
MECHANICAL FUNCTION G
FEEDBACK H

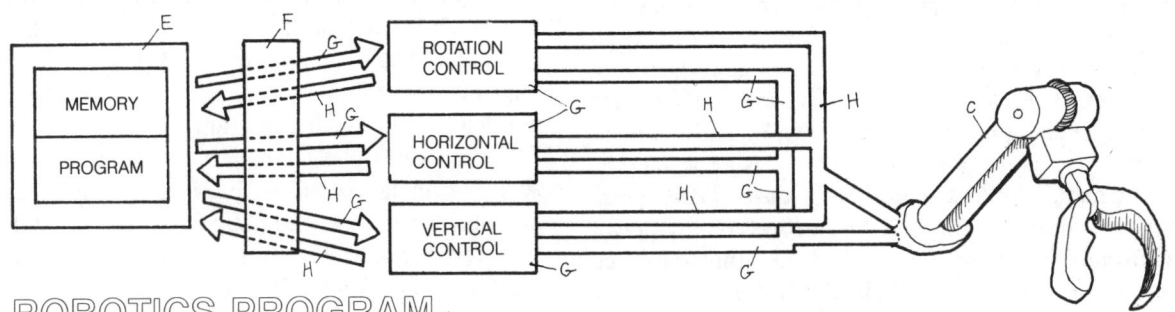

ROBOTICS PROGRAM ★
PROGRAM LINE I,J,K,L
POSITION I^1, J^1, K^1, L^1
OBJECT M

FORWARD 10 — I
DOWN 10 — J
FORWARD 10 — K
CLOSE HAND — L

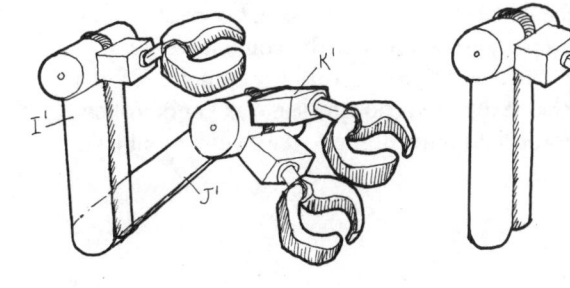

42
COMPUTER GAMES AND SIMULATIONS

Quite possibly, one of your first encounters with a computer was playing an arcade game in a store or on a home video game system. In a computer game you shoot at something, move a chess piece on the screen, follow a path through a dark castle, or perform some variation of these themes. Special game playing programs direct the computer's response to your move. The programs are similar to those of artificial intelligence and robotics. Let's take a look at the creation of a simple game program. The game is having the computer guess a number that you have written down on paper.

Color the Numbers and Branches headings and titles A through D. Write an integer between 1 and 10 (inclusive) in the oval marked "your choice." Start the illustration by coloring the number 5 in the root node of the tree diagram. This represents the computer's first guess. If this number matches your choice, stop and read the following paragraph. If this number does not match your choice, color the arrow representing the relationship between your number and the computer's guess (computer guess too high or computer guess too low). Color the number in the node at the end of the arrow. Continue to color the arrows and numbers until the node contains the correct guess. Then read the following paragraph.

When manufacturers or programmers want to develop a game playing program, they often start with a branching pattern of organization, called a *tree*. The tree is like a flowchart, written on paper, to outline the steps that the game playing program is to follow. Once the tree is completed, the programmer translates the diagram into program lines. The tree is used to organize the data for searching, making decisions, and general data base management systems. Each part of the tree has a special purpose and name. The first point is called the *root node* (even though it is drawn at the top). The arrows coming downward from the root node are called the branches. Each location where the branches split is called a *node*. A tree like that in the example, with two or fewer branches at each node, is called a binary tree. In the example the root node contains the computer's first guess, 5. If this guess is correct, the game stops there. If it is not correct, follow the branch representing whether the computer's *guess is too high* or *too low* compared with *your choice*. If the number in the next node is not the same as yours, follow the next appropriate branch. Stop when your number is reached.

This type of tree is the basis of more sophisticated and complicated games such as chess and fantasy role playing. The rules of the game are similar to the rule base of artificial intelligence programs. Once a set of rules has been written in the form of a tree (or flowchart), the programmer writes the required source program.

Color the Number Guessing Game Program heading and titles E through H. For simplicity, only the lines representing the right half of the tree have been shown. As you color each line, locate the corresponding node or branch in the tree diagram. You may wish to choose another number (5 or less) as your guess for the program.

The lines of the program represent the types of lines used throughout the guessing game. The computer's first guess, 5, is displayed (line 10). The human game player (you) enters the response to the computer's guess (line 20). If the guess is correct (okay), the program stops (line 30). The computer has correctly guessed your number to be 5. If the guess is too low, the computer is directed to the portion of the program (not shown in the program listing) that deals with the right half of the tree (line 40). If the guess is not okay and not too low, then it must be too high. So the computer makes another guess, 3 (line 50). Again you are asked for a response (line 60). If 3 is correct, the program stops (line 70). If 3 is too large, the computer prints out its next guess, 2 (line 110). Otherwise, the guess is 4, the only possible number at this branch of the tree. If 5, 3, and 2 are too large, the program reaches its last guess of 1. The remaining branch (left side of the tree) is implemented a similar way. You may want to write the omitted portion of the program.

For more complicated games, the tree is more complex. A little calculation shows that in the game of chess, the first player has a choice of 20 moves. The second has this same number of opening moves, so the total possible paths is 20 times 20, or 400. The number of nodes and possible branches becomes so large that some tree trimming is done by the programmer. Just as in an artificial intelligence program, the writer lists the antecedent conditions for a particular move and then the possible consequent moves. Such a list may be created after interviewing chess masters or reviewing historic chess games. The program reflects these conditions for a particular move. When a move is to be made, it searches for a particular recognized pattern and makes the indicated move.

COMPUTER GAMES.

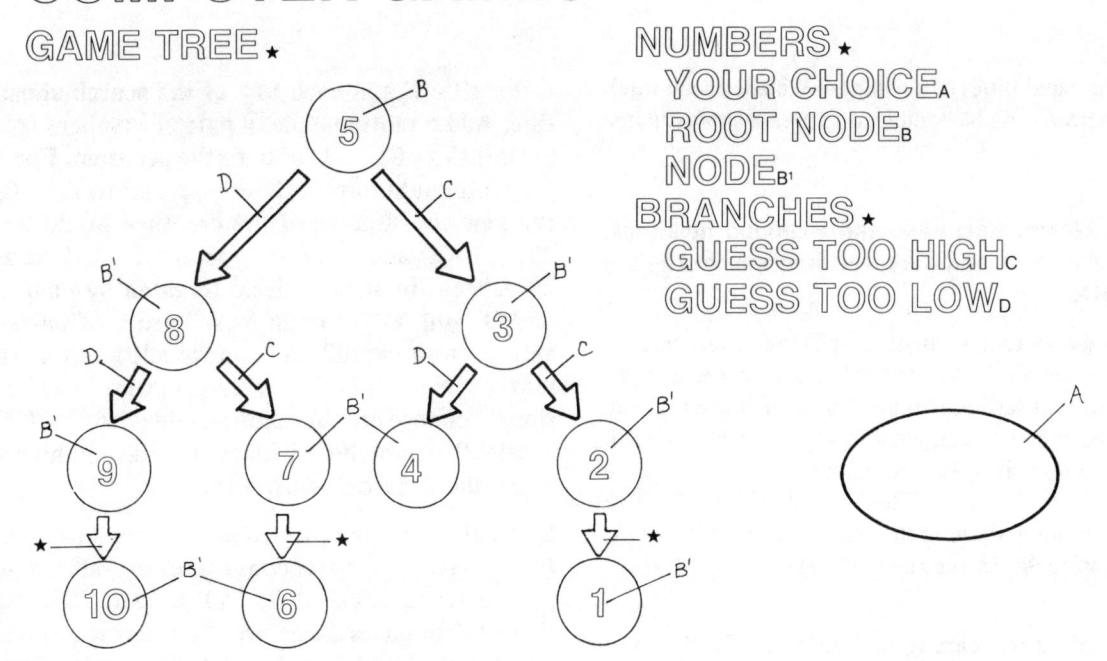

GAME TREE.

- 5 (B)
  - D → 8 (B')
    - D → 9 (B')
      - ★ → 10 (B')
    - C → 7 (B')
      - → 6 (B') ★
  - C → 3 (B')
    - D → 4 (B')
    - C → 2 (B')
      - ★ → 1 (B')

NUMBERS ★
- YOUR CHOICE _A_
- ROOT NODE _B_
- NODE _B'_

BRANCHES ★
- GUESS TOO HIGH _C_
- GUESS TOO LOW _D_

NUMBER GUESSING GAME PROGRAM ★
- PRINT INSTRUCTION _E_
- INPUT INSTRUCTION _F_
- IF...THEN...INSTRUCTION _G_
- STOP INSTRUCTION _H_

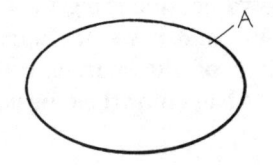

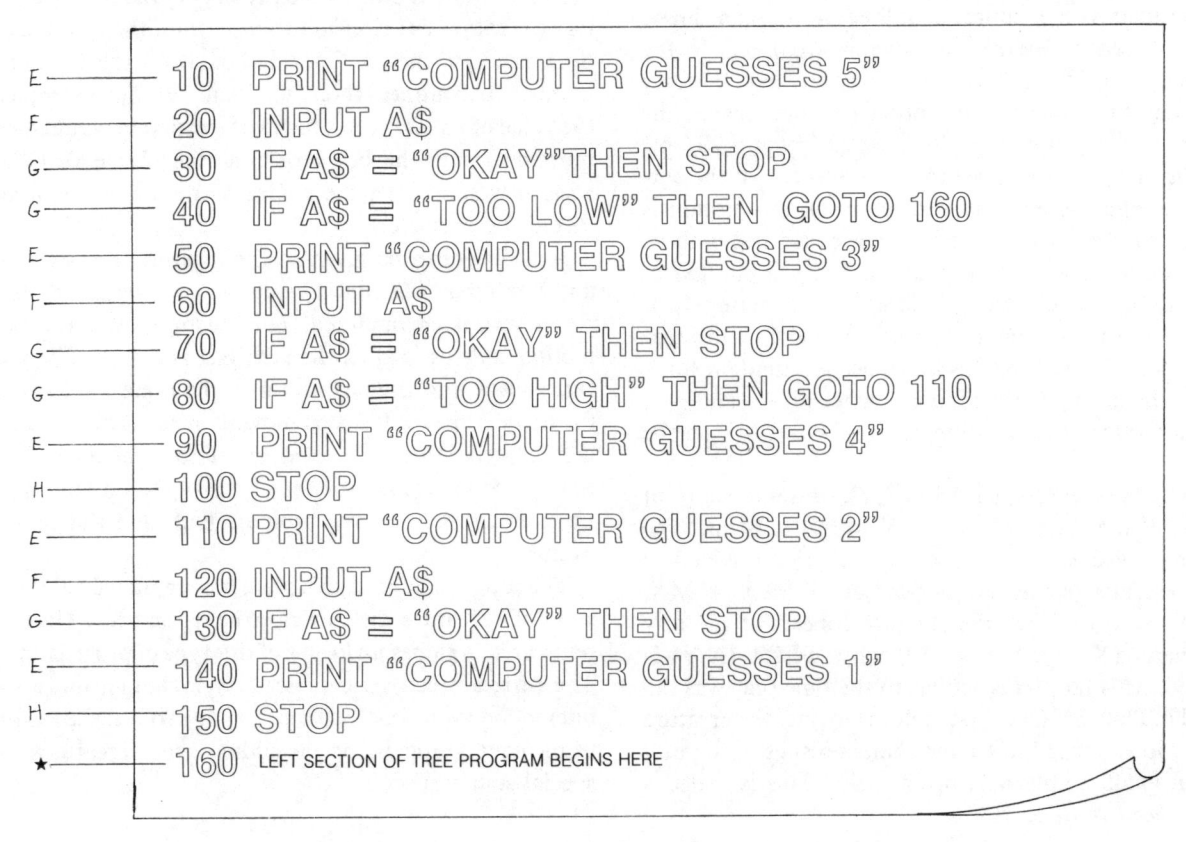

```
E — 10    PRINT "COMPUTER GUESSES 5"
F — 20    INPUT A$
G — 30    IF A$ = "OKAY" THEN STOP
G — 40    IF A$ = "TOO LOW" THEN GOTO 160
E — 50    PRINT "COMPUTER GUESSES 3"
F — 60    INPUT A$
G — 70    IF A$ = "OKAY" THEN STOP
G — 80    IF A$ = "TOO HIGH" THEN GOTO 110
E — 90    PRINT "COMPUTER GUESSES 4"
H — 100   STOP
E — 110   PRINT "COMPUTER GUESSES 2"
F — 120   INPUT A$
G — 130   IF A$ = "OKAY" THEN STOP
E — 140   PRINT "COMPUTER GUESSES 1"
H — 150   STOP
★ — 160   LEFT SECTION OF TREE PROGRAM BEGINS HERE
```

43
INTELLIGENCE SIMULATING GAMES

The graphic capabilities of a computer and artificial intelligence programs can be combined to create sophisticated games.

Color the Game, Eat, Flee, and Rebound headings, titles A through D, and the three diagrams at the top of the plate.

Imagine a game that consists of placing a *creature* (a mouse, frog, or any other animal) inside a rectangular environment and letting it roam about. If it contacts an *obstacle*, the creature can eat the object or continue in another direction. If a *wall* is encountered, the creature chooses another direction. The goal of this game is to choose the *initial position* of the creature so that it will eat the edible obstacles in the shortest time.

Color the Motion heading and titles E, E^1, C^1, and C^2. Locate the initial position (C^1) of the creature in the grid. Color gray the row and column coordinates that are shown outside the grid (for simplicity, only three columns and rows are numbered). Color the program lines of the motion routine as you read about them. Also, color the new position of the creature (C^2).

In order to move a creature about the screen, a coordinate system is used with a *motion program (routine)*. In the example, the grid is chosen to be forty columns by forty rows. The first line of the motion program places the creature in the center, X = 20: Y = 20 (column 20, row 20). The creature is allowed to move into any of the surrounding eight boxes. This restriction on the motion is used so that the creature need only be concerned with its immediate (eight-box) surroundings. The *new position* of the creature is calculated by adding 1, subtracting 1, or adding 0 to the horizontal (X) and vertical (Y) position. The choice of −1, 1, or 0 is made using a random function. In the example, the random choice of −1 and −1, called a *motion code*, is assigned to MX and MY in the program.

Erasing the creature, ERASE (X,Y), causes the current position of the screen (X = 20, Y = 20) to blank. The randomly selected motion codes (−1,−1) are added to the coordinates of the current position (X = X + MX, Y = Y + MY). Then the creature appears at the new coordinates (X = 19, Y = 19) when PLOT (X,Y) is executed. This motion is similar to the type that was described in Plate 32. Of course, before moving, the creature should "look ahead" to see the characteristics of the new position (wall, empty box, or obstacle). This is called a *search ahead routine*.

Color title F and each line of the search ahead routine. Add a motion code, a pair of numbers from the posibilities of 1, −1, or 0, to the program. For example, you could have MX = −1 and MY = 0; then the new coordinates of the creature would be X = 20 + (−1) and Y = 20 + 0 or X = 19 and Y = 20. Check the new position (created by your choice of MX and MY) for the possibilities of obstacle or empty (wall would be a possibility after several moves). Note that in a real program "motion routine," "choose another motion code" and "RND subroutine" would be replaced by line numbers that begin the required subroutine.

Before the creature is moved into the new box, a series of IF . . . THEN . . . instructions checks the value of the box. Here a function called WHAT is used. The value of WHAT determines the nature of the new box (0 = empty box, 1 = wall, and 2 = obstacle). The function and codes depend on the particular computer's graphics routines. If the box is empty, the motion routine is used to place the creature in the new box. If the box is a wall, a new motion code is chosen and the search procedure starts again. If the box ahead is an obstacle, then the creature must decide to eat it or choose another motion code. If the creature is hungry, it moves into the box replacing the obstacle with its own color. The decision to move into the box is made by a random choice. One method is to use a random number subroutine, RND (see Plate 29). For example, if the value of RND is less than .5, the program would direct movement into the box (consume the obstacle). Otherwise, it would direct the choice of another motion code (avoid the obstacle).

A "habit" can be given to the creature. For example, a new motion code would be chosen only when an obstacle or wall is encountered. The creature keeps the same motion code as long as the next box is empty. The creature moves into the box and uses the same motion code for its next move. It keeps moving in the same direction until it strikes a wall or obstacle. Then it changes direction. A count could be kept of the obstacles left. When the count reaches 0, the program ends and the game is over.

The programming in this plate has simulated the movement of a creature within a closed environment. The computer arcade games make use of this type of programming. The program can be enhanced by including more user interaction (you shoot at, capture, or avoid the creature), using finer graphics, or by adding more creatures and special sound effects.

INTELLIGENCE SIMULATING GAMES.

GAME ★
WALL_A
OBSTACLE_B
CREATURE_C
PATH_D

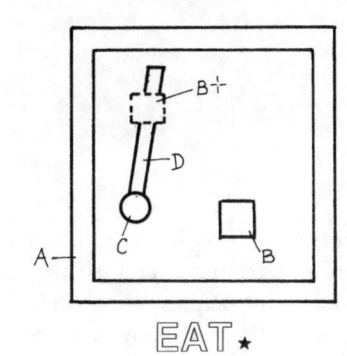

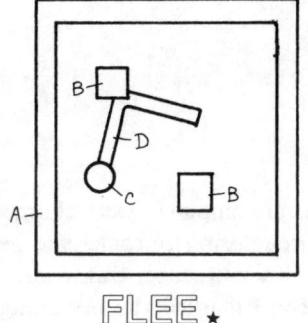

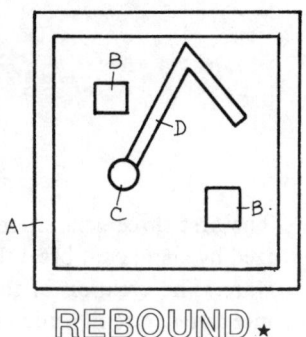

EAT ★   FLEE ★   REBOUND ★

MOTION ★

$$E \begin{cases} X = 20: Y = 20 \\ MX = -1 \quad {}^{E'} \\ MY = -1 \\ ERASE\ (X, Y) \\ X = X + MX \\ Y = Y + MY \\ PLOT\ (X, Y) \end{cases} E$$

MOTION ROUTINE_E
MOTION CODE_{E^1}
INITIAL POSITION_{C^1}
NEW POSITION_{C^2}

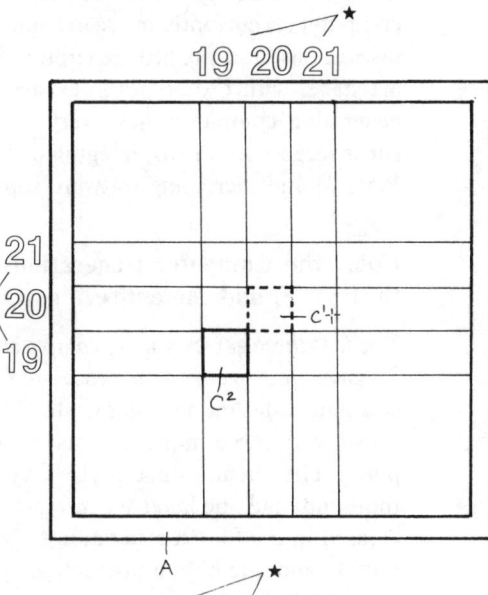

19 20 21

21
20
19

C^1
C^2

SEARCH AHEAD ROUTINE_F

$$F \begin{cases} X = 20: Y = 20 \\ MX = \\ MY = \\ IF\ WHAT\ (X + MX, Y + MY) = 0 \end{cases}$$

★ (THEN GOTO MOTION
    ROUTINE
F — IF WHAT (X + MX, Y + MY) = 1
  ★ (THEN CHOOSE ANOTHER
      MOTION CODE
F — IF WHAT (X + MX, Y + MY) = 2
  ★ (THEN GOTO RND
      SUBROUTINE

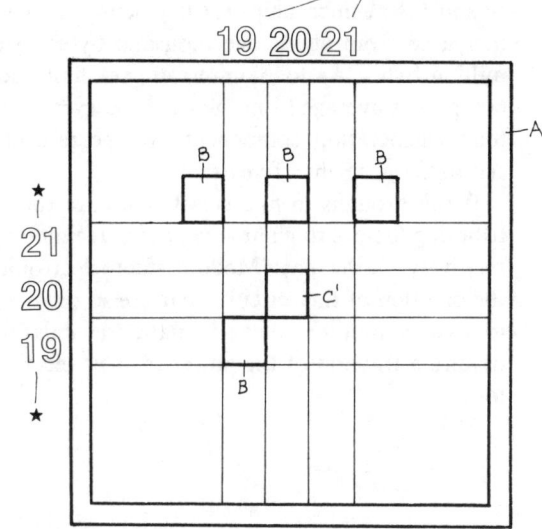

19 20 21

21
20
19

44 THE FUTURE OF COMPUTERS

The first three generations of computers were characterized by significant breakthroughs in electronics and hardware. The creation of the vacuum tube, transistor, and integrated circuit (microchip) marked the beginning of these first three generations. The fourth generation of computers is currently in use in commercial and academic institutions, and the fifth generation is at the state of the art stage, with prototypes in existence. Fourth and fifth generation computers have very-large-scale (VLSI) and super-large-scale (SLSI) integrated circuits (see Appendix Plate 3) and increasing software sophistication.

Color the Computer Generations heading, titles A through F, and the entire illustration.

The *first three generations of computers* demonstrated progressive improvement in processing speed and memory size and a decline in failure rate. The *fourth generation* shows very large improvements in all aspects of a computer. The vacuum-tube processing speed of about two thousand machine language instructions per second is increased in the fourth generation to between one hundred million and one billion instructions per second. Memory size in RAM microchips (or its vacuum-tube equivalent) increased from about one thousand bytes to over three million bytes. As for failure rate, the first vacuum tube computers averaged one blown tube every minute. The fourth generation component average rate of failure is estimated in terms of years.

Breakthroughs in microelectronics are the major contributing factors to giant advances in technology within a relatively short time. Modern microelectronics permits the creation of tiny circuits that are so closely packed as to have a minimal delay in data transmission and yet require a fraction of the power of their electronic ancestors.

The *fifth generation* will show even greater advances in circuitry and software capability. Parallel processing, principles of artificial intelligence (AI), and natural (human) language processing are used in the creation of super-high-speed computer systems.

The hardware component of the fifth generation is to have up to one thousand times the processing power and speed of the fourth generation computer. In order to achieve this level of speed, parallel processing techniques are used. This involves using many microprocessors operating at the same time on different aspects of a particular problem. Each is synchronized to finish at the correct time to produce a rapid result.

The software component of the fifth generation is that of sophisticated knowledge-based management systems and problem-solving software. Artificial intelligence techniques are to be adapted to manage the computer system's architecture, improve human–computer interfacing, and help the user formulate methods of creating data base systems. Changes in types of languages are implemented in this generation. The languages are more natural (human) and formal logic oriented rather than rigid in syntax (such as you have seen with BASIC programming).

Another important component of the fifth generation is the human interface segment. Humans communicate with systems of this generation in natural language, either spoken or entered at a keyboard. Graphic input, as in the form of written pages, can be used as input. The computer responds by use of voice synthesis with a vocabulary beyond that of the synthesizers of the fourth generation.

The evolution of the computer has completed four generations, with the fifth beginning at this point. A prediction can be made at this point of perhaps many more generations of computer systems. Perhaps biological ("living" substances) computers will characterize one of these generations.

THE FUTURE OF COMPUTERS.

COMPUTER GENERATIONS ★
- FIRST A
- SECOND B
- THIRD C
- FOURTH D
- FIFTH E
- IMPROVEMENTS F

- A — VACUUM TUBE
- B — TRANSISTOR
- C — I.C.
- D — V.L.S.I. / IMPROVED SOFTWARE
- E — S.L.S.I. / A.I. / HUMAN INTERFACE
- F — PROCESSING SPEED ↑
- F — MEMORY SIZE ↑
- F — FAILURE RATE ↓

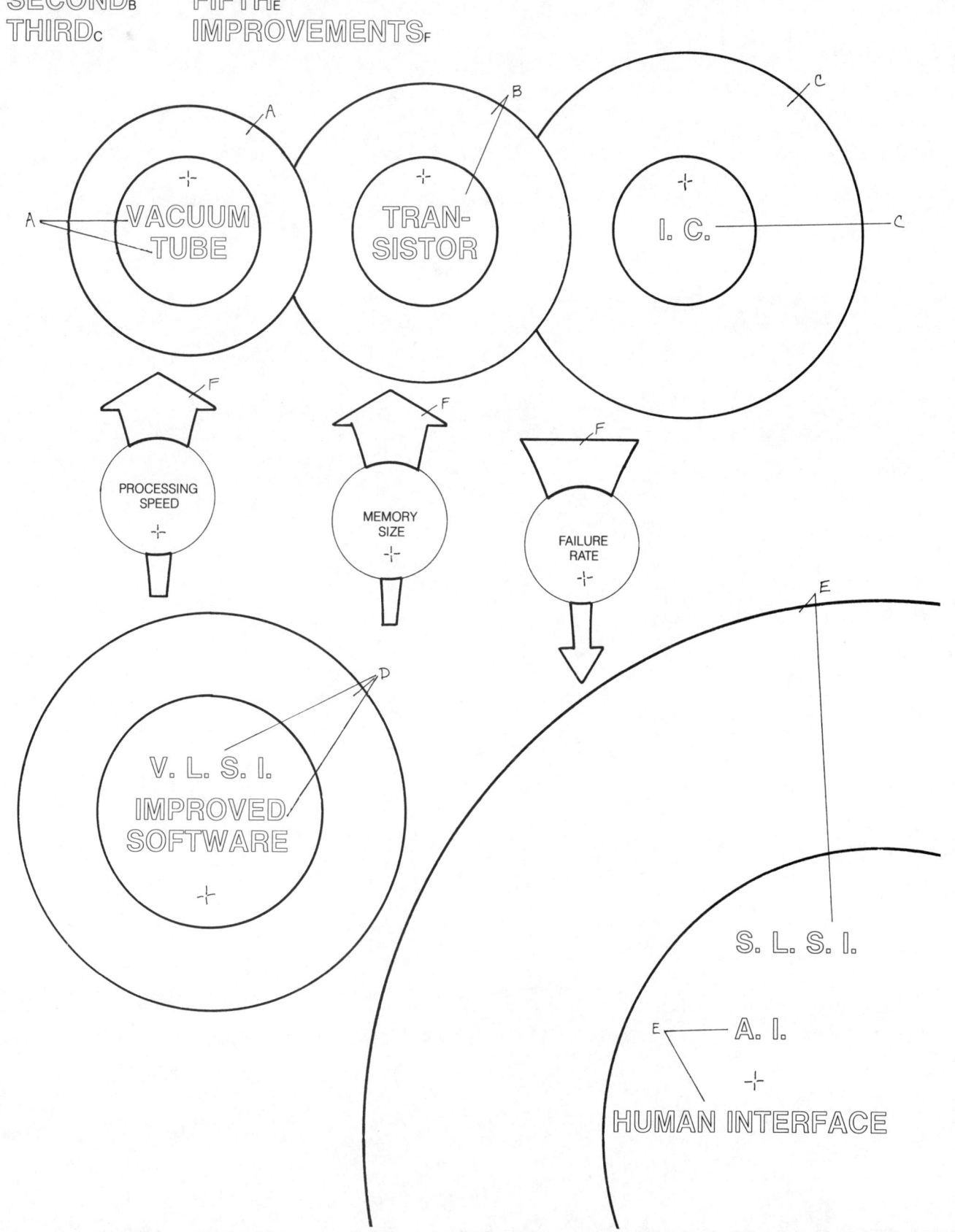

APPENDIX

A1
NUMBER SYSTEMS AND BINARY NUMBERS

Every computer stores and processes numbers, letters, and other characters in a coded form. The computer's circuits respond to two voltage levels representing a 0 or 1. The number system the computer is using is called a binary system. We use a decimal system of numeration. In this plate you will see that these systems are just variations on the same type of numeration system. The systems are described in terms of the positive integers (counting numbers).

Color the Number System and Roman headings, titles A and D, the Roman numerals, and their decimal equivalent underneath.

The *Roman numeral system* uses an additive approach. The system uses a symbol to represent the same value regardless of its position in the number. The value of the numeral is determined by adding up the values of each of the symbols in its representation. The symbol "X" always represents 10 no matter where it appears in the numeral. So, in the diagram, XXX represents three 10s (30). The letter I represents 1, V represents 5, and L represents 50. In order to write 88, the system uses an L, three Xs, a V, and three Is (written LXXXVIII).

Color the Decimal heading, title B, the decimal number, and the value of each digit underneath.

The system of numeration that we use for counting and arithmetic is a positional system. Not only does a symbol represent a particular number, but its position causes a uniform change of value. In our system of numerals each position, except the rightmost, is given ten times the value of the position to its right. In the example, the numerals used are 8s. The rightmost 8 stands for eight 1s. The position to its left represents the number of 10s, in this example eight 10s, or 80. A position to the left of the 10s would represent 100s, and so on. The numerals combined represent 88. Each column represents a power of 10 greater than that of the column to its right. The symbol (0,1,2,3, ... 8,9) in a column indicates how many of that particular power of ten is to be considered as part of the number that is being represented. Ten is the basis of our number system. For this reason, it is called a base 10 or *decimal* (deci = ten) *system*.

Color the Binary heading, titles C and D[1], the binary numeral, and the value of each digit position underneath. Color the equation showing the corresponding decimal value of the binary numeral.

In the *binary* (base 2) *system*, position has a meaning analogous to that used in the base 10 system. The position of a numeral (0 or 1) from rightmost to leftmost determines its value. Each position, except the first, represents a value two times the value of each position to its right. In the example, the rightmost position represents 1. The position to its left represents 2 and the position to its left represents one second power of 2, or $2 \times 2 = 4$. To its left is the $2 \times 2 \times 2$ position, and so on—in this example, to the $2 \times 2 \times 2 \times 2 \times 2 \times 2$ (= 64) position. The binary system is a positional system. Although only two numerals, 0 and 1, are used, their position in the numeral indicates what power of 2 is to be used in the value of the represented number. The decimal equivalent 88 is represented by binary number 1011000 ($1 \times 64 + 0 \times 32 + 1 \times 16 + 1 \times 8 + 0 \times 4 + 0 \times 2 + 0 \times 1 = 88$).

The representation of a number by binary numerals is, in most cases, longer than its representation in decimal numerals. However, the binary system is easily adapted to the on/off (high/low) states of an electronic circuit and so has become the number system used to represent data in the electronic computer. Although you enter a letter, number, or special symbol from the keyboard, the operating system translates it into a binary code number. You have seen that your instructions written in a high-level language are translated into and stored as electronic signals that represent binary numeral patterns. The only drawback is that it is hard for the user to remember a long binary numeral. In the next plate you will learn how other number systems are used to help the user program in machine language and quickly translate from long binary into shorter octal or hexadecimal numerals.

NUMBER SYSTEMS AND BINARY NUMBERS.

NUMBER SYSTEM.
  ROMAN_A
  DECIMAL_B
  BINARY_C
    POSITION DECIMAL VALUE_D'
DECIMAL EQUIVALENT_D

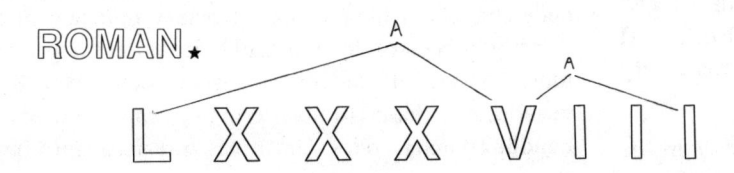

ROMAN.

L X X X V I I I

50 + 10 + 10 + 10 + 5 + 1 + 1 + 1 = 88

DECIMAL.

88

80 + 8

BINARY.

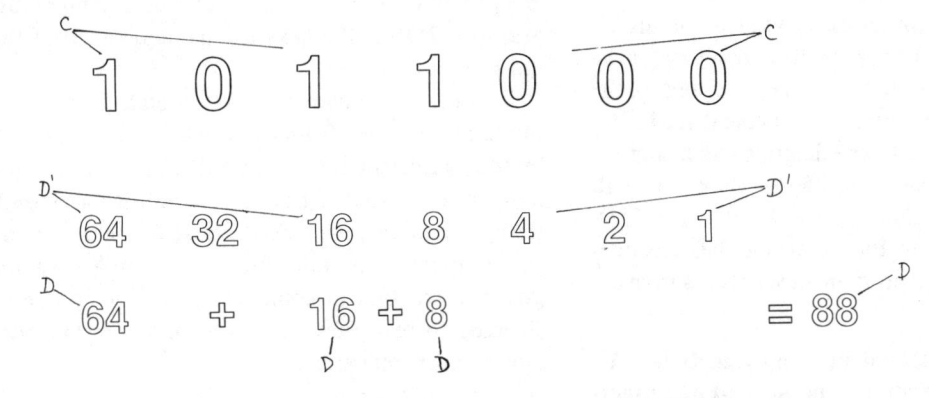

1 0 1 1 0 0 0

64   32   16   8   4   2   1

64 + 16 + 8 = 88

A2
OCTAL AND HEXADECIMAL NUMBERS

In the previous plates you have learned how the operating system uses the electronic equivalents (on/off or high/low voltage) of the binary digits 0 and 1 to process and store a program or data. The binary system uses base 2, while you use the decimal system, base 10. Both, as you have seen, are positional systems. In order for you to communicate with the computer, special program segments of the operating system translate decimal to binary on input and from binary to decimal on output.

Color the Number System and Octal headings and titles A, D, E, and F only. Color the octal numeral at the top of the plate and the equation immediately below it.

The *octal numeral system* uses the base 8. Just as in the case of decimal or binary numerals, the *position value* of the number increases by one power of the base as you go from right to left. The power increase is by 8 in the octal system. In the diagram, the numeral 1333 (base 8) represents $1 \times 512 + 3 \times 64 + 3 \times 8 + 3 \times 1 = 731$ (base 10). The only allowed numerals in each position are 0, 1, 2, 3, 4, 5, 6, or 7.

Color the Hexadecimal heading, title B, the hexadecimal numeral, and the equation below it.

Just like the base 2, 8, and 10 systems, the *hexadecimal system* is positional. The value of a position increases by a power of 16 as you go from right to left. Remember, in each position there can be only one symbol displayed. This presents no problem for base 2, 8, or 10. However, in hexadecimal, the number of single symbol numerals allowed in each position must be 16. In order to allow for the extra six symbols (beyond 0, 1, 2, 3, 4, 5, 6, 7, 8, and 9), the letters A, B, C, D, E, and F are used to represent 10, 11, 12, 13, 14, and 15, respectively. In the diagram the hexadecimal numeral 2DB represents $2 \times 256 + D \times 16 + B$, which is equivalent to $2 \times 256 + 13 \times 16 + 11 (= 731)$. At this point let's see why the octal and hexadecimal systems are used in writing a program or set of data items.

Color the Binary Translated heading and titles A^1, and B^1, and C. Color the binary, octal, and hexadecimal equivalent numerals. Color the brackets showing the grouping of binary digits for octal and hexadecimal. Color the position decimal values under the binary numerals. You can use these to establish for yourself that the decimal equivalent of the binary numeral is 731.

Under usual circumstances, you see only decimal input and output. However, you may wish to have the computer display data during processing, as well as the object code instructions themselves. Machine language code consists of long strings of binary numbers that are directly processed by the CPU. In order to provide a more convenient numeration system, octal (base 8) and hexadecimal (base 16) numbering systems are used when handling binary codes. Until it is translated into binary, the computer does not operate on or process (other than translating into binary) data or instructions written in these bases.

Notationally, every triple of *binary digits* can be expressed as a single equivalent octal digit (0, 1, 2, 3, 4, 5, 6, or 7). In the diagram, the twelve-digit binary number (001011011011) can be written as a four-digit octal numeral (1333). This notation lets the user write programs in languages between machine and higher-level languages. It also permits the user to instruct the computer to display data in a more easily readable form.

Hexadecimal notation makes reading binary digits still easier. Every quartet of binary digits can be expressed as a single hexadecimal digit (0, 1, 2, 3, 4, 5, 6, 7, 8, 9, A, B, C, D, E, or F). The original twelve-digit binary numeral is represented as a three-digit hexadecimal numeral. In the example, 2DB is the hexadecimal equivalent of the original binary numeral.

In order to convert binary to octal, group the binary numerals by threes from right to left and replace the triple by the equivalent octal numeral. In the case of hexadecimal, group by fours from right to left. Replace each quartet by the equivalent hexadecimal numeral. In this way, the computer user can write down complex machine language instruction in compact form. The computer is instructed to read these numerals and translate them into binary electronic signals.

OCTAL AND HEXADECIMAL NUMBERS.

NUMBER SYSTEM.
  OCTAL_A
    GROUPING_A1
  HEXADECIMAL_B
    GROUPING_B1
  BINARY_C
POSITION CONTENT_D
POSITION DECIMAL VALUE_E
DECIMAL EQUIVALENT_F

OCTAL.

1   3   3   3

$1 \times 512 + 3 \times 64 + 3 \times 8 + 3 \times 1 = 731$

HEXADECIMAL.

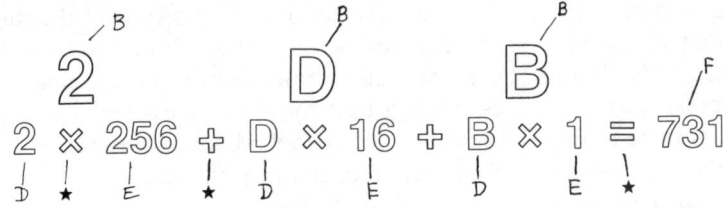

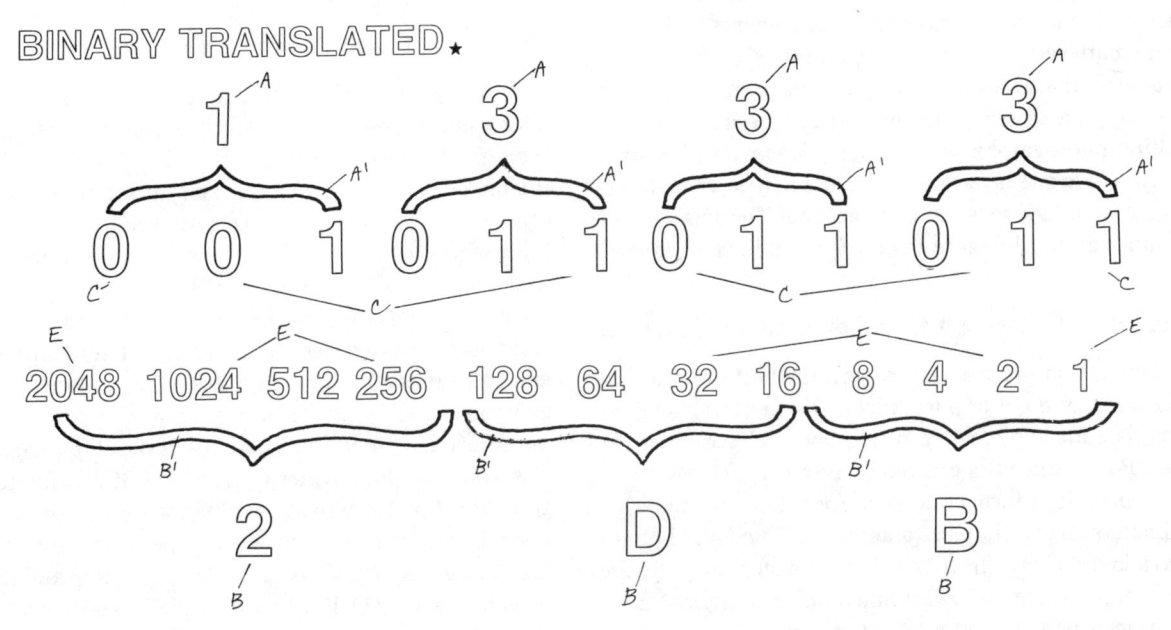

2   D   B

$2 \times 256 + D \times 16 + B \times 1 = 731$

BINARY TRANSLATED.

1   3   3   3

0 0 1 0 1 1 0 1 1 0 1 1

2048   1024   512   256   128   64   32   16   8   4   2   1

2   D   B

A3
BUILDING A MICROCHIP

The first general-purpose electronic computer was ENIAC. It was created by John Mauchly and J. Presper Ekert as a secret wartime project during the early 1940s. It weighed thirty tons and took up 1500 square feet of space. Its eighteen thousand vacuum tubes required a separate air-conditioning unit. Since the creation of that physically tremendous installation, the size of the equivalent electronic computer has shrunk to a few square millimeters, the size of a small microchip containing thousands of circuits.

The term integrated circuit is used to refer to a microchip because it contains many components all designed to work together. Further distinction is made, determined by the number of components on the microchip. Small-scale (SS) integrated circuits have a maximum of 10 components; medium-scale (MS), a maximum of 500; large-scale (LS) a maximum of 20,000; very-large-scale (VLS) a maximum of 100,000; and super-large-scale (SLS) over 1,000,000 components per integrated circuit. In this plate you will learn of the process for constructing the microchip.

Color titles A, B, and C and the upper illustration. Use light colors for A and C.

The process of creating a microchip begins on the drawing board. The engineers design the circuits that will go into the microchip. Here the microchip's *pattern* is shown viewed from above (A). Designing is a very complex process, as there are thousands of components to be drawn and interconnected for one small microchip. Each logic block (see Appendix Plates 4 and 5) is composed of many transistors and other electrical components. The designer's pattern is used as the beginning of a *photoreduction process* that reduces the original diagram to a precise exact copy on specially designed photographic film. The resulting photographic mask plate (*photomask*) becomes the layout for one layer of the microchip. For each different layer, another mask plate is needed. The final size of the film may not be more than a few millimeters square.

Color titles C[1] through G and diagrams 1, 2, and 3.

The fabrication process begins with the cutting of a thin wafer from an ingot of pure silicon. An impurity, such as boron, is added to create a deficiency of electrons in the wafer. *P-type silicon* is created (diagram 1). The wafer is then *heated* in a furnace to produce a thin (about .0005 millimeters) layer of oxide (diagram 2). The layer is similar to a layer of rust (iron oxide) on an iron plate, only the layer here is *silicon dioxide*. Silicon dioxide (glass) is an insulator, a nonconductor of electricity.

A thin coating of a special *photoresist,* a photosensitive emulsion (plastic), is applied to the surface of the wafer. Then the photomask is placed in close contact with the surface of the wafer (diagram 3).

Color titles G[1] through K and diagrams 4 through 7.

The sandwich (silicon wafer with oxide, photoresist, and photomask) is exposed to *ultraviolet light.* The light *hardens* the plastic film of photoresist except for those areas masked by *opaque spots* in the photomask (diagram 4). A *developer solution* of chemicals is used to remove the unprotected *soft plastic.* The oxide is also dissolved in the unprotected areas (diagram 5). This process exposes, through the oxide layer, precisely determined regions in the original silicon layer. The hardened plastic is then removed by chemical means.

The next stage in the fabrication process is that of *infusing* a second type of impurity (*phosphorus*) into the exposed regions. The infusion of the impurity is precisely controlled in a furnace. The result is a region having an excess of electrons (*N-type silicon*) imbedded within the original P-type silicon (diagram 6). This process creates a PN junction that will allow electrical current to flow in only one direction.

A new layer of oxide is grown over the surface of the wafer, covering the N-type silicon (diagram 7). Remember, the oxide formed here is glass, a non-conductor of electricity (insulator). If more PN junctions or other components are to be formed, the process is repeated, forming many layers of circuit junctions.

Color title L and diagrams 8 and 9.

After the process of implementing the components on the microchip is completed, electrical connections, between the separate regions on the microchip itself as well as to the outside world (connector pads) must be formed. Another photomasking step is used to open holes in the oxide layer wherever the *metal connector* (usually aluminum) is to contact the silicon junctions (step not shown, note the break in the silicon dioxide surface in diagram 8). A thin layer of metal is applied to the surface (diagram 8). Plastic and photomask are applied, ultraviolet exposure is made, and the metal is washed away from the predetermined unprotected regions on the surface of the chip (diagram 9).

At this point the wafer is inspected. If it is found to be good, it is bonded into the cavity of its protective package (usually ceramic, see Plate 7). Fine wires are attached between the connector pads on the microchip and the pins of the package (DIP). The package is sealed and tested again. Now the microchip is ready to be incorporated into the circuitry of the computer.

BUILDING A MICROCHIP.

DESIGNER PATTERN_A
PHOTOREDUCTION PROCESS_B
PHOTOMASK_C
  CLEAR_{C1}
  OPAQUE_{C2}
P-TYPE SILICON_D
HEAT_E
SILICON DIOXIDE_F

PHOTORESIST_G
HARDENED PLASTIC_{G1}
SOFT PLASTIC_{G2}
ULTRAVIOLET LIGHT_H
DEVELOPER SOLUTION_I
PHOSPHORUS INFUSION_J
N-TYPE SILICON_K
METAL CONNECTOR_L

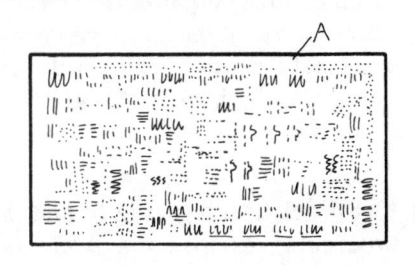

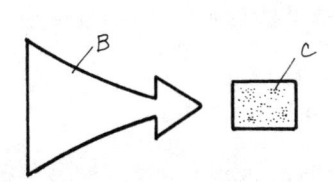

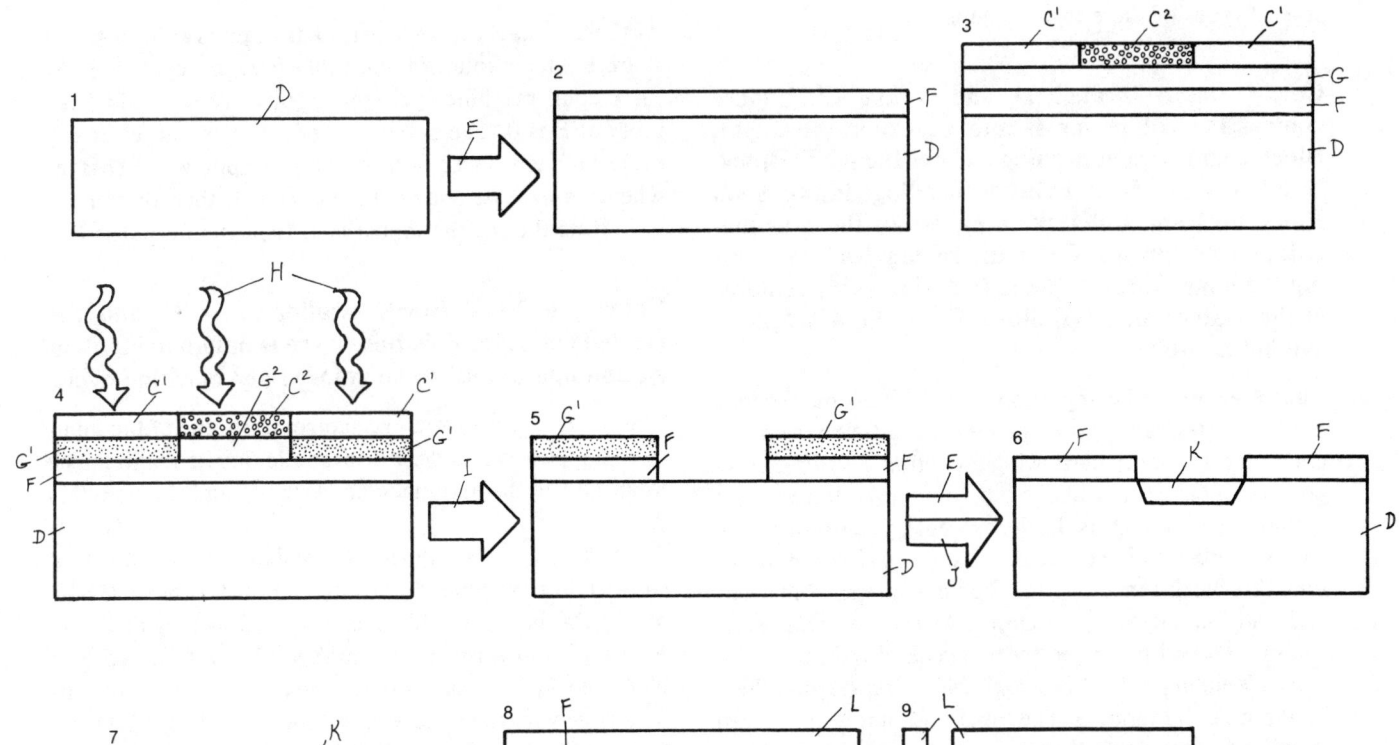

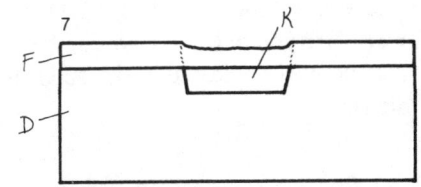

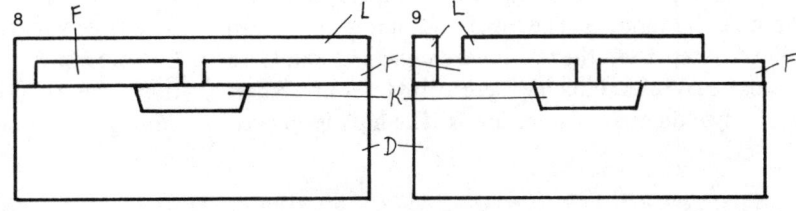

A3
BUILDING A MICROCHIP
CN 12

A4 LOGIC BLOCKS

The circuits that perform the arithmetic and make the decisions in a computer are combinations of still smaller logic circuits. These smaller circuits, composed of transistors and other components, can be thought of as tiny building blocks used to create larger special function circuits. Each microchip in the modern computer contains tens of thousands of these circuits. The computer uses these circuits to compare the bit (binary digit) patterns stored in memory. In this way, the computer can compare a symbol entered by the user at the keyboard and stored by the operating system in RAM with a bit pattern in ROM. If the two match, then certain tasks can be performed. The computer performs and recognizes commands by simple bit pattern comparisons and processing. In this plate you will see the functional characteristics of several types of these logic circuits.

Color titles A through D, and B¹ and C¹. Choose contrasting colors for B and C. Color the Input, Blocks, and Output headings. Color the AND Block, Input A, Input B, and Output headings in the AND Block diagram. Color the numbers of the four machine cycle periods. Color the rectangles representing the input states at A and B, and the output states at the right of the AND block. Color the AND block symbol as well.

The inspection and comparison of each bit of binary coded numbers is fundamental to the processing functions of the computer. Rather than showing the actual electronic components of circuits, symbolic blocks are used to represent certain types of circuits. In the example, you see one such circuit representation called an *AND block*. In order to see how this block functions, the four possible combinations of 1 and 0 input pairs are shown. At each *machine cycle* (timing interval generated by the clock circuit) a pair of values is input to the AND logic block, represented here by input A and input B. The input and output have been simplified to represent the two *binary states of 1 and 0*. In the actual electronic circuits these two states are represented by two different voltage levels. The high level (say, five volts) represents the binary digit 1. The low level (say, two volts) represents the binary digit 0. During the first machine cycle, in the diagram, the inputs at A and B are both 1. The first machine cycle output of the AND block is 1 also. At the second machine cycle, input A is 1 and B is 0. At this point, the output of the AND block is 0. When you have colored all the inputs and corresponding outputs, you see that for each machine cycle the only way the output is 1 is when both inputs A and B are 1. Otherwise, the output is 0.

Color the OR Block heading, title E, and the related diagram, proceeding as with the AND Block diagram.

At the first machine cycle period, the inputs at both A and B are 1. The output of the *OR block* at this cycle is 1. At the second machine cycle the input at A is 1, while the input at B is 0. The output is again 1. The output at any cycle is 1 whenever both or either input is 1. That is, whenever at least one of the inputs is 1, then the output is 1. If neither of the inputs is 1, then the output is 0.

Color the NOT Block heading, title F, and the related diagram. This time there is only one input, at A, and one output to be colored per machine cycle.

The *NOT circuit* inverts or changes the value of the input to the oppositive value. For example, in the diagram the input during the first machine cycle is 1 and the output is 0.

There are many types of combination blocks (not shown). For example, the negation of the OR block (NOR block) consists of an OR block followed by a NOT block. A NAND block consists of an AND block followed by a NOT block. Both of these combination blocks give outputs which are the reverse of the corresponding AND and OR blocks. In the next plate you will see how combinations can be used for more complicated tasks such as adding two binary digits.

LOGIC BLOCKS.

MACHINE CYCLE NUMBERA
INPUT★
  1 STATEB
  0 STATEC
BLOCKS★
  ANDD
  ORE
  NOTF

OUTPUT★
  1 STATEB'
  0 STATEC'

AND BLOCK★

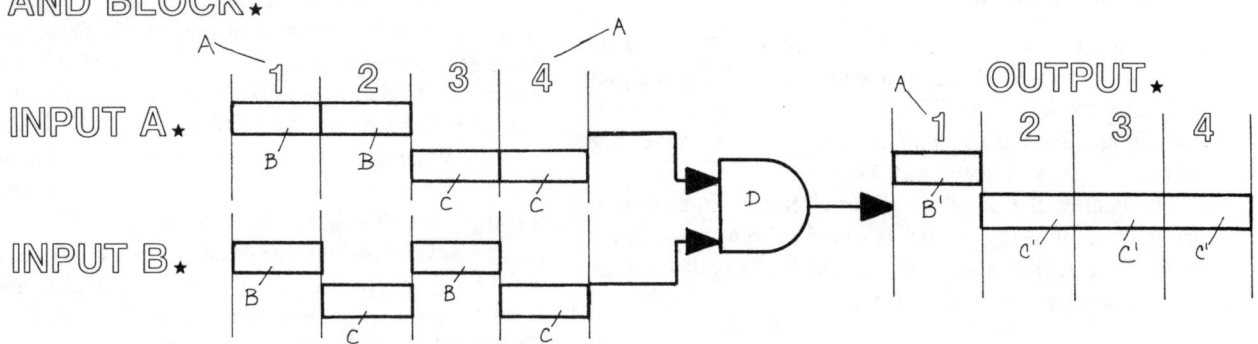

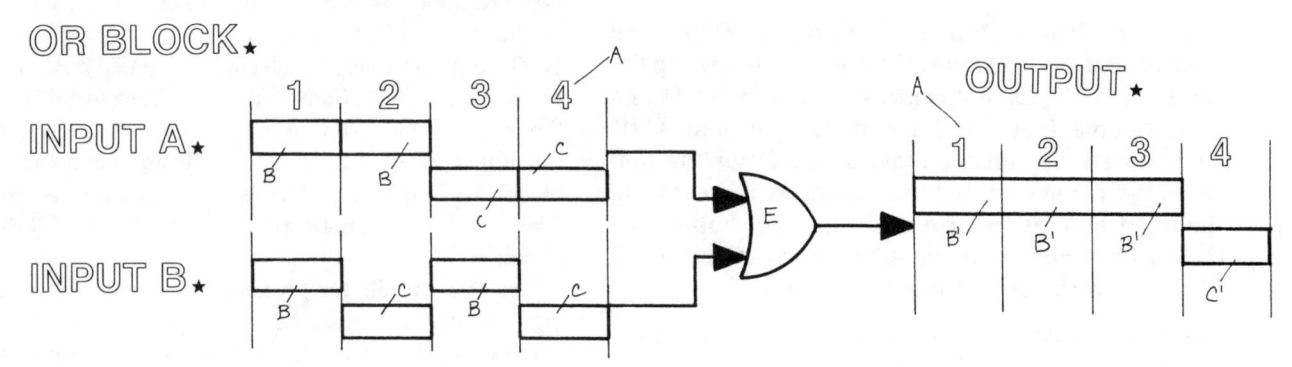

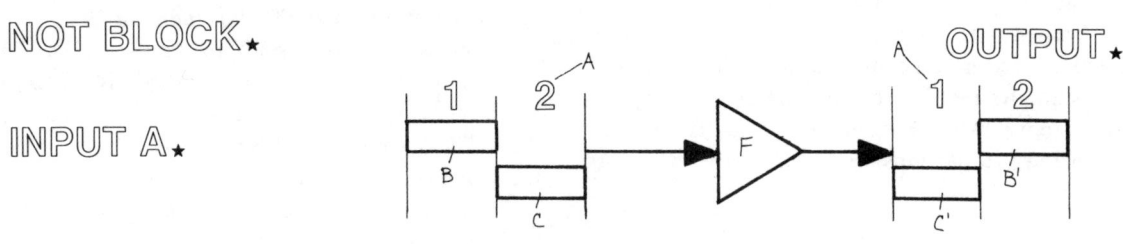

OR BLOCK★

NOT BLOCK★

A5
LOGIC BLOCKS: BINARY ADDITION

In the previous plate you saw how the major logic blocks of a computer circuit function. In this plate you will see how these blocks are used to perform processing operations. Remember, the operating system sends a series of binary coded numbers to each particular circuit when a specific operation is to be performed. Here, you will see, as one small segment of a circuit, how two binary digits (bits) can be added.

Color the Binary One-Digit Addition, Input A, Input B, and Sum headings, titles A and B, and the table at the top of the plate.

You can see from the table that the sum *1s digit* (rightmost position) is 1 whenever one but not both input digits is 1. Otherwise, it is 0. The sum *2s digit* is 1 only when both input digits are 1. You can check this by reviewing binary numbers in Appendix Plate 1.

The goal of the one-digit adder circuit is to duplicate, using logic blocks, the simple one-digit binary addition table. That is, the value of the 1s and 2s digits of the sum is the output of the adder circuits.

Color the Input, Output, 2s Digit, 1s Digit, and Blocks headings and titles C through F, including D^1, D^2, E^1, and E^2. Choose contrasting colors for D and E. Color the Input A, Input B, Output, and AND Circuit headings on the illustration. Color the machine cycle numbers and the rectangles representing the input bits (at Input A and Input B). Follow the circuit lines and color the AND block of the AND Circuit and the output bits (2s digit).

The *AND logic block* is the same as you have seen in the previous plate. Here, the block is used to produce an output of 1 when both input numbers are 1. The output of this block is used in the computation of the 2s digit of the binary sum. As required by the one-digit binary addition table above, when both inputs are 1, the output representing the 2s digit must be 1. Otherwise, the output is 0.

Color the EXCLUSIVE-OR Circuit heading and titles G and H. Color as above, following the circuit lines from the input bits through each of the blocks of the EXCLUSIVE-OR circuit to the output bits (1s digit).

The circuit to produce the required 1s digit is more complicated than that used for the 2s digit. By referring to the table you can see that in the case of the 1s digit, the output is 0 if both inputs are 1 or both inputs are 0. Otherwise, the output is 1. This type of output requirement is met by use of an *EXCLUSIVE-OR circuit*. That is, the *OR block* produces a 1 output if either or possibly both inputs are 1. The EXCLUSIVE-OR block produces a 1 output if either but not both inputs are 1.

Let's take a walk through the circuit. At the first *machine cycle*, both inputs, A and B, are 1. The upper *NOT block* (connected only to A) inverts A so that the input to the upper AND block is 0 (for A) and 1 (for B). So, the output for the upper AND block is 0. The lower NOT block (connected only to B) inverts B (to 0). The input to the lower AND block is 1 (for A) and 0 (for B). Therefore, its output is 0. Neither AND block output is 1. At this first machine cycle, the output of the OR block is 0. This is just the 1s digit output required when both inputs are 1.

At the second machine cycle, A has a value of 1 and B is 0. The upper NOT block inverts A as before. The output of the upper AND circuit is still 0. However, the lower NOT circuit inverts B (to have a value of 1). Both inputs to the lower AND circuit are now 1. The output from this block is 1. Finally, the input to the OR block is 0 (from the upper AND block) and 1 (from the lower AND block). Its output is 1. This is the output that is required when one but not both inputs to the EXCLUSIVE-OR circuit is 1.

The two circuits for producing the required 1s and 2s digit output are combined by using a common input to both (Input A and Input B). When the operating system requires the addition of two one-digit binary numbers, each number is input to both the AND and EXCLUSIVE-OR circuit blocks. The output of the EXCLUSIVE-OR is interpreted, by the operating system, as the value of the 1s digit. The output of the AND block is interpreted to mean the value of the 2s digit.

The block diagram helps the engineer design the actual microchip. These special-purpose circuits are combined to produce the desired logic and arithmetic operations that are used by the operating system in carrying out the instructions of the user's program.

BINARY ADDITION.
BINARY ONE-DIGIT ADDITION.
   1s DIGIT_A
   2s DIGIT_B

INPUT A.	1—A	1—A	0—A	0—A
INPUT B.	1—A	0—A	1—A	0—A
SUM.	B—1 0—A	B—0 1—A	B—0 1—A	B—0 0—A

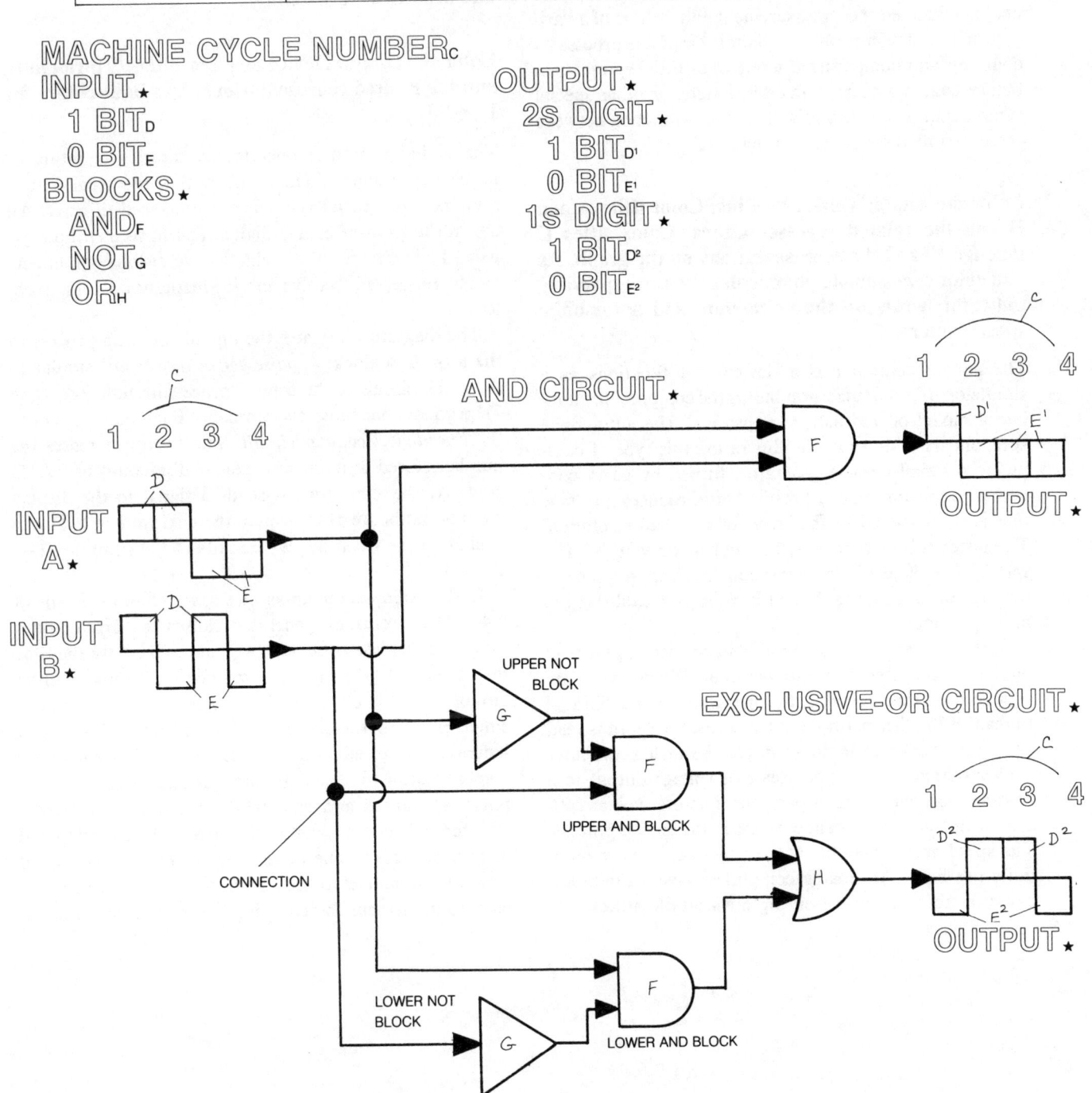

MACHINE CYCLE NUMBER_C
INPUT.
   1 BIT_D
   0 BIT_E
BLOCKS.
   AND_F
   NOT_G
   OR_H

OUTPUT.
   2s DIGIT.
      1 BIT_{D1}
      0 BIT_{E1}
   1s DIGIT.
      1 BIT_{D2}
      0 BIT_{E2}

AND CIRCUIT.

INPUT A.

INPUT B.

UPPER NOT BLOCK

UPPER AND BLOCK

CONNECTION

LOWER NOT BLOCK

LOWER AND BLOCK

EXCLUSIVE-OR CIRCUIT.

OUTPUT.

A6
ANALOG AND DIGITAL COMPUTERS

The types of data and methods of its processing determine the classification of a computer as analog or digital. Analog computers are designed to process physical events (temperature, voltage, distance, etc.) and make use of the analogy between their measurement and a value of a variable in a particular problem. Digital computers process by counting and comparing discrete data that represent, in binary code, numbers, numerals, letters, or other special symbols. In this plate you will see the distinction between these two methods of processing data.

Color the Analog Device heading. Color titles A and B and the related representations. Color titles C through F^2 and the representations on the graph. As you color each sample point, color the corresponding indicator arrow on the voltmeters and automobile speedometers.

The analog computer is a device that functions as a simulator. The manufacturer builds the computer to simulate a model of a situation or process. The automobile speedometer is an example illustrating this type of computer. A small electric generator, turned by gears connected to the automobile's drive shaft, produces a *voltage* that is proportional to the *speed* of the shaft's rotation. The faster the shaft rotates, the higher the voltage. The speedometer is just a voltmeter connected to this generator. Instead of being calibrated in volts, it is calibrated in miles per hour.

In the diagram, 0 volts (automobile not moving) is read on the speedometer as 0 miles per hour. When 6 volts are produced by the generator, the speedometer is calibrated to read as 30 miles per hour. At 12 volts, the speed is read as 60 miles per hour. In this example, the analog computer converts from a continuous scale of voltage output to a reading representing miles per hour. Factors such as calibration and adjustment allow errors in the analog process. The speedometer may be in error by one, two, or more miles per hour. All analog computers have a limitation based on accuracy in measuring physical quantities.

Applications of analog computers include the monitoring of flow rate, temperature, and pressure in chemical or oil pipe lines. The computer activates required control mechanisms when necessary.

Color the Digital Device heading, titles G through L, and the related representations. Use light colors for I and J.

The digital computer operates by directly counting or processing numbers. The numbers that represent letters, numerals, or special symbols are processed directly. All are in the form of binary digits. You have seen how, by using logic circuits, the digits in several binary numbers can be processed to solve an arithmetic or decision problem.

The diagram illustrates the digital counting process in the form of a clock. A *pulse generator circuit,* similar to the clock circuit of the central processing unit (see Plate 7), produces one *pulse* every second. Each pulse is sent to the *first digital counter circuit.* The circuit increases the number stored in its memory (a small amount of RAM) by 1. At the same time it sends a signal to the display circuits (not shown) to display the next numeral. This is similar to the video display circuits of the computer (see Plate 3).

In the example, the upper *clock face* shows the time of 9:48. The next pulse generated causes the first counter circuit to increase the count by 1 and to increase the time displayed to 9:49. At the following pulse, the first counter circuit resets its corresponding display to 0 and sends a single pulse to the *second counter circuit*. This circuit increases its stored value to 5 and sends a signal to the display circuit to show the numeral 5. In this way each pulse is counted and calculation is done to increase a counter and send a signal to a display. The counting and display are exact. The processing method of the digital computer is similar to this illustration. Logic circuits are used to implement the counting and comparing process.

ANALOG AND DIGITAL COMPUTERS.

ANALOG DEVICE ★
VOLTAGE $_A$
SPEED $_B$
LINEAR FUNCTION $_C$
SAMPLE POINT 1 $_D$
  VOLTAGE ARROW $_{D^1}$
  SPEED ARROW $_{D^2}$
SAMPLE POINT 2 $_E$
  VOLTAGE ARROW $_{E^1}$
  SPEED ARROW $_{E^2}$
SAMPLE POINT 3 $_F$
  VOLTAGE ARROW $_{F^1}$
  SPEED ARROW $_{F^2}$
VOLTMETER (VOLTS) ★ 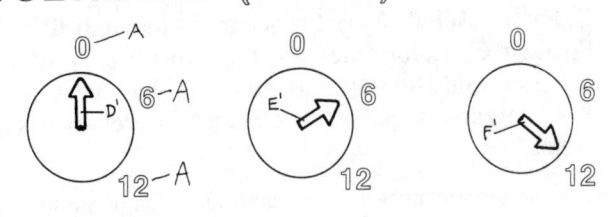
SPEEDOMETER (MPH) ★

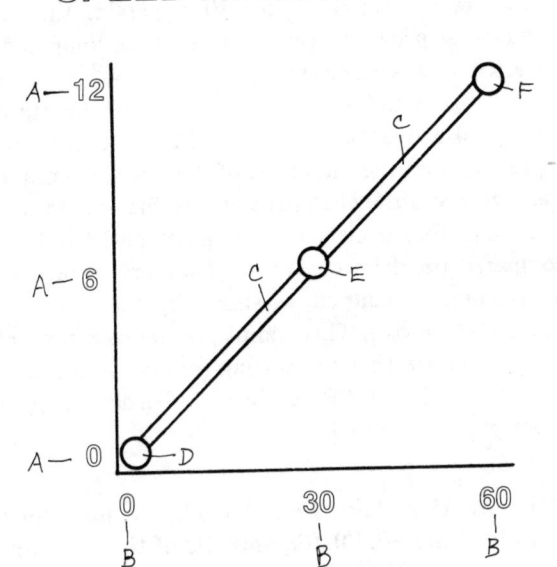

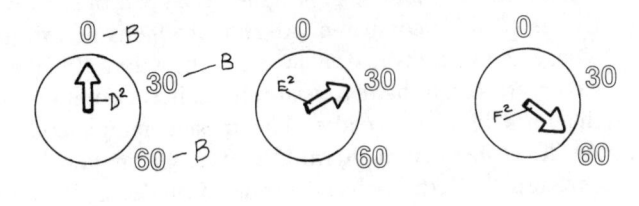

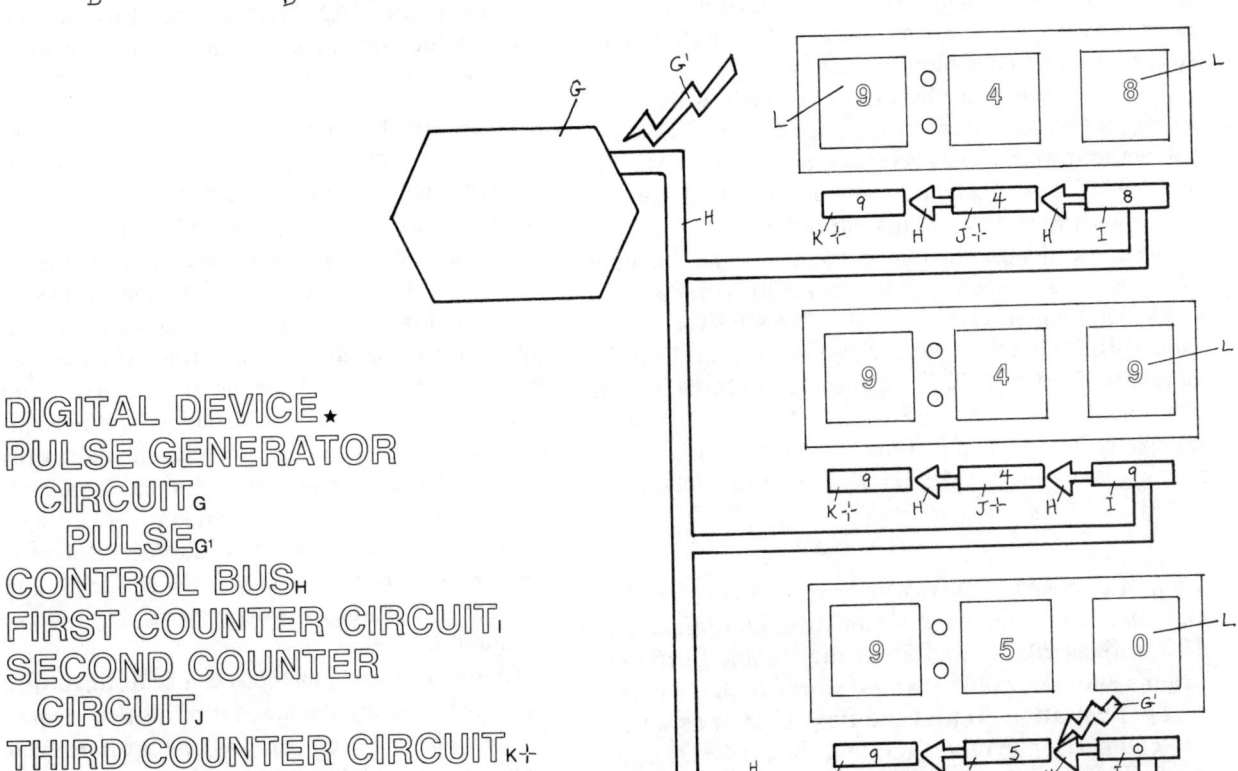

DIGITAL DEVICE ★
PULSE GENERATOR
  CIRCUIT $_G$
    PULSE $_{G^1}$
CONTROL BUS $_H$
FIRST COUNTER CIRCUIT $_I$
SECOND COUNTER
  CIRCUIT $_J$
THIRD COUNTER CIRCUIT $_K$
CLOCK FACE DIGIT $_L$

A7
SORTING

One of the functions of a data base management system is sorting data. Sorting a data list consists of arranging the elements in a predefined order. A list of names may be sorted into alphabetical order; a list of team scores may be arranged in ascending or descending order. There are many methods of sorting a set of elements. In this plate you will learn of one method called a Bubble Sort, so called because the largest or smallest element (depending on ordering selected) floats to the top of the array like a bubble in water.

Color the Bubble Sort Program heading and titles A through C. Color lines 40, 50, and 60 only of the program and the adjacent diagram. This portion of the program is called an element interchange segment.

The bubble sort program task is to sort a list of names into alphabetical order. The list of names is stored in a one-dimensional array called NAME$ (see the initial list, below). In the bubble sort program, each pair of consecutive elements is compared. An interchange is performed whenever two elements' values are in the wrong alphabetical order. Recall that letters are stored in the computer in the form of binary codes. The most common code is ASCII (American Standard Code for Information Interchange). The letter A has the code 65 (in decimal), B has the code 66, and so on up to Z, whose code is 90. In order to alphabetize, the computer places A before B, because A has a smaller code number than B.

A key segment of the bubble sort program is the interchange of two consecutive elements of the array. Here the two consecutive elements being compared are NAME$(I) and NAME$(I + 1). Line 30 has compared BAKER and ABLE and has ascertained that the order is incorrect. The element interchange program segment will alter the order of the two array values. Adjacent to line 40 in the diagram, NAME$(I) contains BAKER, while NAME$(I + 1) contains ABLE. First BAKER is stored in a variable HOLD$ (line 40). Then, ABLE is assigned to NAME$(I), (line 50). Finally, BAKER is assigned to NAME$(I + 1) to complete the interchange (line 60). Now ABLE is correctly placed in NAME$(I) and BAKER follows in NAME$(I + 1).

Color the NAME$ Array as Sorting Proceeds, Initial, and Pass 1 headings. Color titles D, E, F, G, and H and lines 20, 30, and 80 of the Bubble Sort Program. Color the values (names) stored in the NAME$ array illustrations Initial and Pass 1 below as well as the comparison symbols (G) and the arrow (H). The arrow indicates that an interchange is made.

In the bubble sort program a *comparison* is made between one entry and the one right after. If the pair is out of order, an *interchange* is made. If the pair is in the correct order, the sort program goes on to the next pair. That is, element 1 and 2 are compared, then 2 and 3, and so on until the end of the list is reached.

The first two elements of the initial array are compared by the program. The values ART and BAKER stored in the first two elements are in correct order, so no interchange is made after the comparison. (In line 30, ART is shown to belong in front of BAKER, so the program flow is directed to line 80, bypassing the element interchange program segment.) The next compared pair, BAKER and ABLE, are out of order. At this point an interchange is made by lines 40 to 60, as described and illustrated above. Interchange of BAKER and ABLE is represented on the initial list of the lower illustration by the *arrow* and the changed order of the second list. The third and fourth elements, BAKER and CAROL, are compared (in the second list). They are in order so no interchange is required, as shown by the absence of an interchange arrow. This completes one pass through the array. You see that the sorting process is not complete because ART and ABLE are out of order. At least one more pass is required.

Color the Pass 2 and Pass 3 headings and titles I and J. Color lines 10, 70, 90, and 100 of the program, the values in the NAME$ array for Passes 2 and 3, as well as the comparisons, the arrow, and the counter values shown below.

In order to determine whether or not another pass is required, an interchange *counter* is used. If at least one interchange is made, as in the first pass of the example, the interchange counter is increased by 1 (line 70, which follows the element interchange segment). At the end of the pass (line 90) if at least one interchange has occurred, program flow is passed to line 10 to begin the comparison pass through the list one more time. If an interchange is not required, line 30 directs the program to line 80, bypassing line 70 and not incrementing the counter. The process continues until the interchange counter remains at 0 at the end of a complete pass through the array, indicating that the list is finally in sorted order. In the example program, "ALL DONE" would be displayed. "ALL DONE" symbolizes the point at which additional processing, such as printing the array or storing it on disk, can be initiated.

Computer sorting methods can be distinguished by the time they take, by the amount of memory required, and by the number of comparisons that must be made before the sort is completed. The bubble sort is one of the simplest of the many sorting methods. It is used when the computer does not have very much RAM available.

SORTING.

ASSIGNMENT INSTRUCTION_A
ARRAY NAME_B
  SUBSCRIPT_B'
ARRAY VALUE_C
FOR INSTRUCTION_D
IF...THEN...INSTRUCTION_E
NEXT INSTRUCTION_F
COMPARISON_G
INTERCHANGE ARROW_H
COUNTER VALUE_I
PRINT INSTRUCTION_J

BUBBLE SORT PROGRAM.

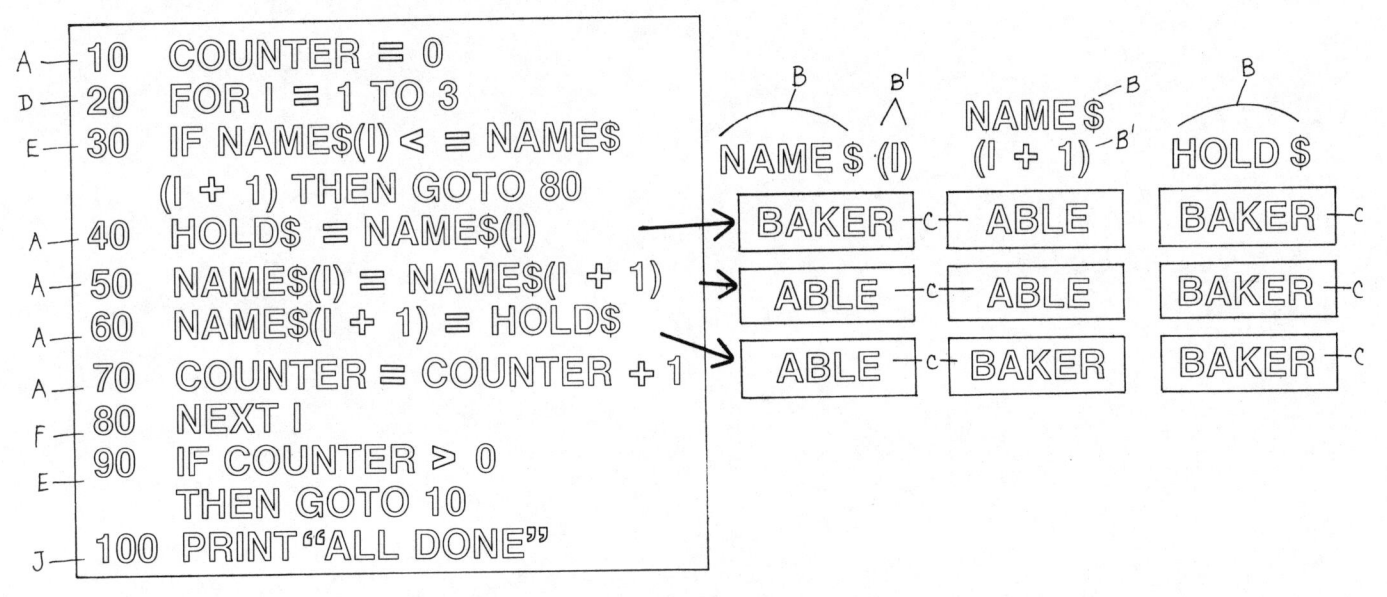

```
A — 10   COUNTER = 0
D — 20   FOR I = 1 TO 3
E — 30   IF NAME$(I) <= NAME$
         (I + 1) THEN GOTO 80
A — 40   HOLD$ = NAME$(I)
A — 50   NAME$(I) = NAME$(I + 1)
A — 60   NAME$(I + 1) = HOLD$
A — 70   COUNTER = COUNTER + 1
F — 80   NEXT I
E — 90   IF COUNTER > 0
         THEN GOTO 10
J — 100  PRINT "ALL DONE"
```

NAME$ ARRAY AS SORTING PROCEEDS.

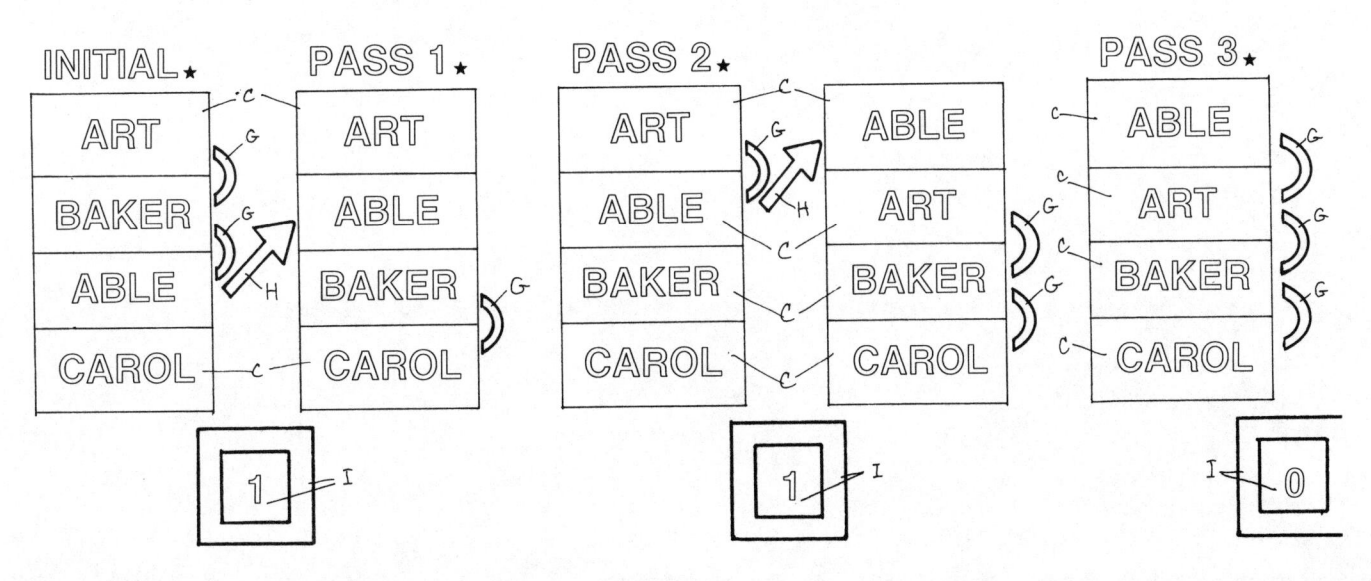

INITIAL. | PASS 1. | PASS 2. | PASS 3.

CONVERSION TABLE

DECIMAL	HEXADECIMAL	OCTAL	BINARY	ASCII	DECIMAL	HEXADECIMAL	OCTAL	BINARY	ASCII
0	00	000	00000000	NUL	64	40	100	01000000	@
1	01	001	00000001	SOH	65	41	101	01000001	A
2	02	002	00000010	STX	66	42	102	01000010	B
3	03	003	00000011	ETX	67	43	103	01000011	C
4	04	004	00000100	EOT	68	44	104	01000100	D
5	05	005	00000101	ENQ	69	45	105	01000101	E
6	06	006	00000110	ACK	70	46	106	01000110	F
7	07	007	00000111	BEL	71	47	107	01000111	G
8	08	010	00001000	BS	72	48	110	01001000	H
9	09	011	00001001	HT	73	49	111	01001001	I
10	0A	012	00001010	LF	74	4A	112	01001010	J
11	0B	013	00001011	VT	75	4B	113	01001011	K
12	0C	014	00001100	FF	76	4C	114	01001100	L
13	0D	015	00001101	CR	77	4D	115	01001101	M
14	0E	016	00001110	SO	78	4E	116	01001110	N
15	0F	017	00001111	SI	79	4F	117	01001111	O
16	10	020	00010000	DLE	80	50	120	01010000	P
17	11	021	00010001	DC1	81	51	121	01010001	Q
18	12	022	00010010	DC2	82	52	122	01010010	R
19	13	023	00010011	DC3	83	53	123	01010011	S
20	14	024	00010100	DC4	84	54	124	01010100	T
21	15	025	00010101	NAK	85	55	125	01010101	U
22	16	026	00010110	SYN	86	56	126	01010110	V
23	17	027	00010111	ETB	87	57	127	01010111	W
24	18	030	00011000	CAN	88	58	130	01011000	X
25	19	031	00011001	EM	89	59	131	01011001	Y
26	1A	032	00011010	SUB	90	5A	132	01011010	Z
27	1B	033	00011011	ESC	91	5B	133	01011011	[
28	1C	034	00011100	FS	92	5C	134	01011100	\
29	1D	035	00011101	GS	93	5D	135	01011101	]
30	1E	036	00011110	RS	94	5E	136	01011110	^
31	1F	037	00011111	US	95	5F	137	01011111	_
32	20	040	00100000	SPACE	96	60	140	01100000	`
33	21	041	00100001	!	97	61	141	01100001	a
34	22	042	00100010	"	98	62	142	01100010	b
35	23	043	00100011	#	99	63	143	01100011	c
36	24	044	00100100	$	100	64	144	01100100	d
37	25	045	00100101	%	101	65	145	01100101	e
38	26	046	00100110	&	102	66	146	01100110	f
39	27	047	00100111	'	103	67	147	01100111	g
40	28	050	00101000	(	104	68	150	01101000	h
41	29	051	00101001	)	105	69	151	01101001	i
42	2A	052	00101010	*	106	6A	152	01101010	j
43	2B	053	00101011	+	107	6B	153	01101011	k
44	2C	054	00101100	,	108	6C	154	01101100	l
45	2D	055	00101101	-	109	6D	155	01101101	m
46	2E	056	00101110	.	110	6E	156	01101110	n
47	2F	057	00101111	/	111	6F	157	01101111	o
48	30	060	00110000	0	112	70	160	01110000	p
49	31	061	00110001	1	113	71	161	01110001	q
50	32	062	00110010	2	114	72	162	01110010	r
51	33	063	00110011	3	115	73	163	01110011	s
52	34	064	00110100	4	116	74	164	01110100	t
53	35	065	00110101	5	117	75	165	01110101	u
54	36	066	00110110	6	118	76	166	01110110	v
55	37	067	00110111	7	119	77	167	01110111	w
56	38	070	00111000	8	120	78	170	01111000	x
57	39	071	00111001	9	121	79	171	01111001	y
58	3A	072	00111010	:	122	7A	172	01111010	z
59	3B	073	00111011	;	123	7B	173	01111011	{
60	3C	074	00111100	<	124	7C	174	01111100		
61	3D	075	00111101	=	125	7D	175	01111101	}
62	3E	076	00111110	>	126	7E	176	01111110	~
63	3F	077	00111111	?	127	7F	177	01111111	

GLOSSARY

ACOUSTIC COUPLER   A device that provides a mechanical means of securing a telephone receiver to a modem.

ADDRESS   A label (number or name) that designates a location in the computer's memory (RAM or ROM).

ALGORITHM   An orderly procedure that consists of a list of instructions for accomplishing a particular task.

ALPHANUMERIC   A set of symbols (letters, numerals, and special symbols).

ANALOG COMPUTER   A computer that uses physical quantities as a model to represent mathematical values.

ANIMATION   The simulation of graphic movement on a video display under software control.

APPLICATION PROGRAM   A program designed to perform a given task or solve a particular problem.

ARCHITECTURE   The internal preset arrangement of the components of a computer which determines how the computer operates.

ARITHMETIC LOGIC UNIT (ALU)   The section of the CPU that performs arithmetic and logical operations on the data passing through it.

ARRAY   A table of values (numeric or string). Each entry of the table is referenced by the array name and a subscript.

ARTIFICIAL INTELLIGENCE   The simulation of human thought processes by a computer to solve a particular problem.

ASCII   American Standard Code for Information Interchange. Code used to store and transmit data.

ASSIGNMENT INSTRUCTION   An instruction used to assign a value to a variable.

AUXILIARY STORAGE   Storage available in a computer in addition to its own main memory (RAM or ROM). Usually auxiliary storage is in the form of a disk or tape.

BASIC   Basic All-purpose Symbolic Instruction Code. A computer language invented by Kemeny and Kurtz at Dartmouth College in 1963. First designed as a language to teach programming. It was later implemented on microcomputers to provide an interactive programming language.

BATCH PROCESSING   Processing information in logical groups.

BAUD   A rate of information flow given in bits per second.

BELT PRINTER   A printer which uses a belt with character impressions.

BINARY NUMBER SYSTEM   A number system that uses base 2 and the numerals 0 and 1.

BIT   Binary digIT. The smallest unit of digital information. It has only two states, on or off (1 or 0).

BRANCHING   The action of transferring from a current sequence of instructions to a different sequence.

BUBBLE SORT   One of many types of sorting methods. Sometimes called an interchange sort.

BUFFER   A portion of RAM where data is held until the slower input/output devices are ready to receive the data.

BUG   An error in a program that causes the incorrect performance of a task or incorrect output.

BUS   An electronic connection of parallel wires providing a communication line along which data, addresses, or control signals can be sent.

BYTE   The basic unit of information storage in a computer. Commonly, it consists of eight bits considered as one unit.

CATHODE-RAY TUBE (CRT)   The screen portion of the video display. It is similar to the picture tube of a television set.

CENTRAL PROCESSING UNIT (CPU)   The major circuit section of the computer. It includes the arithmetic, control, and logic sections. It performs the computations and directs the functioning of the rest of the computer hardware.

CLOCK   An electronic circuit that times the operations of the CPU and associated support circuits.

CODING   Process of preparing a set of computer instructions.

COMPILER   A program that translates instruction written in a high-level language (source code) into machine language (object code).

CONTROL UNIT   Section of the CPU which directs the operations of the computer and initiates the proper signals to the other computer circuits to execute specific instructions.

CURSOR   Movable indicator on the video display that indicates a specific character or space that is being displayed. The cursor indicates where the next typed character will appear on the screen.

DAISY WHEEL PRINTER   A printer that has a wheel mechanism with characters on the perimeter of the wheel at the end of spokes. The wheel rotates to place the appropriate character in a printing position.

DATA   The information given to or received from a computer.

DATA BASE   A collection of data items that are used by applications programs to produce reports, effect searches, and analyze.

DEBUG Process of finding and correcting mistakes or errors in a program.

DECIMAL NUMBER SYSTEM A number system using base 10 and the numerals 0, 1, 2, 3, 4, 5, 6, 7, 8, and 9.

DEFERRED MODE A method of entering a program into RAM without having the computer execute the instructions. Execution is deferred until a command such as RUN is entered by the user.

DIGIT A numeral.

DIGITAL COMPUTER A computer that operates on specific data coded as digits.

DISK (DISC) A circular piece of plastic coated with magnetic material or plastic coated metal that is used for auxiliary storage.

DOT MATRIX PRINTER A printer that forms characters by converting a symbol into a suitable group of dots imprinted on paper.

DUPLEX Process of establishing two-way communication simultaneously between computers (usually by means of a modem).

EDITOR A program which allows the user to enter text. It allows the user to write and modify instructions of a program.

EPROM Electronically (or Erasable) Programmable **ROM**. ROM which can be erased either by an electrical signal or by ultraviolet light.

EXECUTE The running of a program.

FETCHING Process by which the CPU obtains an instruction that it will execute.

FIFTH GENERATION Stage in the history of computers characterized by the use of artificial intelligence programs, large-scale integrated circuits, and parallel processing of data.

FILE A collection of related data items usually stored in auxiliary storage (disk or tape).

FIRMWARE Programs that are permanently stored in ROM which allow the computer to perform certain predetermined tasks.

FIRST GENERATION Stage in the history of computers characterized by vacuum-tube circuits.

FLOPPY DISK DRIVE A device used to store information on a disk. The disk is called "floppy" because it is a thin platter of plastic, coated with magnetic material.

FLOWCHART A diagram indicating the steps in the flow of a program's performance of a task or solution of a problem.

FORTRAN FORmula TRANslator. A high-level language that is science and mathematics oriented. BASIC can be considered as a subset of FORTRAN.

FOURTH GENERATION Stage in the history of computers characterized by large-scale integrated circuits and sophisticated operating systems achieving a much higher speed of calculation than previous generations.

FULL DUPLEX System of transmission in which transmission and reception can occur at the same time.

GRAPHICS MODE A state of video display in which diagrams or pictures are displayed under the control of a program.

HALF DUPLEX System of transmission in which either transmission or reception can occur, but not both at the same time.

HARD COPY Data or information printed on paper.

HARDWARE Mechanical, magnetic, or electronic devices that make up a computer. The physical equipment of the computer system.

HEXADECIMAL NUMBER SYSTEM A number system that uses base 16 and makes use of the numerals 0, 1, 2, 3, 4, 5, 6, 7, 8, and 9 and the letters A, B, C, D, E, and F.

HIGH-LEVEL LANGUAGE A computer language that uses human language (e.g., English) words to specify the steps in performing a task.

INK JET PRINTER A printer that uses a high-speed stream of electrically charged ink droplets fired through a magnetic field to form letters on paper.

INPUT Information that is entered into the computer.

INSTRUCTION A set of symbols which are interpreted by the computer as a command to perform a particular task.

INTEGRATED CIRCUIT (IC) An electronic circuit on a single microchip that contains many electronic components and is designed to perform several functions in a computing system.

INTERACTIVE A system capable of two-way communication with a user during the execution of a program.

INTERFACE An electronic circuit used to connect one electrical computer component to another. For example, a disk drive must be interfaced to the processor unit to receive or supply data.

INTERPRETER A program that translates each line of a program into machine code.

K In the context of computers, it is a symbol that stands for 1024. For example, 64K bytes means 64 times 1024 bytes.

KEYBOARD A device for typing information into a computer system.

LIBRARY ROUTINES A set of programs that is supplied with the computer operating system to perform a given set of tasks such as finding the square root of a number.

MACHINE LANGUAGE A programming language whose instructions are written in binary, octal, or hexadecimal code by the user. Programs written in machine language are closest to the level at which the computer can process an instruction.

MAIN MEMORY The memory which is directly accessible to the CPU. It is composed of RAM and ROM.

MEMORY CHIP A microchip which stores data. Either RAM or ROM.

MICROCHIP A section of a semiconductor, such as silicon, that has been specially manufactured to contain a number of electronic circuits.

MICROPROCESSOR An integrated circuit that can execute instructions. It is also known as the CPU.

MODEM MOdulator DEModulator. A piece of hardware

that permits computers to transmit information over regular telephone lines.

MONITOR A video display unit which uses a cathode-ray tube to display characters.

MONITOR A program that oversees the operation of other programs. It is part of the operating system of a computer.

NETWORK The interconnection of several computers to each other or to a single host computer system.

NON-VOLATILE MEMORY A type of memory that does not require electronic current to retain stored data. Tape and disks are examples of such memory.

OCTAL NUMBER SYSTEM A numbering system that uses base 8 and makes use of the numerals 0, 1, 2, 3, 4, 5, 6, and 7.

OPERATING SYSTEM A set of programs that control the functioning of other programs in a computer. It is the software that runs the computer system and performs functions needed to control system operations. Such functions include input/output, storage assignment tasks, and compiling (or interpreting).

OUTPUT Information produced by the computer as a result of a set of instructions.

PERIPHERAL A device that is an accessory to the computer. Examples include printers, auxiliary storage devices, and plotters.

PIXEL The smallest unit of video display that is accessible by the software of a computer.

PLOTTER A peripheral device that draws diagrams under the direction of a computer program.

PRINTER A peripheral device that produces hard copy of output of a program.

PROGRAM A series of instructions to a computer that, when executed, result in the computer performing a task or solving a problem.

PROGRAMMABLE LOGIC ARRAY Portion of ROM used by the control unit to decode an instruction in the instruction register of the CPU.

RANDOM ACCESS MEMORY (RAM) Any memory that can be written on (information stored) or read from (information retrieved) by the computer under the direction of a program.

RASTER A technique of video display in which an electronic beam is moved across a screen in a horizontal pattern of lines.

READ The process of retrieving data from memory or from a peripheral input device (such as a keyboard or disk).

READ ONLY MEMORY (ROM) Memory on which data or instructions are programmed at the time of manufacture. It cannot be erased or reprogrammed by computer operations.

RESERVED WORD A sequence of symbols recognized by the operating system, compiler, or interpreter that indicates a particular function is to be performed.

ROUTINE A series of instructions within a program that perform a specific task.

RS232C The name of a type of output port that permits serial transmission of data to a peripheral device.

RUN The instruction to a computer to execute a program.

SECOND GENERATION Stage in the history of computers characterized by the use of transistor circuits.

SOFTWARE Any program used by the computer to perform a given function.

SORTING Process of arranging data in a predetermined sequence.

SOURCE PROGRAM A program written in a language requiring translation or compilation into a machine language program (object program).

STORE The process of placing data onto some type of storage device (auxiliary or RAM).

SYNTHESIZER A piece of software or hardware that is used to create music or words by generating small portions of sound.

SYSTEM COMMANDS Instructions that cause the computer to perform specific operations relating to such functions as storage, video display, or printer operations.

TAPE Magnetic or paper media used to store data or programs.

TERMINAL A peripheral device that consists of a keyboard and video display connected (by modem or direct wire) to a computer. Terminals are usually used in timesharing or network systems.

THERMAL PRINTER Printer that uses a specially designed print head that heats specifically treated paper to form a character for hard copy.

THIRD GENERATION Stage in the history of computers characterized by the use of integrated circuits (microchips).

TIME SHARING One or more computers or terminals that make use of a common central storage unit or computer.

TURTLE GRAPHICS Drawings created by a computer using the LOGO computer language. Commands move a cursor (turtle) around the screen to create diagrams or pictures.

VIDEO DISPLAY UNIT A peripheral device on which is displayed input and output.

VOLATILE MEMORY Memory that does not retain information after power is lost. RAM is an example of volatile memory.

WORD A group of bits (usually 8 or 16) that are treated as one addressable memory unit.

WORD PROCESSOR A program that allows the entry and manipulation of text to produce such output as reports, lists, or even labels.

WRITE The placement of data into a memory device or display on a peripheral unit.

INDEX

accoustic coupler, 11, 12
address, 8
address bus, 8
algorithm, 13
alphanumeric, 3
amplitude, 37
analog computer, A6
AND logic block, 7, A4, A5
animation, 32
antecedent, 40
applications program, 9, 37
arithmetic logic unit (ALU), 6, 7, 17
arithmetic operation symbols, 15, 16
array, 25, 26
artificial intelligence, 40, 42, 43, 44
ASCII, 3, 10, A7
assignment, 15
assignment instruction, 17, 21, 23, 24
auxiliary storage, 2

bar graph, 32
base, A1
BASIC, 8, 14
baud, 11
binary addition, A5
binary numbers, 8, A1
branching, 20
bubble sort, A7
buffer, 12
bus, 8

cathode ray tube (CRT), 2
central processing unit (CPU), 2, 4, 7, 8, 9
character generator, 33
characters per second (CPS), 4
CLEAR, 15
clock unit, 7
CLS, 15
column, 26
communication processor, 12
compiler, 8, 9, 10
conditional branching, 20
consequent, 40
control bus, 8
control unit (CU), 6, 7
counter variable, 24, 25
counting, 21
cursor, 3

daisy wheel printer, 4, 35
data base, 37
data base file, 37
data base management, A7
data base management program, 37
data bus, 8
data instruction, 23
decimal numbers, A1
decoding, 7
dedicated machine, 14
DEF FN instruction, 28

deferred mode, 15
define function, 28
delimiter, 17, 18
demodulator, 11
digital computer, A6
DIM instruction, 25, 26
disk drive, 5
dot matrix, 3
dot matrix printer, 4, 35
double-sided disk, 5
dual in-line pin (DIP), 7
duration, 38

editor, 36
EXCLUSIVE-OR logic circuit, A5

feedback, 41
fetching, 7, 8
fifth generation, 44
first generation, 1, 44
floppy disk, 5
flowchart, 13, 14
FOR instruction, 24, 25
FORWARD instruction, 34
fourth generation, 44
frequency, 37
function, 28, 29
function argument, 28

games, 42, 43
GOSUB instruction, 30
GOTO instruction, 19, 24
graphics mode, 31

hard disk, 5
hard sector, 5
hardware, 9
hertz, 38
hexadecimal numbers, A2
high-level languages, 10
high-resolution graphic (HIRES), 33
HOME, 15

IF . . . THEN . . . instruction, 19, 20, 21, 22, 23, 24
immediate mode, 15, 16
impact printer, 4
input, 2
INPUT instruction, 18, 19, 22, 23
input/output board, 6
instruction register, 8
INT function, 28
integer function, 28
integrated circuit, 44
interactive programming, 18
interface: human, 44
internal memory, 2
interpreter, 8, 9, 10

key word, 10
keyboard, 2, 3

keyboard code, 3
keyboard input, 14
knowledge based expert system, 40

language prompt, 3
LEFT instruction, 34
line number, 15
logic block, A3, A4, A5
LOGO, 34
loop, 19, 24
low-resolution graphic (LORES), 31, 32

machine code, 8
machine cycle, A4
machine language, 10
magnetic tape, 5
main computer board, 6
main memory, 6
mainframe computer, 1
memory management, 9
menu, 36
microchip, 1, 7, A3
microcomputer, 1
minicomputer, 1
modem, 11, 12
modulator, 11
music application program, 38
music synthesis, 38

N-type silicon, A3
NAND logic block, A4
natural language, 44
networking, 12
NEW, 15
NEXT instruction, 24, 25
node, 42
non-impact printer, 4
NOR logic block, A4
NOT logic block, A4, A5
number systems, A1
numeric datum, 17

object program, 8
octal numbers, A2
one-dimensional array, 25, 26
operating system (OS), 9
OR logic block, 7, A4, A5

P-type silicon, A3
parallel processing, 44
parameter, 28
parent board, 6
peripheral management, 9
phoneme, 39
photomask, A3
photoreduction, A3
photoresist, A3
pixel, 31, 32, 33

plotter, 35
plotting instruction, 31
PN-junction, A3
PRINT instruction, 16, 17, 18
printer, 2, 4
printer code, 4
processor unit, 3
program, 14, 15
program counter, 8
programmable logic array (PLA), 8
pseudorandom number, 29

query language, 37
QWERTY, 3

random access memory (RAM), 6, 7, 9, 23
random number, 29
random number generation, 29
raster, 33, 35
READ instruction, 23
read only memory (ROM), 6, 7, 9
read/write head, 5
register, 7
REM, 15
REPEAT instruction, 34
reserved word, 10
return, 15
RETURN instruction, 30
RIGHT instruction, 34
RND instruction, 29

robot, 41
robotics, 41
root node, 42
row, 26
rule interpreter, 40
RUN, 12, 15, 19

scanning, 2
SCRATCH, 15
second generation, 1, 44
sector, 5
silicon dioxide, A3
single-sided, 5
soft sector, 5
software, 9
software pixel, 33
sorting, A7
sound wave, 37
source program, 8
SQR function, 28
square-root function, 28
STEP, 24
STOP instruction, 20
string datum, 17
subroutine, 28, 30
subscript, 25, 26, 27
subscripted variable, 25
syntax, 14
synthesis: music, 38
synthesis: voice, 39
synthesizer: sound, 38

system commands, 15
systems software, 9

text mode, 31
thermal printer, 4
third generation, 1, 44
timesharing, 12
TO instruction, 34
tone generator, 38
track, 5
transistor, 1, 44
tree, 42
trolley, 35
turtle graphics, 34
two-dimensional array, 26, 27

user friendly, 19

vacuum tube, 1, 44
variable, 15, 17
variable name, 17
vector graphics, 34
video display, 2, 3, 31, 33
video display pixel, 33
video display screen, 3
video refresh, 33

waveform, 38
waveform digitization, 39
word processing, 36
write protect, 5